Computational Linguistics: An Introduction

Computational Linguistics: An Introduction

Chloe Barnes

STATES
ACADEMIC PRESS
www.statesacademicpress.com

Computational Linguistics: An Introduction
Chloe Barnes
ISBN: 978-1-63989-122-1 (Hardback)

STATES
ACADEMIC PRESS

Published by States Academic Press,
109 South 5th Street,
Brooklyn, NY 11249, USA

Cataloging-in-Publication Data

Computational linguistics : an introduction / Chloe Barnes.
p. cm.
Includes bibliographical references and index.
ISBN 978-1-63989-122-1
1. Computational linguistics. 2. Cross-language information retrieval. 3. Multilingual computing.
4. Applied linguistics. I. Barnes, Chloe.
P98 .C66 2022
410.285--dc23

Table of Contents

Preface

The field of science concerned with the computational modeling of natural language is referred to as computational linguistics. It is an inter-disciplinary field which draws upon the principles of computer science, mathematics, philosophy, psychology and anthropology. It also focuses on building artifacts which are useful in processing and producing language. The sub-fields of computational linguistics are theoretical computational linguistics and applied computational linguistics. The key objectives of computational linguistics involve the formulation of grammatical and semantic frameworks for characterizing languages. Various approaches used for research in this field encompass developmental approaches, structural approaches, production approaches and comprehension approaches. This book is a valuable compilation of topics, ranging from the basic to the most complex theories and principles in the field of computational linguistics. Most of the topics introduced herein cover new techniques and the applications of this field. For someone with an interest and eye for detail, this book covers the most significant topics in the field of computational linguistics.

To facilitate a deeper understanding of the contents of this book a short introduction of every chapter is written below:

Chapter 1- The discipline which focuses on the computational modeling of natural language is known as computational linguistics. It also involves the study of appropriate computational approaches to linguistic questions. The topics elaborated in this chapter will provide a brief introduction to the different facets of computational linguistics such as morphological processing and computational semantics.

Chapter 2- The area of study within computer science which seeks to provide computers with the ability to understand text and speech similar to the way humans understand them is known as natural language processing. This chapter closely examines the key concepts of natural language processing such as corpus linguistics, finite automata and natural language generation to provide an extensive understanding of the subject.

Chapter 3- The analysis of string of symbols in computer languages, data structures or natural language, which conform to the rules of formal grammar, is known as parsing. The topics elaborated in this chapter will help in gaining a better perspective about language theory and parsing as well as context-free languages and top-down parsing.

Chapter 4- Machine translation deals with the usage of software for the purpose of translating text or speech from one language to another. The method of machine translation which uses various machine translation approaches within a single machine translation system is known as hybrid machine translation. This chapter discusses in detail the different aspects of machine translation such as hybrid machine translation and dialogue systems.

Chapter 5- The methodologies and technologies which allow the recognition and translation of speech into text by computers are known as speech recognition. Most of the general-purpose speech recognition systems are developed through Hidden Markov Models. This chapter has been carefully written to provide an easy understanding of the varied facets of speech recognition and processing such as text to speech synthesis and Hidden Markov Model.

Chapter 6- Some of the prominent aspects of computational linguistics are chunking and shallow parsing, syntactic parsing, word sense disambiguation, etymological annotation, extratextual annotation and computational lexicology. The chapter closely examines these aspects of computational linguistics to provide an extensive understanding of the subject.

I owe the completion of this book to the never-ending support of my family, who supported me throughout the project.

Chloe Barnes

1

Introduction to Computational Linguistics

The discipline which focuses on the computational modeling of natural language is known as computational linguistics. It also involves the study of appropriate computational approaches to linguistic questions. The topics elaborated in this chapter will provide a brief introduction to the different facets of computational linguistics such as morphological processing and computational semantics.

Computational linguistics (CL) is a trans-disciplinary field of study that combines Computer Science and Linguistics. CL is primarily concerned with studying how linguistic knowledge underlying natural languages can be computationally modeled. Based on this, technological solutions can be developed for certain practical problems involving human languages. In that sense, making computer systems that are capable of processing and generating human languages is the goal of Computational Linguistics. Computational Linguistics also provides methods for accessing and analysing large data in natural languages that can be used by linguists for abstraction and generalizations.

The field goes back to 1950s when syntactic parsing and machine translation started. The theoretical linguistic perspectives of Syntax itself emerged alongside the evolution of formal languages and automata in Computer Science. Until 1990s CL was closely connected to linguistics with the linguists writing grammars and the computational linguists implementing them. But with the statistics revolution in 1990s, probabilistic models started to be adopted in natural language processing systems. This brought about a shift in the way linguistic knowledge is used in CL. Creation of corpora, annotated with linguistic knowledge, became one of the major efforts. A major concern here is about consistency in annotation. This involved understanding of linguistic issues and what level of granularity should one go while developing schemes for corpora annotation.

Computational linguistics, thus, deals with developing methods for analysing a text in a linguistic meaningful way, developing linguistic resources for this purpose and developing quality estimation methods for the developed tools and data resources. This involves making implicit linguistic information in a text explicit, hence organizing the data such that the machine uses it for processing.

Types of Analysis

Computational linguistics, works towards developing computational approaches to meaningfully interact with natural language data. A natural language utterance can be in the form of spoken or written data. Therefore, broadly, there are two types of analysis that need to be done on a natural language data:

- Analysis of phonetics/phonology: This involves speech recognition and speech synthesis from a raw speech signal. All the sub-problems such as phoneme identification, prosody, language detection etc. broadly fall under this category.
- Analysis of text: Analysing written texts at different levels of linguistic analysis constitutes text analysis. Since the analysis involves orthographic representation of the texts, phonological level of analysis is left out here.

Speech processing analyses sounds and text processing attempts to extract meaning from a text. For making the machines talk to humans, the machines need to recognize speech sounds and be able to speak. These processes are referred to as speech recognition and speech synthesis. The process of Speech recognition involves recognition of speech sounds and converting them into text. Whereas, speech synthesis involves conversion from text to speech.

Before any higher level application of text processing can actually be performed say summarization of a given natural language text the raw text which is basically a series of alphabets interspersed with delimiters (a space, punctuation, nonsense characters etc.) has to be processed through various stages of linguistic analysis. The analysis involves understanding of various aspects of language. What kind of knowledge about language is required to process a text? Lexical knowledge, morphological knowledge, syntactic knowledge and semantic and pragmatic knowledge. All the linguistic components of a text need to be handled in various stages of analysis.

Sentence Splitting and Tokenization

Any running text has to be identified as made up of multiple sentences which in turn is made up of multiple tokens. Computationally, a token is generally understood to be a string separated by delimiters. A sentence, therefore, is conceived to be a sequence of tokens. Tokens can be lexical words but not always so because unknown characters, acronyms, punctuation marks, compound words etc. also are text entries which are a part of textual analysis. Clearly, it is not simply sufficient to label anything which is delimited by a space is a token since spaces are not consistently used in natural texts between punctuation marks, even between words in morphologically rich languages. Also compound words are sometimes written using hyphen in between parts of the compound, whereas in other scenarios the same hyphen might just imply continuity of one word across two lines. Treating space and hyphen invariably as delimiters is not as straightforward and simple as it seems. Sentence splitting involves Identifying and learning the sentence delimiters which demarcate one sentence from another. Identifying full stops and treating them as sentence delimiters doesn't always works. Full stops generally mark a sentence boundary. However, it can also occur in abbreviations, hesitation of utterance in direct speech marked by multiple full stops in sequence, numbers and fraction etc. The challenges that underlie these sentence boundary and token boundary identification is the first step before any further processing can be done. Tokenizer module is designed to take care of these issues in text processing.

Parts of Speech Tagging

A part of Speech Tagger is a module that takes the output of the tokenizer module (which is set of tokens that make up a sentence), and identifies the word classes that a token belongs to. These word classes are identified based on the principles of regular contrasts determined by morphological forms, lexical meaning and syntactic functions that can be demonstrated in empirically verifiable ways. The number of word classes or parts of speech required for a language varies from language to language. A Part of Speech (POS) tagset is a set of tag names that any given token in a raw text can be assigned. A POS tagger takes the tokens as input and outputs the token along with its POS tag label. Example: Raw text: The girl looked towards the hill.

$\rightarrow$ Tokenizer $\rightarrow$ {The} {girl} {looked} {towards} {the} {hill} {.}

$\rightarrow$ POS tagger $\rightarrow$ {The – DT} {girl – NN} {looked – VBD} {towards – IN} {the – DT} {hill – NN}

The labels DT, NN, IN, VBD are the POS tags which are part of the Stanford POS tagset. Deciding what and how many word classes should be assigned for a given language is a policy decision that varies from language to language.

Morph Analysis

For the given set of tokens belonging to a particular word class, there could be various inflectional variations of the same lexical stem to convey distinctions in meaningful components that make up a word. For example 'give' is a stem/root word which inflects as 'gave, gives, giving, given' that shows variations of aspect and tense of the action denoted by the verb 'give'. Some languages which use circumfixes (for instance, Chikasaw language) have interesting morphological properties that a lot more than tense and aspect are encoded within a single word. E.g. chokma (he is good) + ik-o (negative) $\Rightarrow$ ik-chokm-o (he is not good). Understanding these meaningful internal components of a token belonging to a word class is called Morph analysis. Thus morph analyzer can be modeled as a component that takes a token to determine the basic meaning units that make up the word. It provides multiple outputs for a word which may have more than one analysis. For example, 'chairs' in English is both, a noun and a verb. An English morph analyser would, therefore, provide following possible analyses for the word 'Chairs',

$$\text{Chairs} \rightarrow < \text{root} = \text{chair, category} = \text{n, number} = \text{plural, person} = 3 >;$$
$$< \text{root} = \text{chair, category} = \text{verb, number} = \text{singular, tense} = \text{present} > \text{etc.}$$

Chunking

Once you have identified that a given input sentence is made up of a set of words and what the internal make-up of the word itself is, we are ready to do a syntactic analysis of the words. To put it differently, we are now interested in how the given words are stringed together and structurally organized to form a correct sentence (syntactic analysis). Computationally, we want to learn what are the non-overlapping, internally-structured units that make up a sentence and how they are organized structurally. These non-overlapping, internally-structured units that make up a sentence are what we call as chunks. In other words, a chunk is a simple constituent which does not have a nested structure internally. A chunk may have a single word as its member or a chunk can encompass more than a word where one of the words would be the head of the chunk. Therefore, every chunk would have a 'head'.

Parsing

Syntactic Parsing of a sentence involves providing its grammatical analysis. In NLP, this can be done at two levels, shallow and deep.

- Shallow Parsing: If a raw text is split into tokens, POS tagged and chunked we have broadly analyzed what the structure of a sentence is at its outset. Now the sentences are said to be shallow parsed. Further dependency or constituency structures can be learnt from the shallow parser output. For Indian languages, morph analyser is also added in the shallow parsing pipeline as several Indian languages have rich morphology and even POS tagging needs morph information for more accurate outputs.

- Full/Deep Parsing: Parsing is the automatic analysis of the grammatical structure of a sentence by a machine. A Parser takes a sentence as its inputs and outputs its grammatical analysis in terms of what grammatical functions different words play in a sentence.

Parsing needs a mathematical model where the syntax of a language is encoded. This assumes a grammar. The grammar may contain rules which have purely syntactic information or may also incorporate certain level of semantic information, e.g., lexical semantics. There are several grammatical frameworks which may be used for the computational modeling. These frameworks depend on different linguistic theories. Two frameworks which are quite commonly used in the field are: Constituency analysis (following Phrase Structure Grammars) and dependency analysis (following dependency grammars). Constituency analysis takes a sentence as an input and analyses it in terms of its phrase structures. Phrase structure expresses hierarchical relations among group of words. Dependency structure is an alternative way of analysing a sentence which represents grammatical relations between words in a sentence.

Examples: Harry bought a book.

- Phrase Structure analysis:

  (ROOT

  (S

  (NP (NNP Harry))

  (VP (VBD bought)

  (NP (DT a) (NN book))

  (NP (NN yesterday)))))

- Dependency analysis:

  Nsubj (bought-2, Harry-1)

  root (ROOT-0, bought-2)

  det (book-4, a-3)

  dobj (bought-2, book-4)

  nmod:tmod (bought-2, yesterday-5)

In the dependency analysis, two lexical nodes are related to each other by a dependency relation. Bought forms the root of the tree structure. Word Harry is related to bought by the relation 'nsubj'. Determiner a is related to the noun book by the relation 'det'. Book is related to bought as 'dobj'. Yesterday is related to bought by the relation 'nmod:tmod'. For languages that have relatively free word order, a dependency analysis between the linguistic units that make up a sentence is more suitable for syntactic analysis than constituency analysis. Since Indian languages are also relatively free word order languages, a dependency grammatical framework suits them better.

Semantics, Discourse, Pragmatic analysis: Other computational tasks that are essential for NLP are understanding the semantics of the parsed sentence structure, understanding the text beyond the sentence level, usually at the level of a text fragment, sentiment and opinion analysis of a text etc. For example, the Penn Discourse Treebank (PDTB -REF) is based on the idea that discourse connectives such as and, but, then, while etc. can be thought of as predicates with associated argument structures. Analysis of this structure of a text constitutes discourse analysis. Other than understanding the nature and function of discourse connectives and the way they relate two events, one also needs to identify anaphoric references or multiple references of the same entity and event in a given discourse. This is called as coreference chain resolution.

Computational Machineries

The natural language processing and even the theoretical perspectives on syntax evolved alongside the development of theoretical perspectives on formal language and automata theory in Computer Science. We will briefly discuss about some of these ideas to understand how traditionally linguistic structures are understood from a computational point of view.

In the context of a formal language theory, a language is a set of strings over some alphabet ∑. Formal languages are defined with respect to a given alphabet, which is a finite set of symbols, each of which is called a letter. This notation however does not mean that elements of the alphabet must be "ordinary" letters; they can be any symbol, such as numbers, or digits, or words. A finite sequence of letters is called a string, or a word. For example, let ∑ = {0,1} be an alphabet. Then all binary numbers are strings over ∑. Now formal languages are sets of strings, subsets of ∑* (set of all strings of ∑). When these languages are fairly simple, they can be characterized by means of rules. Some languages are specified by grammars, which are themselves finite objects whose semantics is defined by a grammar framework. Familiar grammar frameworks are: context sensitive grammars, definite clause grammars, tree adjoining grammars, context-free grammars, and non-deterministic finite state automata. Within a given grammar framework F, any grammar G recognizes a unique language L(G), namely, the set of strings accepted by G. Instead of a rigorous formal description of every one of these frameworks in general, we just point out how some of the common natural language tasks can be processed computationally through these models.

Take for instance the computational device called as Finite State Automata (FSA). Informally, it consists of a finite set of states (imagine them as vertices of a graph), connected by a finite number of transitions (treat them as edges of a graph). Each of the transitions is labeled by a letter, from some finite alphabet ∑. A computation starts at a designated state, the start state or initial state, and it moves from one state to another along the pre-defined transitions. As it moves, it prints the letter which labels the transition. Thus, during a computation, a string of letters is printed out. Some of the states of the machine are designated as final states, or accepting states. Whenever the computation reaches a final state, the string that was printed so far is said to be accepted by the machine. Since each computation defines a string, the set of all possible computations defines a set of strings or, in other words, a language. We can then say that this language is accepted or generated by the machine. Example: In NLP tasks, storing the lexical entries of a language in a dictionary is important and FSAs provide an efficient means for storing and accessing dictionaries. If Hindi words like laDaka, laDake, laDakoM, laDakiyAM which have a common root laDak have to be stored, one can use a finite state automata to recognize them as valid strings in the language.

The organization of the lexicon as outlined above is extremely simplistic. A possible extension can involve attaching additional information pertaining to the words to the final states of the FSA. Such information can include definitions, morphological information, translations, etc. FSA are thus suitable for representing various kinds of dictionaries, in addition to simple lexicons. While Finite State Automata may be useful for some natural language applications as shown above, it is often useful to be able to relate two formal languages through some mechanism. Take for example an NLP task such as POS tagger. This component can be viewed as an application that takes a set of input tokens (a source formal language) and establishes relation with a set of POS tags (a target formal language). On similar lines, one can view a morph analyzer as a relation between natural language strings and their internal morphological structure. Formally, this means we are trying to establish relations between two languages and we should have some machinery to achieve this. Such a computational machinery is called as Finite State Transducer. Transducers are similar to automata, the only difference being that the edges are not labeled by single letters, but rather by pairs of symbols: one symbol from input alphabet (∑1) and one symbol from output alphabet (∑2) i.e. a regular relations are defined over two sets of alphabets ∑1 and ∑2. Take for example the morph analysis of a word like 'bacche' (children).

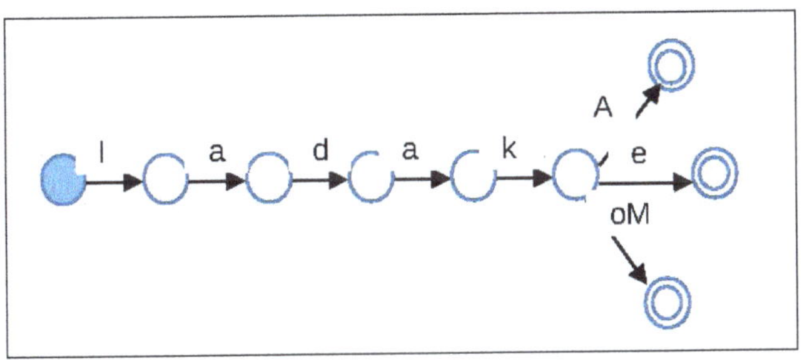

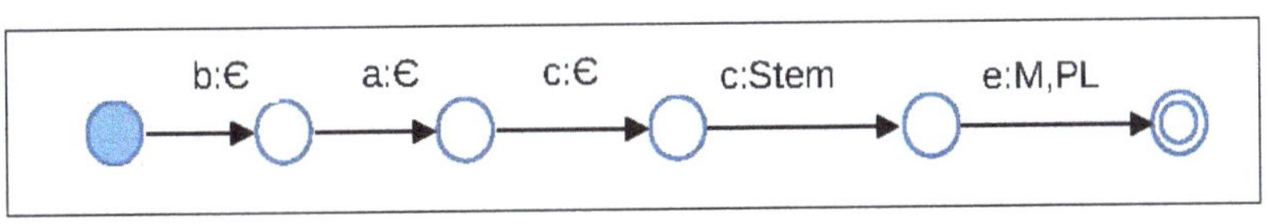

Till 'bacc' the transducer produces the corresponding morph output 'Stem' by mapping the relation between the string in language 1 i.e. 'bacc' to string in language 2 i.e. 'Stem'. Once the morpheme 'e' is encountered after the stem, the transducer is mapped to another string 'M,PL' which indicates that the analysis of the encountered morpheme 'e' is that the stem to which this morpheme is attached is masculine in gender and plural in number.

The Finite state automata and the transducer that we have informally discussed so far can handle only regular languages and regular relations respectively. Informally, regular languages can be understood in this way: all sufficiently long words in a regular language may be pumped to generate a new word that also lies within the same language. By pumping we mean that the strings of the language have a middle section of the word repeated an arbitrary number of times. Usually the regular languages are expressed in a concise manner by means of regular expressions.

E.g. Imagine that you define a language that accepts only those strings in which the input symbols belong to the set $\Sigma = \{a, b\}$ and also that there should be one or more number of 'a's before you encounter a 'b' and then any letter may follow it or just end there. We can express this language as a regular expression:

(a) +b ((a)*(b)*)*.

Here * represents that the expression to which it is attached can occur zero or more times and + indicates that the expression to which it is attached can repeat one or more times. Thus strings like aaab, ababab, aaaaaaabbbbbb, aaabababababa, ab, abbbbbb are all acceptable strings in this language but not baba, baaaaa etc. because there are no 'a's before the first b.

Regular languages and relations are useful for various applications of natural language processing, but there is a limit to what can be achieved with such means. Not all languages over some alphabet Σ are regular. To exemplify a non-regular language assume a language defined over an alphabet $\Sigma = \{a, b\}$ whose members are strings that consist of some number of 'a's followed by the same number of 'b's. Formally this can be represented as $\{a^n.b^n \mid n > 0\}$. There is no regular expression can be used to capture this language. Such a language cannot be defined by a finite state automaton. There are many such languages and there is a well-known technique called pumping lemma for proving that certain languages are not regular.

In order to deal with a class of more complex languages, people came up with the idea of grammar. Intuitively speaking, a grammar is a set of rules that operate on a set of symbols. For the formal grammars, distinction is made between two kinds of symbols: a terminal symbol and a nonterminal symbol. Terminal symbols should be understood as the set of symbols that are elements of the target language and non-terminals are the symbols that facilitate the specification of rules of manipulation. In the case of natural languages, which are of course non-regular in nature, the syntactic categories such as Noun, Noun phrase, Verb phrase are non-terminal symbols and the actual words, phrases are terminal symbols. It should be understood that strictly speaking, the non-terminals have no external or special interpretations as far as formal languages are concerned. Now with this understanding, you can define rules as a non-empty sequence of symbols both terminals and non-terminals with the constraint that the first element should be a non-terminal symbol. e.g. if your language can generate definitely determined noun phrases from given set of nouns, then you can define the terminal symbols as the set of nouns namely {car, horse, mountain} and non-terminals as set of syntactic categories needed namely {DEF, NN, NP, PL, NNS }. Now you can define your rules as follows:

NN → car, horse, mountain

PL → s

NNS → NN.PL

DEF → the

NP → DEF NN

Now this grammar allows you to analyze strings such as the cars, the mountain, the mountains as valid linguistic expressions. This is a very simplistic language that is pointed out for illustration. Much other sophisticated formalism has been developed for analyzing and processing natural language utterances. Context-free grammars were formalized and they were used for deriving the phrase structure representation of English sentences. However it was widely believed that natural languages show properties which were beyond the expressive powers of a Context-free grammar. It was in 1980s it was proven that Dutch language and another dialect of Swiss German could not be handled by the expressive powers of Context-free grammars i.e. the two languages were transcontext-free. This led to the formulation of mildly context-sensitive languages. Several linguistic formalisms were proposed as adequate for expressing the class of natural languages. Some noteworthy ones are Tree Adjoining Grammars, Head grammars, Linear indexed grammars, Combinatory Categorical Grammars etc.

Thus in this way, languages were analyzed and computed as implementations of formal grammars before 1990s where linguists describe the grammar and computer scientists implemented these grammars. But with the advent of statistical methods in artificial intelligence, the methodology to compute the linguistic tasks such as recognizing sentences, identifying their structure, extracting their meaning have been treated as statistical machine learning problems. For example, POS tagging can be formalized as establishing a regular relation between two set of languages. As POS tag of a word depends on its context, there is no methodology of showing this context dependence through regular expressions. Instead, the problem of learning a POS tag of a given word is modeled as a sequence learning task in statistical machine learning where the probabilities for the given word in a context of surrounding words to belong to a word class is calculated and the highest probability class is assigned as its POS tag. To learn these probabilities, typically we need to annotate a significant amount of data (call it gold annotation), providing a set of examples for the machine to learn from. This is called supervised machine learning. Look at the below example:

The	DT
boy	NN
went	VBD
into	IN
the	DT
room	NN

We have shown that there are some tokens on the left and their tags are manually annotated on the right. By tagging thousands of words like this, we can generate a reliably good probabilistic model which asserts that the probability that a given word which follows the is a Noun is high. This kind of supervised learning involves learning by examples and typically requires annotation of large amount of data. Instead of annotating the data of POS tags for a new language, if you observe that there are regular templates or patterns into which you can manipulate the already existing annotation for another language, basically you are projecting the knowledge from existing annotation onto a new language and aligning the knowledge to converge with the properties of the target language POS properties. Basically, in supervised learning you are grouping objects into a predetermined set of categories say in this example it is a set of POS tags.

Learning not based on examples but based on some computational patterns is unsupervised learning. Typically, unsupervised machine learning involves dividing a set of objects into clusters so that objects in the same cluster are similar to each other based on some observable properties and those in different clusters are dissimilar to each other. A variety of clustering algorithms are used to achieve this. Identifying unsupervised techniques to solve many of the NLP tasks is an active research activity.

Relevant Linguistic Issues

NLP problems such as POS tagging, morph analysis have been addressed in many languages across the world through supervised learning and reasonably saturated accurate performances have been achieved through these techniques. Now, as the linguistic complexity of the NLP task at hand increases, the cost and labor involved with the annotation task increases. Consider the task of syntactic parsing where the grammatical structure of sentence needs to be automatically processed by the machine. Large treebank projects with syntactic parse annotation have been carried out. A syntactic treebank is a large corpus of parsed text with annotation of the syntactic structure of a sentence. Developing a treebank requires a large data (typically thousands of sentences) and a dedicated group of annotators who have to be trained to parse the sentence following a chosen annotation scheme. Annotation scheme could be based on the kind of linguistic framework adopted for the analysis of sentences. For instance, Indian languages are annotated for dependency analysis in the Computational Paninian Grammar (CPG) framework.

In this way, instead of engineering the grammars of the yesteryears by hand, large grammars could be derived automatically from treebanks. Similarly people build treebanks for semantic role labeling, discourse analysis etc. In statistical machine translation systems, parallel corpus is used to automatically identify how phrases or expressions from one language translate to another language. Current-ly, for syntactic parsers, the data are sets of sentences annotated with syntactic trees or dependency graphs, the largest of which are currently around 1M words in size in English. SMT systems require a large amount of parallel text for training. The parallel text is usually created by human translators, of which the largest publicly available set contains approximately 200M words. But still there are issues to be fixed despite the large training data, computational power and statistical techniques.

Morphology

Given the basic design of human spoken language, the levels of phonology, syntax, semantics and pragmatics are arguably unavoidable. They needn't look exactly the way that they do, perhaps, but there has to be something to do the work of cach of these levels. But morphology is basically gratuitous, as well as complex and irregular: anything that a language does with morphology, it usually can also do more straightforwardly with syntax; and there is always some other language that does the same thing with syntax. For instance, English morphology inflects nouns to specify plurality: thus dogs means "more than one dog". This inflection lets us be specific, in a compact way, about the distinction between one and more-than-one. Of course, we could always say the same thing in a more elaborated way, using the resources of syntax rather than morphology: more than one dog. If we want to be vague, we have to be long winded: one or more dogs.

Modern Standard Chinese (also known as "Mandarin" or "Putonghua") makes exactly the opposite choice: there is no morphological marking for plurality, so we can be succinctly vague about whether we mean one or more of something, while we need to be more long-winded if we want to be specific. Thus (in Pinyin orthography with tone numbers after each syllable):

na4er5	you3	gou3
there	have	dog
"there's a dog or dogs there."		

na4er5	you3	ji3	zhi1	gou3
there	have	several	CLASSIFIER	dog
"there's dogs there"				

As an example of another kind of morphological packaging, English can make iconify from icon and -ify, meaning "make into an icon." Perhaps it's nice to have a single word for it, but we could always have said "make into an icon." And many languages lack any general way to turn a noun X into a verb meaning "to make into (an) X", and so must use the longer-winded mode of expression. Indeed, the process in English is rather erratic: we say vaporize not *vaporify, and emulsify not *emulsionify, and so on.

In fact, one of the ways that morphology typically differs from syntax is its combinatoric irregularity. Words are mostly combined logically and systematically. So when you exchange money for something you can be said to "buy" it or to "purchase" it, we'd be surprised if (say) groceries, telephones and timepieces could only be "purchased," while clothing, automobiles and pencils could only be "bought," and things denoted by words of one syllable could only be "acquired in exchange for money." Yet irrational combinatoric nonsense of this type happens all the time in morphology. Consider the adjectival forms of the names of countries or regions in English. There are at least a half a dozen different endings and also many variations in how much of the name of the country is retained before the ending is added.

-ese	Bhutanese, Chinese, Guyanese, Japanese, Lebanese, Maltese, Portuguese, Taiwanese
-an	African, Alaskan, American, Angolan, Cuban, Jamaican, Mexican, Nicaraguan
-ian	Argentinian, Armenian, Australian, Brazilian, Canadian, Egyptian, Ethiopian, Iranian, Jordanian, Palestinian, Serbian
-ish	Irish, British, Flemish, Polish, Scottish, Swedish
-i	Afghani, Iraqi, Israeli, Kuwaiti, Pakistani
-?	French, German, Greek

And you can't mix 'n match stems and endings here: *Taiwanian, *Egyptese, and so on just don't work. To make it worse, the word for citizen of X and the general adjectival form meaning associated with locality X are usually but not always the same. Exceptions include Pole/Polish, Swede/Swedish, Scot/Scottish, Greenlandic/Greenlander. And there are some oddities about pluralization: we talk about "the French" and "the Chinese" but "the Greeks" and "the Canadians". The plural forms "the Frenches" and "the Chineses" are not even possible, and the singular forms "the Greek" and "the Canadian" mean something entirely different.

It's worse in some ways than having to memorize a completely different word in every case (like "The Netherlands" and "Dutch"), because there are just enough partial regularities to be confusing. This brings up George W. Bush. For years, there has been a web feature at Slate magazine devoted to "Bushisms", many if not most of them arising from his individual approach to English morphology. Some of the early and famous examples, from the 1999 presidential campaign, focus on the particular case:

- "If the East Timorians decide to revolt, I'm sure I'll have a statement".
- "Keep good relations with the Grecians".
- "Kosovians can move back in".

President Bush, if these quotes are accurate, quite sensibly decided that -ian should be the default ending, after deletion of a final vowel if present. This follows the common model of Brazil::Brazilians and Canada::Canadians, and gives Bush's East Timor::East Timorians, Greece::Grecians and Kosovo::Kosovians, instead of the correct (but unpredictable) forms East Timorese, Greeks and Kosovars. And why not? The President's method is more logical than the way the English language handles it. Despite these derivational anfractuosities, English morphology is simple and regular compared to the morphological systems of many other languages. One question we need to ask ourselves is: why do languages inflict morphology on their users.

What is a Word?

We've started talking blithely about words and morphemes as if it were obvious that these categories exist and that we know them when we see them. This assumption comes naturally to literate speakers of English, because we've learned through reading and writing where white space goes, which defines word boundaries for us; and we soon see many cases where English words have internal parts with separate meanings or grammatical functions, which must be morphemes. In some languages, the application of these terms is even clearer. In languages like Latin, for example, words can usually be "scrambled" into nearly any order in a phrase. "In connected discourse the word most prominent in the speaker's mind comes first, and so on in order of prominence."

Thus the simple two-word sentence facis amice "you act kindly" also occurs as amice facis with essentially the same meaning, but some difference in emphasis. However, the morphemes that make up each of these two words must occur in a fixed order and without anything inserted between them. The word amice combines the stem /amic-/ "loving, friendly, kind" and the adverbial ending /-e/; we can't change the order of these, or put another word in between them. Likewise the verb stem /fac-/ "do, make, act" and the inflectional ending /-is/ (second person singular present tense active) are fixed in their relationship in the word facis, and can't be reordered or separated. Among many others, the modern Slavic languages such as Czech and Russian show a similar contrast between words freely circulating within phrases, and morphemes rigidly arranged within words. In such languages, the basic concepts of word and morpheme are natural and inevitable analytic categories.

In a language like English, where word order is much less free, we can still find evidence of a similar kind for the distinction between morphemes and words. For example, between two words we can usually insert some other words (without changing the basic meaning and relationship of the originals), while between two morphemes we usually can't. Thus in the phrase "she has arrived", we treat she and has as separate words, while the /-ed/ ending of arrived is treated as part of a larger word. In accordance with this, we can introduce other material into the white space between the words: "she apparently has already arrived." But there is no way to put anything at all in between /arrive/ and /-ed/. And there are other forms of the sentence in which the word order is different "has she arrived?"; "arrived, has she?" but no form in which the morphemes in arrived are re-ordered.

Tests of this kind don't entirely agree with the conventions of English writing. For example, we can't really stick other words in the middle of compound words like swim team and picture frame, at least not while maintaining the meanings and relationships of the words we started with. In this sense they are not very different from the morphemes in complex words like re+calibrate or consumer+ism, which we write "solid", i.e. without spaces. A recent (and controversial) official spelling reform of German make changes in both directions splitting some compounds orthographically while merging others: old radfahren became new Rad fahren, but old Samstag morgen became new Samstag-morgen.

As this change emphasizes, the question of whether a morpheme sequence is written "solid" is largely a matter of orthographic convention, and in any case may be variable even in a particular writing system. English speakers feel that many noun-noun compounds are words, even though they clearly contain other words, and may often be written with a space or a hyphen between them: "sparkplug", "shot glass". These are common combinations with a meaning that is not entirely predictable from the meanings of their parts, and therefore they can be found as entries in most English dictionaries. But where should we draw the line? are all noun compounds to be considered words, including those where compounds are compounded? What about (say) government tobacco price support program? In ordinary usage, we'd be more inclined to call this a phrase, though it is technically correct to call it a "compound noun" and thus in some sense a single though complex word. Of course, in German, the corresponding compound would probably be written solid, making its "wordhood" plainer.

There are a number of interesting theories out there about why morphology exists, and why it has the properties that it does. If these theories turn out to be correct, then maybe linguistics will be as lucky with the complexities of morphology as physics was with "Greek alphabet soup" of elementary particles discovered in the fifties and sixties, which turned out to be complex composites of quarks and leptons, composed according to the elegant laws of quantum chromodynamics.

Universality of the Concepts "Word" and "Morpheme"

Do the concepts of word and morpheme then apply in all languages? The answer is "(probably) yes". Certainly the concept of morpheme, the minimal unit of form and meaning arises naturally in the analysis of every language. The concept of word is trickier. There are at least two troublesome issues: making the distinction between words and phrases, and the status of certain grammatical formatives known as clitics.

Words vs. Phrases

Since words can be made up of several morphemes, and may include several other words, it is easy to find cases where a particular sequence of elements might arguably be considered either a word or a phrase. In some languages, this boundary is even harder to draw. 'Not every language has a kind of unit which behaves in most (not to speak all) respects as does the unit called "word". It is therefore a matter of fiat and not a question of fact whether to apply the word "word" to a type of subunit in the Chinese sentence.' On the other hand, other linguists have argued that the distinction between words and phrases is both definable and useful in Chinese grammar. The Chinese writing system has no tradition of using spaces or other delimiters to mark word boundaries; and in fact the whole issue of how (and whether) to define "words" in Chinese does not seem to have arisen until 1907, although the Chinese grammatical tradition goes back a couple of millennia.

Status of Clitics

In most languages, there is a set of elements whose status as separate words seems ambiguous. Examples in English include the 'd (reduced form of "would"), the infinitival to, and the article a, in I'd like to buy a dog. These forms certainly can't "stand alone as a complete utterance", as some definitions of word would have it. The sound pattern of these "little words" is also usually extremely reduced, in a way that makes them act like part of the words adjacent to them. There isn't any difference in pronunciation between the noun phrase a tack and the verb attack. However, these forms are like separate words in some other ways, especially in terms of how they combine with other words. Members of this class of "little words" are known as clitics. Their peculiar properties can be explained by assuming that they are independent elements at the syntactic level of analysis, but not at the phonological level. In other words, they both are and are not words. Some languages write clitics as separate words, while others write them together with their adjacent "host" words. English writes most clitics separate, but uses the special "apostrophe" separator for some clitics, such as the reduced forms of is, have and would ('s 've 'd), and possessive 's. The possessive 's in English is an instructive example, because we can contrast its behavior with that of the plurals. These two morphemes are pronounced in exactly the same variable way, dependent on the sounds that precede them:

Noun	Noun + s (plural)	Noun + s (possessive)	Pronunciation (both)
thrush	thrushes	thrush's	iz
toy	toys	toy's	z
block	blocks	block's	s

And neither the plural nor the possessive can be used by itself. So from this point of view, the possessive acts like a part of the noun, just as the plural does. However, the plural and possessive behave very differently in some other ways:

- If we add a following modifier to a noun, the possessive follows the modifier, but the plural sticks with the head noun.

	Morpheme stays with head noun	Morpheme follows modifier
Plural	The toys I bought yesterday were on sale.	*The toy I bought yesterdays were on sale.
Possessive	*The toy's I bought yesterday price was special.	The toy I bought yesterday's price was special.

In other words, the plural continues like part of the noun, but the possessive acts like a separate word, which follows the whole phrase containing the noun (even though it is merged in terms of sound with the last word of that noun phrase).

Table: There are lots of nouns with irregular plurals, but none with irregular possessives.

Plural (irregular in these cases)	Possessive (always regular)
oxen	ox's
spectra	spectrum's
mice	mouse's

Actually, English does have few irregular possessives: his, her, my, your, their. But these exceptions prove the rule: these pronominal possessives act like inflections, so that the possessor is always the referent of the pronoun itself, not of some larger phrase that it happens to be at the end of.

So the possessive 's in English is like a word in some ways, and like an inflectional morpheme in some others. This kind of mixed status is commonly found with words that express grammatical functions. It is one of the ways that morphology develops historically. As a historical matter, a clitic is likely to start out as a fully separate word, and then "weaken" so as to merge phonologically with its hosts. In many cases, inflectional affixes may have been clitics at an earlier historical stage, and then lost their syntactic independence. Important distinctions are often difficult to define for cases near the boundary. This is among the reasons that we have lawyers and courts. The relative difficulty of making a distinction is not a strong argument, one way or the other, for the value of that distinction: it's not always easy, for example, to distinguish homicide from other (and less serious) kinds of involvement in someone's death. Despite the difficulties of distinguishing word from phrase on one side and from morpheme on the other, most linguists find the concept of word useful and even essential in analyzing most languages. In the end, we wind up with two definitions of word: the ordinary usage, where that exists (as it does for English or Spanish, and does not for Chinese); and a technical definition, emerging from a particular theory about language structure as applied to a specific language.

Relationship Between Words and Morphemes

What is the relationship between words and morphemes? It's a hierarchical one: A word is made up of one or more morphemes. Most commonly, these morphemes are strung together, or concatenated, in a line. However, it is not uncommon to find non-concatenative morphemes. Thus the Arabic root /ktb/ "write" has (among many other forms):

katab	pefective active
kutib	perfective passive
aktub	imperfective active
uktab	imperfective passive

The three consonants of the root are not simply concatenated with other morphemes meaning things like "imperfective" or "passive", but rather are shuffled among the vowels and syllable positions that define the various forms. Still, a given word is still made up of a set of morphemes, it's just that the set is not combined by simple concatenation in all cases. Simpler examples of non-concatenative morphology include infixes, like the insertion of emphatic words in English cases like "un-frigging-believable", or Tagalog.

bili	'buy'	binili	'bought'
basa	'read'	binasa	'read' (past)
sulat	'write'	sinulat	'wrote'

Categories and Subcategories of Words and Morphemes

The different types of words are variously called parts of speech, word classes, or lexical categories. The Cambridge Encyclopedia of Language gives this list of 8 for English:

- Noun
- Pronoun
- Verb
- Adjective
- Adverb
- Conjunction
- Preposition
- Interjection

This set might be further subdivided. Most of the increase (from 8 to 36) is by subdivision (e.g. "noun" divided into "singular common noun," "plural common noun," "singular proper noun," "plural proper noun," etc., but there are a few extra odds and ends, such as "cardinal number."

Other descriptions of English have used slightly different ways of dividing the pie, but it is generally easy to see how one scheme translates into another. Looking across languages, we can see somewhat greater differences. For instance, some languages don't really distinguish between verbs and adjectives. In such languages, we can think of adjectives as a kind of verb: "the grass greens," rather than "the grass is green." Other differences reflect different structural choices. For instance, English words like in, on, under, with are called prepositions, and this name makes sense given that they precede the noun phrase they introduce: with a stick. In many languages, the words that correspond to English prepositions follow their noun phrase rather than preceding it, and are thus more properly called postpositions, as in the following Hindi example:

- Ram cari-se kutte-ko mara.
- Ram stick-with dog hit.
- "Ram hit the dog with an stick."

Types of Morphemes

- Bound Morphemes: Cannot occur on their own, e.g. de- in detoxify, -tion in creation, -s in dogs, cran- in cranberry.
- Free Morphemes: Can occur as separate words, e.g. car, yes.

In a morphologically complex word, a word composed of more than one morpheme, one constituent may be considered as the basic one, the core of the form, with the others treated as being added on. The basic or core morpheme in such cases is referred to as the stem, root, or base, while the add-ons are affixes. Affixes that precede the stem are of course prefixes, while those that follow the stem are suffixes. Thus in rearranged, re- is a prefix, arrange is a stem, and -d is a suffix. Morphemes can also be infixes, which are inserted within another form. English doesn't really have any infixes, except perhaps for certain expletives in expressions like un-effing-believable or Kalama-effing-zoo.

Prefixes and suffixes are almost always bound, but what about the stems? Are they always free? In English, some stems that occur with negative prefixes are not free, such as -kempt and -sheveled. Bad jokes about some of these missing bound morphemes have become so frequent that they may re-enter common usage. Morphemes can also be divided into the two categories of content and function morphemes, a distinction that is conceptually distinct from the free-bound distinction but that partially overlaps with it in practice.

The idea behind this distinction is that some morphemes express some general sort of referential or informational content, in a way that is as independent as possible of the grammatical system of a particular language, while other morphemes are heavily tied to a grammatical function, expressing syntactic relationships between units in a sentence, or obligatorily-marked categories such as number or tense. Thus (the stems of) nouns, verbs, adjectives are typically content morphemes: "throw," "green," "Kim," and "sand" are all English content morphemes. Content morphemes are also often called open-class morphemes, because they belong to categories that are open to the invention of arbitrary new items. People are always making up or borrowing new morphemes in these categories: "smurf," "nuke," "byte," "grok."

By contrast, prepositions ("to", "by"), articles ("the", "a"), pronouns ("she", "his"), and conjunctions are typically function morphemes, since they either serve to tie elements together grammatically ("hit by a truck," "Kim and Leslie," "Lee saw his dog"), or express obligatory morphological features like definiteness ("she found a table" or "she found the table" but not "*she found table"). Function morphemes are also called "closed-class" morphemes, because they belong to categories that are essentially closed to invention or borrowing it is very difficult to add a new preposition, article or pronoun. For years, some people have tried to introduce non-gendered pronouns into English, for instance "sie" (meaning either "he" or "she", but not "it"). This is much harder to do than to get people to adopt a new noun or verb.

Try making up a new article. For instance, we could try to borrow from the Manding languages an article (written "le") that means something like "I'm focusing on this phrase as opposed to anything else I could have mentioned." We'll just slip in this new article after the definite or indefinite "the" or "a" that's where it goes in Manding, though the rest of the order is completely different. Thus we would say "Kim bought an apple at the-le fruit stand," meaning "it's the fruit stand (as opposed to anyplace else) where Kim bought an apple;" or "Kim bought an-le apple at the fruit stand," meaning "it's an apple (as opposed to any other kind of fruit) that Kim bought at the fruit stand."

This is a perfectly sensible kind of morpheme to have. Millions of West Africans use it every day. However, the chances of persuading the rest of the English-speaking community to adopt it are negligible. In some ways the open/closed terminology is clearer than content/function, since obviously function morphemes also always have some content. The concept of the morpheme does not directly map onto the units of sound that represent morphemes in speech. To do this, linguists developed the concept of the allomorph. Here is the definition given:

- Allomorphs: Non-distinctive realizations of a particular morpheme that have the same function and are phonetically similar. For example, the English plural morpheme can appear as [s] as in cats, [z] as in dogs, or ['z] as in churches. Each of these three pronunciations is said to be an allomorph of the same morpheme.

Inflectional vs. Derivational Morphology

Another common distinction is the one between derivational and inflectional affixes. Derivational morphemes makes new words from old ones. Thus creation is formed from create by adding a morpheme that makes nouns out of (some) verbs. Derivational morphemes generally:

- Change the part of speech or the basic meaning of a word. Thus -ment added to a verb forms a noun (judg-ment). Re-activate means "activate again".

- Are not required by syntactic relations outside the word. Thus un-kind combines un- and kind into a single new word, but has no particular syntactic connections outside the word we can say he is unkind or he is kind or they are unkind or they are kind, depending on what we mean.

- Are often not productive or regular in form or meaning derivational morphemes can be selective about what they'll combine with, and may also have erratic effects on meaning. Thus the suffix -hood occurs with just a few nouns such as brother, neighbor, and knight, but not with most others. E.g., *friendhood, *daughterhood, or *candlehood. Furthermore "brotherhood" can mean "the state or relationship of being brothers," but "neighborhood" cannot mean "the state or relationship of being neighbors." note however that some derivational affixes are quite regular in form and meaning, e.g. -ism.
- Typically occur "inside" any inflectional affixes. Thus in governments, -ment, a derivational suffix, precedes -s, an inflectional suffix.
- In english, may appear either as prefixes or suffixes: pre-arrange, arrange-ment.

Inflectional morphemes vary (or "inflect") the form of words in order to express the grammatical features that a given language chooses, such as singular/plural or past/present tense. Thus Boy and boys, for example, are two different forms of the "same" word. In English, we must choose the singular form or the plural form; if we choose the basic form with no affix, we have chosen the singular. Inflectional Morphemes generally:

- Do not change basic syntactic category: Thus big, bigg-er, bigg-est are all adjectives.
- Express grammatically-required features or indicate relations between different words in the sentence. Thus in lee love-s kim, -s marks the 3rd person singular present form of the verb, and also relates it to the 3rd singular subject lee.
- Occur outside any derivational morphemes. Thus in ration-al-iz-ation-s the final -s is inflectional, and appears at the very end of the word, outside the derivational morphemes -al, -iz, -ation.
- In english, are suffixes only.

Table: Some examples of English derivational and inflectional morphemes.

derivational	inflectional
-ation	-s Plural
-ize	-ed Past
-ic	-ing Progressive
-y	-er Comparative
-ous	-est Superlative

Table: Properties of some derivational affixes in English.

-ation	is added to a verb	to give a noun
	finalize confirm	finalization confirmation

un-	is added to a verb	to give a verb
	Tie wind	untie unwind
un-	is added to an adjective	to give an adjective
	happy wise	unhappy unwise
-al	is added to a noun	to give an adjective
	Institution universe	Institutional universal
-ize	is added to an adjective	to give a verb
	concrete solar	concretize solarize

Most morphemes are neither derivational nor inflectional. For instance, the English morphemes Melissa, twist, tele-, and ouch. Also, most linguists feel that the inflectional/derivational distinction is not a fundamental or foundational question at all, but just a sometimes-useful piece of terminology whose definitions involve a somewhat complex combination of more basic properties. Therefore we will not be surprised to find cases for which the application of the distinction is unclear. For example, the English suffix -ing has several uses that are arguably on the borderline between inflection and derivation (along with other uses that are not). One very regular use of -ing is to indicate progressive aspect in verbs, following forms of "to be": She is going; he will be leaving; they had been asking. This use is generally considered an inflectional suffix, part of the system for marking tense and aspect in English verbs.

Another, closely related use is to make present participles of verbs, which are used like adjectives: Falling water; stinking mess; glowing embers. According to the rule that inflection doesn't change the lexical category, this should be a form of morphological derivation, since it changes verbs to adjectives. But in fact it is probably the same process, at least historically as is involved in marking progressive aspect on verbs, since "being in the process of doing X" is one of the natural meanings of the adjectival form X-ing.

There is another, regular use of -ing to make verbal nouns: Flying can be dangerous; losing is painful. The -ing forms in these cases are often called gerunds. By the "changes lexical categories" rule, this should also be a derivational affix, since it turns a verb into a noun. However, many people feel that such cases are determined by grammatical context, so that a phrase like Kim peeking around the corner surprised me actually is related to, or derived from, a tenseless form of the sentence Kim peeked around the corner. On this view, the affix -ing is a kind of inflection, since it creates a form of the verb appropriate for a particular grammatical situation, rather than making a new, independent word. Thus the decision about whether -ing is an inflection in this case depends on your analysis of the syntactic relationships involved. It's for reasons like this that the distinction between inflectional and derivational affixes is just a sometimes-convenient descriptive one, and not a basic distinction in theory.

What is the Meaning of an Affix?

The meanings of derivational affixes are sometimes clear, but often are obscured by changes that occur over time. The following two sets of examples show that the prefix un- is easily interpreted as "not" when applied to adjectives, and as a reversing action when applied to verbs, but the prefix con- is more opaque.

un-	untie
	unshackle
	unharness
	unhappy
	untimely
	unthinkable
	unmentionable

con-	constitution
	confess
	connect
	contract
	contend
	conspire
	complete

Are Derivational Affixes Sensitive to the Historical Source of the Roots they Attach to?

Although English is a Germanic language, and most of its basic vocabulary derives from Old English, there is also a sizeable vocabulary that derives from Romance (Latin and French). Some English affixes, such as re-, attach freely to vocabulary from both sources. Other affixes, such as "-ation", are more limited.

Root	tie	consider
	free form	free form
	Germanic root	Latinate root
Source	Old English tygan, "to tie"	Latin considerare, "to examine"
Prefix	retie	reconsider
Suffix	reties	reconsiders
	retying	reconsideration
	retyings	reconsiderations

The suffix -ize, which some prescriptivists object to in words like hospitalize, has a long and venerable history. The suffix -ize comes originally from the Greek -izo. Many words ending with this suffix passed from Ecclesiastical Greek into Latin, where, by the fourth century, they had become established as verbs with the ending -izare, such as barbarizare, catechizare, christianizare. In Old French we find many such verbs, belonging primarily to the ecclesistical sphere: baptiser, canoniser, exorciser.

The first -ize words to be found in English are loans with both a French and Latin pattern such as baptize, catechize, and organize. Towards the end of the 16th century, however, we come across many new formations in English, such as bastardize, equalize, popularize, and womanize. The formal and semantic patterns were the same as those from the borrowed French and Latin forms, but owing to the renewed study of Greek, the educated had become more familiar with its vocabulary and used the patterns of Old Greek word formation freely. Between 1580 and 1700, the disciplines of literature, medicine, natural science and theology introduced a great deal of new terminology into the language. Some of the terms still in use today include criticize, fertilize, humanize, naturalize, satirize, sterilize, and symbolize. The growth of science contributed vast numbers of -ize formations through the 19th century and into the 20th. The -ize words collected by students in in this class nine years ago show that -ize is almost entirely restricted to Romance vocabulary, the only exceptions we found being womanize and winterize. Even though most contemporary English speakers are not consciously aware of which words in their vocabulary are from which source, they have respected this distinction in coining new words.

Constituent Structure of Words

The constituent morphemes of a word can be organized into a branching or hierarchical structure, sometimes called a tree structure. Consider the word unusable. It contains three morphemes:

- Prefix "un-".
- Verb stem "use".
- Suffix "-able".

What is the structure? Is it first "use" + "-able" to make "usable", then combined with "un-" to make "unusable"? or is it first "un-" + "use" to make "unuse", then combined with "-able" to make "unusable"? Since "unuse" doesn't exist in English, while "usable" does, we prefer the first structure, which corresponds to the tree shown below:

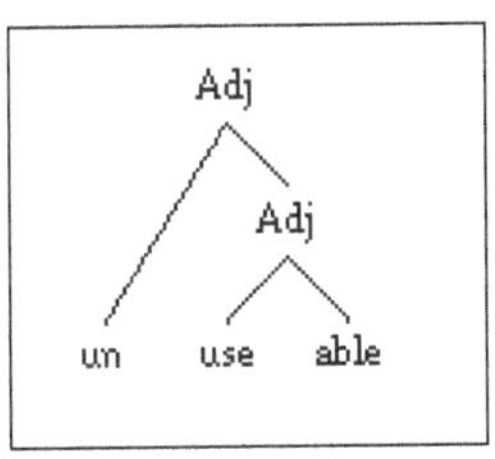

This analysis is supported by the general behavior of these affixes. There is a prefix "un-" that attaches to adjectives to make adjectives with a negative meaning ("unhurt", "untrue", "unhandy", etc.). And there is a suffix "-able" that attaches to verbs and forms adjectives ("believable", "fixable", "readable"). There is no way to combine a prefix "un-" directly with the verb "use", so the other logically-possible structure won't work. Now let's consider the word "unlockable". This also consists of three morphemes:

- Prefix "un-".
- Verb stem "lock".
- Suffix "-able".

This time, though, a little thought shows us that there are two different meanings for this word: one corresponding to the left-hand figure, meaning "not lockable," and a second one corresponding to the right-hand figure, meaning "able to be unlocked." In fact, un- can indeed attach to (some) verbs: untie, unbutton, uncover, uncage, unwrap. The verbs that permit prefixation with un- are those that effect a change in state in some object, the form with un- denoting the undoing of that change.

This lets us account for the two senses of "unlockable". We can combine the suffix -able with the verb lock to form an adjective lockable, and then combine the prefix un- with lockable to make a new adjective unlockable, meaning "not able to be locked". Or we can combine the prefix un- with the verb lock to form a new verb unlock, and the com-bine the suffix -able with unlock to form an adjective unlockable, meaning "able to be unlocked". By making explicit the different possible hierarchies for a single word, we can better understand why its meaning might be ambiguous.

Morphology FAQ

These questions and answers are based on some patterns of error observed.

Example: Can a word = a morpheme?

Solution: Yes, at least in the sense that a word may contain exactly one morpheme:

Word (=Morpheme)	Word Class
car	noun
thank	verb
true	adjective
succotash	noun
gosh	interjection
under	preposition
she	pronoun
so	conjunction
often	adverb

Example: Are there morphemes that are not words?

Solution: Yes, none of the following morphemes is a word:

Morpheme	Category
un-	prefix
dis-	prefix
-ness	suffix
-s	suffix
kempt (as in unkempt)	bound morpheme

Example: Can a word = a syllable?

Solution: Yes, at least in the sense that a word may consist of exactly one syllable:

Word	Word Class
car	noun
work	verb
in	preposition
whoops	interjection

Example: Are there morphemes that are not syllables?

Solution: Yes, some of the following morphemes consist of more than one syllable; some of them are less than a syllable:

Morpheme	Word Class
under	preposition (> syll.)
spider	noun (> syll.)
-s	'plural' (< syll.)

Example: Are there syllables that are not morphemes?

Solution: Yes, many syllables are "less" than morphemes. Just because you can break a word into two or more syllables does not mean it must consist of more than one morpheme.

Word	Syllables	Comments
kayak	(ka.yak)	neither ka nor yak is a morpheme
broccoli	(bro.ko.li) or (brok.li)	neither bro nor brok nor ko nor li is a morpheme
angle	(ang.gle)	neither ang nor gle is a morpheme
jungle	(jung.gle)	neither jung nor gle is a morpheme

So, there is no necessary relationship between syllables, morphemes, and words. Each is an independent unit of structure.

Example: What are the major differences between derivational and inflectional affixes?

Solution: First, it's worth saying that most linguists today consider this distinction as a piece of convenient descriptive terminology, without any fundamental theoretical status. Then we can point to the basic meanings of the terms: derivational affixes "derive" new words from old ones, while inflectional affixes "inflect" words for certain grammatical or semantic properties.

	derivational	inflectional
position	closer to stem	further from stem
addable on to?	yes	not in English
meaning?	(often) unpredictable	predictable
changes word class?	maybe	no

Example: Are clitics inflectional or derivational morphemes?

Solution: The answer would depend on your definitions and as we explained earlier, the categories of "inflection" and "derivation" are descriptive terms that really don't have a strong theoretical basis. However, based on comparison to typical examples of inflectional and derivational affixes, the answer seems to be "neither", in that clitics are not really lexical affixes at all.

Morphological Processing

Morphological processing, in general, involves automatic analysis of components of words according to the grammar used in a language. Technically, it refers to the process of analysing internal structures in words by performing some screening operations on them to find out their components, pattern of their composition as well as their function in formation of words in language. Within this scheme, words are considered as sets of surface constructions where morphemes are used as building blocks to generate the final forms of words following some Word Formation Rules (WFRs) applicable within a language. Characteristically, it differs from Part-of-speech (POS) tagging in the sense that while POS tagging aims at assigning explicit lexical POS tags to words, morphological processing tries to retrieve all grammatical information of morphemes used in a word to understand their functional role in formation of the word.

From computational point of view, the basic method of morphological processing involves automatic extraction of grammatical, syntactic, and semantic information of words to be used at higher levels of text processing. It aims at studying the functional role of morphemes, the minimum meaningful indivisible units of a language. There are several ways for morphological processing where the primary task is to extract grammatical, syntactic and semantic information from words by using expanded lexicon as a separate part of a grammar. For achieving this goal it is necessary to analyse systematically the surface structures words and their lexical, syntactic, morphophonemic, and semantic properties embedded within their structures.

Early Works on Morphological Processing

There exist several morphological processing systems for English and other languages. Among these, the earliest proposed method takes into account the phonological aspects of words in processing. It introduces an approach of concatenation at morpheme level because of which it is regarded as a Two Level Morphological Analysis Scheme, which is widely known as the KIMMO system. Researchers advanced the KIMMO system when they applied it for processing, describing, and annotating English words. This was further modified and augmented togenerate more robust outputs in processing of Finnish words, and was effectively adopted and fruitfully implemented to develop efficient algorithm for automatic morphological processing of French words.

The basic operation involved in processing of words used by KIMMO system is as follows: it follows a special kind of phonological system based on 'finite state machinery (automata)', which is efficient to skim through the morphological components used for formation of words. Within this system, the characters (i.e. letters) are realised to have two levels: surface level and lexical level. For proper representation, each character belonging to its surface level is linked with more than one symbol at lexical level. Thus, for instance, the character <t> converts into <c> at lexical level if it occurs before <i>. It remains <t> at surface level if it does not occur before <i> (i.e., t+i = ci, but t+u = tu). When the system starts to analyse words, it takes all these phonological rules into consideration with due emphasis on the context of phonological change of characters, which eventually determines the link between the surface level and the lexical of words. The structure in which this information is encoded for future implementation in the system is known as 'finite state transducer', an important part of 'finite state machinery'.

After the introduction of language corpora in electronic form, various new approaches and methods are developed and used within a very short span of time to process words morphologically. Here, emphasis is paid on initial manual analysis of words found in corpora and subsequent use of the information as a necessary knowledge base in the development of automatic processor. By using information obtained from analysis of words from corpora, some novel systems for morphological processing are designed, developed and implemented. The robustness and quality of these systems are far better than the earlier systems as these systems are based on exhaustive knowledge base acquired from empirical analysis of words. Language corpora have worked as basic resources of information regarding morphological structure of words as well as test beds for evaluation and authentication of newly developed systems.

Issues in Morphological Processing

From purely technical point of view automatic morphological processing of words is concerned with study of the internal morphemic structure of words. It is a stage where the structure, type, grammatical property, formation, and functional roles of morphemes are empirically analysed. For inflectional languages, the process has the capability to reduce lexical ambiguity by increasing the compactness in lexical representation. Initial analysis of large number of words (both inflected and non-inflected) can show that two types of morphemes are used to construct words:

- Roots and stems, which have independent use with a meaning in texts.
- Affixes, which are tagged with roots and stems for providing new linguistic perspectives to the existing words.

After structural analysis of words collected from corpora it is found that words are generally formed as a result of:

- Conjoining between a stem and an affix.
- Conjoining between an affix and a stem.
- Conjoining of two or more affixes with stems.
- Conjoining between two stems to produce a compound stem.
- Some acceptable combinations of conjoining between a stem and an affix conjoining of two or more affixes with stems.

In general, each constituent morpheme has to contribute towards the overall linguistic property of a word. Based on this criterion, morphemes are partitioned into several subclasses, which discharge specific functions in formation of words. In case of word formation, morphemes are usually governed by the following two rules:

- Rules of morphosyntax, which works to restrict the process of random conjoining among the various morpheme subclasses.
- Rules of generative morphology, which are concerned with the morphophonemic or morpho-graphemic restructuring of symbols at the boundaries of two conjoining morphemes.

The WFRs that generate final forms of words with the help of constituent morphemes are mostly concatenative in nature. No morpheme is allowed to get embedded within other morphemes during word formation. However, due to the affect of spelling rules, forms of some words are not the result of simple concatenation of constituent morphemes. Since, spelling rules for words are quite complex in nature, sometimes, one spelling rule may affect (or be affected by) the decision of rules that may operate at some other morpheme boundaries. Therefore, the major problem of processing of words in a language is proper detection of morphemic boundaries, which are not as explicit as the boundary that exists between words in sentence. At certain context, lexical projection of a word may be derived as a union of projections of constituent morphemes obtained as results of integrated morphosyntactic processing. Therefore, for extracting root and suffix part from inflected words, we should have good command over a language. Generally, a linguist working on his native language can have better results than a non-native user, since in many occasions, the intuitive knowledge of a linguist helps to find out the right root and suffix parts from inflected words, which may be beyond the grasp of a non-native user.

Final determination of POS of a word depends on the role it plays in a sentence. So, by defining syntactic and semantic role of a word in a sentence, we can identify if a word is used as a finite verb or noun in a sentence. But identification of POS of a word, when it is isolated from the contexts of its use is based not on its function but on its morphemic identity. Thus, determination of possible POS that a word can take depends on its structure that carries various grammatical properties, such as, aspect, case, tense, person, gender, number, particle, suffix, and others.

For instance, in case of morphological processing, a finite verb is nothing more than an isolated word where a root is systematically followed by an aspect marker, auxiliary marker, tense marker, person marker, and particle all arranged grammatically following the sequence of their usage permitted in a language.

Methods of Information Storage

Before the task of morphological processing of words begins, it is necessary to have an electronic dictionary for the generation of a lexical database, which will be required at subsequent stages of word processing. The electronic dictionary (ED-I) should have two parts: root part, and suffix part. To distinguish these from standard electronic dictionaries, these are named as the followings:

- Root Lexicon (RL).
- Suffix Lexicon (SL).

While the RL contains in normal and allomorphic variants verb roots, nouns stems, pronoun bases, adjective stems, adverb stems, postpositions, and indeclinable in lemmatised form, the SL contains the total list of suffix with all possible allomorphic variations available in a language.

Table: Proposed structure of the ED-I with RL and SL.

Electronic Dictionary I (ED-I)			
Root Lexicon (RL)		Suffix Lexicon (SL)	
RL_01 (NN)	Nominal stem	SL_01 (NN)	Nominal suffix
RL_02 (PN)	Pronominal base	SL_02 (PN)	Pronominal suffix
RL_03 (FV)	Verbal root	SL_03 (FV)	Verbal suffix

RL_04 (ADJ)	Adjectival stem	SL_04 (ADJ)	Adjectival suffix
RL_05 (ADV)	Adverbial stem	SL_05 (ADV)	Adverbial suffix
RL_06 (IND)	Indeclinable		-
RL_07 (PP)	Postposition		-

At the initial training phase, both RL and SL are compiled manually in a sequential order following the stages stated below:

- All types of words (both inflected and non-inflected forms) are compiled from corpora and sorted in alphabetical order to generate a list of lexemes (lexicon) where all the repetitive forms are allowed to have only a single entry (tokenization).
- All sorted out words are classified based on their part-of-speech, information of which is collected from regular standard dictionaries which assign POS to words.
- Classified words are further sub-divided into two broad groups: inflected and non-inflected.
- All non-inflected words are put in a list of particular POS they belong to (e.g., nouns are sent to RL1).
- Inflected words are first broken into root and suffix part. While roots (and stems) are distributed within RL based on their primary POS, suffixes are further classified and stored within respective list of SL based on their affiliation to particular POS.
- Some representative samples of all types of inflected word belonging to different POS are taken for initial manual analysis to find out the rules of grammatical mapping underlying their surface forms.
- Scheme is made ready to identify relevant suffix parts (e.g., number, person, tense, aspect, honorific, etc.) that are required by particular root or stem to generate valid surface forms.
- Identified grammatical mapping rules are converted into algorithms for designing a system that can identify a word and process it rightly.

Both the RL and the SL are sub-divided into several parts based on the POS of roots and stems. For instance, the RL has seven subparts each one of which is entitled to preserve roots, stems, and bases of words belonging to different POS. Thus, while RL_01 preserves nominal stems, RL_02 stores pronominal bases, RL_03 stores verb roots, RL_04 collects adjectival stems, RL_05 preserves adverbial stems, RL_06 lists up all indeclinable forms and RL_07 lists up all postpositions collected from corpora. On the other hand, the SL has only five subparts of which SL_01 stores nominal suffixes,

SL_02 stores pronominal suffixes, SL_03 stores verbal suffixes, SL_04 preserves adjectival suffixes, and SL_05 lists up all adverbial suffixes collected from analysis of sample inflected words gathered in corpora.

During the initial training period, both the RL and SL are regularly augmented and grammatical mapping algorithms are modified to deal with new words, which are found in corpora but not available in dictionaries. In essence, generation of a dictionary made differently with list of roots and suffixes of various types along with large sets of rules for grammatical mapping is an indispensable part for designing a morphological processing system. The following schema shows how introductory preparations are made for morphological processing of words in a language.

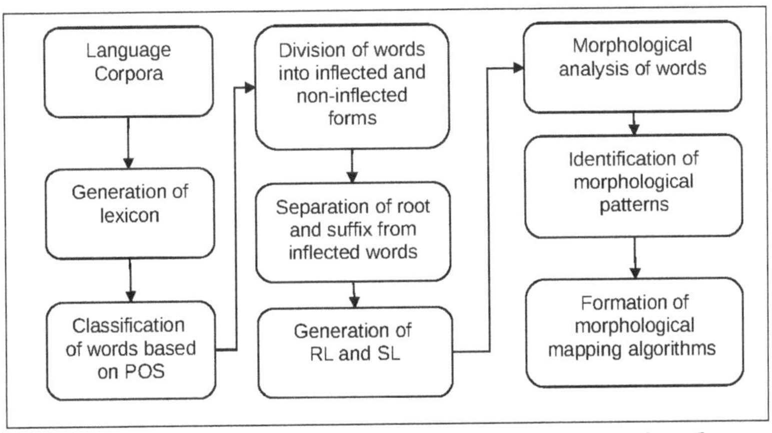

Introductory preparation for morphological processing of words.

The systematised information described above is not generally found within the dictionaries available in the market. What makes it relevant in the present context is its elaborate and formal analysis of morphological structure of words, the information of which is essential for designing a system for automatic morphological processing of words. As a result, algorithm, with the help of root and suffix lists and rules of grammatical mapping, is able to process words rightly to produce a complete output with all the relevant morphological information.

After compilation of information from analysis of words, the data is stored in uniformed manner for processing of words. Thus, in case of nouns, prefixes are stored in NPG (Noun Prefix Group), stems are stored in NRG (Noun Root Group), suffixes are stored in NSG (Noun Suffix Group), and case markers are stored in NCG (Noun Case Group) in a sequential linear order to generate valid outputs. Similarly, in case of pronouns, pronominal roots are stored in PRG (Pronominal Root Group), suffixes are stored in PSG (Pronominal Suffix Group) and case markers are stored in PCG (Pronominal Case Group). Since pronouns are not tagged with prefix, it does not have any prefix group.

In case of adjectives, adjectival prefixes are stored in APG (Adjective Prefix Group), adjectival roots are stored in ARG (Adjective Root Group), and adjectival suffixes are stored in ASG (Adjective Suffix Group). Since adjectives are never tagged with case markers, this particular group is absent here. In case of verbs (both finite and non-finite), verb roots are stored in VRG (Verb Root Group) while verbal suffixes are stored in VSG (Verb Suffix Group). Similarly, adverbial roots are stored in AVRG (Adverb Root Group), while adverbial suffixes are stored in AVSG (Adverb Suffix Group). This method felicitates valid root-suffix mapping for generation of surface words belonging to various POS. The following diagram shows how [(prefix) + root + (suffix) + (case)] information of inflected words belonging to different POS are preserved in ED-I.

Table: Storage of information of (prefix)-root-(suffix)-(case) for morphological processing.

Prefix	+	Root	+	Suffix	+	Case	→	Output
NPG	+	NRG	+	NSG	+	NCG	→	Surface Form
(1...n)		(1...n)		(1...n)		(1...n)		
-	+	PRG (1...n)	+	PSG (1....n)	+	PCG (1...n)	→	Surface Form
APG (1...n)	+	ARG (1...n)	+	ASG (1....n)	+	+	→	Surface Form
-	+	VRG (1....n)	+	VSG (1....n)	+	-	→	Surface Form
-	+	AVRG (1....n)	+	AVSG (1....n)	+	-	→	Surface Form

The process of data storage is further substantiated with electronic dictionary (ED-II) that contains list of words, compounds, reduplicated words collected from corpora and dictionaries. It is modelled after regular dictionaries available so that the regular features of words (e.g., etymology, part-of-speech, meaning, synonyms, usage, etc.) normally available in standard dictionaries are preserved in ED-II. In addition, possible variations of spelling of words are faithfully reproduced in it so that a particular word, due to spelling variation, is not left out or identified as a different one. However, it has no place for inflected compounds and reduplicated forms, since it is possible to generate all these forms by using the same algorithm applied for inflected single words.

Methods of Processing

Processing Non-Inflected Words

Given a sentence, search for a word begins from left-hand direction of the sentence, and it proceeds gradually towards the right-hand terminal end. On its way, the system first encounters a string made of some characters, proceeds further until it finds a blank space at the end of that string, and once found, it stops there considering the string as a single word unit. At this stage the system does not know if the word string is an inflected one or not. Once the word is found, the system tries to find out an exact match of the string from the data stored in RL. If a match is found in RL the word is then identified and all the information relating to the word is produced from ED-II. In case, the word is not found in RL, the system assumes that the word is an inflected one or not entered in RL due to paucity of corpus data. In case of non-inflected words, since these are not passed through further verification, these are first matched in the RL and then processed based on the information available in ED-II.

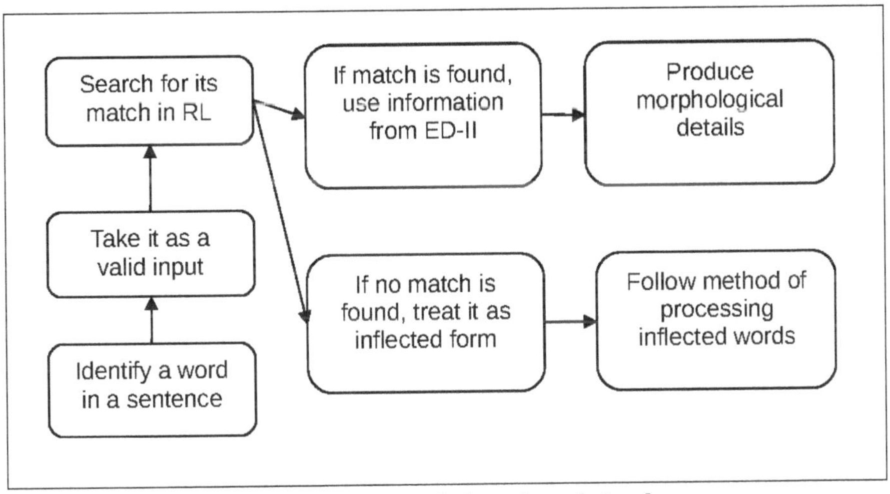

Schema for processing non-inflected words in a language.

Following the schema of processing, the system first encounters a word in sentence, searches for its match in RL, and if a match is found, it immediately goes to ED-II to extract all relevant information for display. If a valid match is not found, it considers the word as an inflected one and initiates the process applicable for inflected words. Thus the system processes all non-inflected words, determines their lexical classes, and tags them accordingly with particular POS. If the system fails, it may be assumed that either the word is not in RL or there is error in spelling of the word.

Processing Inflected Words

Most of the inflected words found in a language belong to noun, pronoun, adjective, finite verb, non-finite verb, and adverb. However, words belonging to each lexical class follow a more or less uniform manner for using inflections due to which morphological processing is a regular and systematic operation for most of the inflected words. The following diagram shows how inflected words are processed by using information obtained from RL and SL.

In general, the method of processing inflected words includes identification of inflected words in a sentence, separation of root and suffix parts, finding out valid root part from RL and suffix part from SL, understanding grammatical agreement between the two, and generation of the processing results. For this, the system has to follow the following steps in a sequential order. After the first step of searching out an inflected word in a sentence is over, the system breaks an inflected word into root part and suffix part by applying information obtained from respective RL and SL. Then the system obtains all relevant morphological and grammatical information from ED-II, and presents these in a separate table.

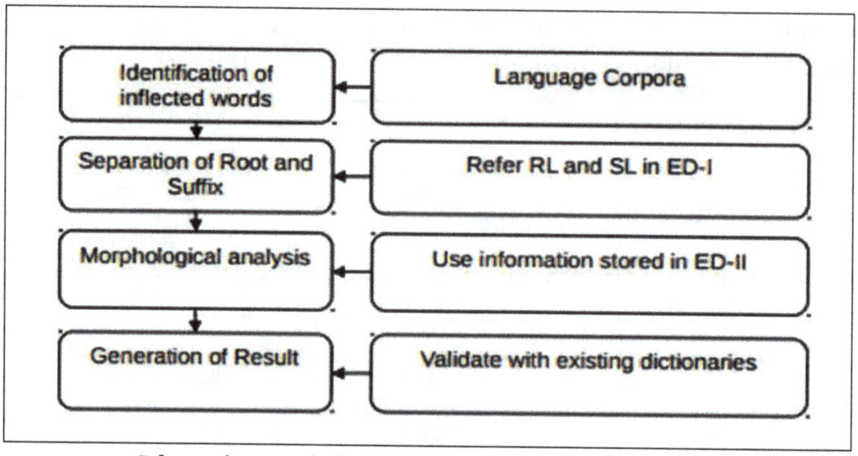

Schema for morphological processing of inflected words.

The most important as well as the most complicated part of the whole process is the Suffix Stripping that involves separation of root and suffix parts from an inflected word. For this, the best way is to apply a trial and error method based on heuristics, the success of which is primarily grounded on the quality of robustness of a system. In this process, the system proceeds from left to right-hand direction following the sequence of characters used within a surface word string. With each character it will form a subset and verify if this subset matches with any of the strings stored within RL. It goes on adding one more character (= C) at each time ($[C_{1+1+1+} \dots C_n]\#$) until it finds out a suitable match in the following way:

First set : $[C_1C_2 \dots C_n]\#$,

Second set : $[C_1C_2C_3 \dots C_n]\#$,

Third set : $[C_1C_2C_3C_4 \dots C_n]\#$,

Fourth set : $[C_1C_2C_3C_4C_5 \dots C_n]\#$,

Fifth set : $[C_1C_2C_3C_4C_5C_6 \dots C_n]\#$,

Sixth set : $[C_1C_2C_3C_4C_5C_6C_7 \dots C_n]\#$,

Seventh set : $[C_1C_2C_3C_4C_5C_6C_7C_8 \dots C_n]\#$, etc.

In all practicalities, the process of subset formation as well as their subsequent matching will follow the algorithm stated below:

- Stage 1: Constitute a substring combining first two characters of a string.
- Stage 2: Verify if the substring matches with a string stored in RL.
- Stage 3: If a match is found, consider it as root and other part as suffix.
- Stage 4: If a no match is found, add one more character to the string.

- Stage 5: Repeat the same process used in Stage 1 and 2.
- Stage 6: Match the suffix part with a suffix stored in SL.
- Stage 7: If a match is found, consider the word as a valid one.
- Stage 8: Apply the grammatical mapping rule for root-suffix combination.
- Stage 9: Match the output string with the input string for validation.
- Stage 10: Collect all grammatical and semantic information from Dic-2.
- Stage 11: Produce the final result.
- Stage 12: Encounter the next word string in the sentence.

The process of matching will eventually identify the valid match with information available in RL and SL. Once the root and suffix parts are matched with their corresponding strings in RL and SL, the system will apply rules of grammatical agreement between the two to approve their validity. After validation, the system will declare the word as an accepted one and retrieve necessary information from ED-II for final presentation. After the initial run of the system on texts, outputs are put to verification and validation. Generally, verification of output shows four types of result:

- Some words are rightly processed.
- Some words are wrongly processed.
- Some words are not processed at all.

To make the process accurate, the system needs augmentation of lexical database stored in RL and SL as well as modification of linguistic rules used for grammatical mapping. It is noted that verification and validation of grammatical agreement depend on information stored in respective lexicons. In addition to this, information about unacceptable subsets of root-suffix pairs also help in a great way to make the system robust, efficient, and accurate.

Part of Speech Tagging

In Natural Language Processing, Language Technology, and Computational Linguistics, the process of Part-of-Speech (POS) tagging is also identified as Grammatical Annotation, the primary goal of which is to disambiguate words at the grammatical level and assign them to particular lexical categories or parts-of-speech. Because of this unique goal, POS tagging is called as Word Category Disambiguation, which in essence, involves the process of marking up words manually or automatically within a corpus as corresponding to particular parts of-speech, based on their forms, functions and contexts (i.e., relationship of words with their adjacent and related words) within the larger syntactic strings like phrases, sentences, and paragraphs.

Although the process of POS tagging is a complicated and error-prone process, it cannot be ignored because research and development works of NLP, LT, and CL cannot advance further with just a list of words obtained from a language corpus without any information about grammatical behaviours of words in various usage-based contexts. In descriptive and applied linguistics on the other hand, POS tagged corpus is equally necessary because words represent different parts-of-speech in different textual contexts and information about parts-of-speech of words provided in traditional dictionaries is fuzzy, implicit, and indeterminate. Words vary in part-of-speech; it is not a new thing to natural languages. We find a large number of words in a language, which are ambiguous in form, meaning, and part-of-speech.

The Challenge

This feature of part-of-speech variation of words is prevalent in any living natural language be it an advanced language like English or an endangered language like Mundari. For instance, in English the word sound can be tagged as a noun (e.g., the sound of music), an adjective (e.g., a sound decision), as well as a verb (e.g., he sounds rational) based on the context of its use in sentences. While a native speaker can identify the words as noun, adjective or finite verb, and can perform grammatical and semantic analysis of the words innately based on their internalised linguistic rules and grammar of the language, a computer system which is being trained to tag words automatically in corpora, needs elaborate linguistic rules and conditions to perform the task of identifying parts-of-speech of words in texts.

Although it is believed that the list of parts-of-speech presented in grammars, dictionaries, and school texts are enough for a language to tag words in texts, in reality, however, we find that there are many fine text categories and text sub-categories in a natural language text, and these fine divisions should be spelt out distinctly if we want to design a POS tagging scheme for words used in a text of a language. For instance, in Bangla, it is usually stated in grammar books that it has only eight parts-of-speech, namely, Noun, Pronoun, Adjective, Adverb, Finite Verb, Non-finite Verb, Postposition, and Indeclinable. It is also believed that only these parts-of-speech are required for the language. It is also assumed that once we learn these categories, we shall have no problem to identify the part-of-speech of each and every word used in the language. In actuality, however, we note that there are many fine text categories, like demonstratives, infinitives, gerunds, conjunctions, enclitics, quantifiers, particles, punctuations, etc., the form and function of which we need to identify, analyse and understand properly, if we want to have a total command over parts-of-speech of words vis-à-vis grammar of the language.

The more complex challenge in POS tagging lies in other areas where we need to mark the distinction between plural and singular nouns and pronouns; tag words marked with case makers and inflections in texts; tag grammatical gender found with words; tag nouns and adjectives marked with gender and number markers; mark verbs attached with person, number, gender, tense, aspect, modality, honourification, and other markers; tag adjectives marked with suffixes of degree; tag adjectives behaving like nouns in texts, etc. These are more complex and therefore challenging issues in POS tagging as there is a chance that we can make mistakes in identification of actual grammatical identity of the words loaded with so many varieties of grammatical information.

Information of tagging of all these types is absolutely necessary for designing algorithm for POS tagging to words in a language text by a computer. Else a POS tagging algorithm will fail to trace varied unique linguistic information of words, while a tagged text will fail to exhibit the finer linguistic functions of words in language the information of which is indispensible in subsequent linguistic research and development activities relating to theoretical linguistics, applied linguistics and computational linguistics. This is a real challenge for those people who are engaged in developing a POS tagger of a language.

Morphological Analysis vs. POS Tagging

Once the basic principles and rules are developed and collectively agreed upon, we can go for tagging a corpus text manually or train a system to tag the text automatically. However, we need to keep in mind that a POS tagging scheme is not a replacement for a tool used for morphological analysis of words, because POS tagging is different in goal and application. While the basic goal of a morphological analyser is to identify the morphemes used in formation of a word, the goal of a POS tagger is to identify grammatical identity or part-of speech of a word used in a text.

A word when used in a sentence usually carries various information, some of which are distinctly evident from its surface form (e.g., number marker, plural marker, gender marker, person marker, case marker, tense marker, emphatic marker, negative marker, etc.), while other information is obtainable from its contextual environment (e.g., part-of-speech or grammatical function of a word in a given context). That means both kinds of morpheme related information of a word can come from morphological and grammatical analysis of a word. This signifies that we should look at a word from two levels:

- Morphological level
- Syntactic level

Information of morphological level is possible to extract from morphological structure of a word analysed individually in isolated context. On the other hand, information of syntactic level is possible to extract from its grammatical function within a syntactic construction. While the first function is carried out by a morphological analyzer, the second function is carried out by a POS tagger (and a parser). Thus, morphological analyzer and POS tagger play two different yet crucial roles in providing morphological and grammatical information of words one at their isolated situation and the other at their sentential frames.

A morphological analyzer primarily looks at a word in isolation and provides all its possible morphology-related information, including multiple parts-of-speech or lexical identities. On the contrary, a POS tagger looks at a word in a sentential context (within small window) and provides the exact part-of-speech of the word in a syntactic frame. Therefore, it can be argued that the task of a POS tagger is primarily to disambiguate the grammatical category information provided by a morphological analyzer and select the most appropriate POS category of words in their specific sentential contexts. Taking this observation as a ground truth a POS tagset for a language is designed primarily with grammatical categories of words in mind. Any other morphological information, which is obtained from a morphological analyzer, is not usually included at the POS tagging level.

One important thing we need to keep in mind that before we apply morphological analysis or POS tagging automatically on a text corpus, we must carry out these tasks manually on some sample texts to gather experience, to reduce amount of error, and to save time. Prior experiments are also required for achieving higher level of accuracy and robustness when morphological analysis and POS tagging are to be carried out automatically on corpora. In essence, prior trial and correction exercise usually generate all the following advantages:

- Experimental morphological analysis and POS tagging of words in a corpus database throw up many new issues and challenges, based on which predetermined tagsets can be revised, modified, and extended.
- Elaborate guidelines for morphological analysis and POS tagging are to be developed during this period based on experimental analysis and tagging exercises.
- Morphologically analysed words and POS tagged corpora may be utilized for training automatic morphological analyzer and POS tagger.
- Prior experiments supply necessary knowledge and insights that are indispensible for enhancing robustness of a morphological analyser and a POS tagger.
- Information obtained from prior experiments may also be used in language description, dictionary compilation, grammar book writing, and language teaching.

Levels of POS Tagging

In principle, part-of-speech (POS) tagging is a process of assigning part-of-speech tags to each and every word used in a piece of text after the word is passed through the stages of morphological analysis and grammatical interpretation. Generally, a set of specially designed codes (known as 'tags') carrying grammatical information are assigned to words to indicate their parts-of-speech in accordance with their usage in the text. In most cases, a well-defined set of linguistic rules are used to identify and assign POS tags to the words to determine their lexico-semantic entities and syntactico-grammatical functions in the text. The immediate advantages of POS tagging are realized in the following three levels:

- Lexical level: It allows to analyse morphological structure of words represented in their surface forms.
- Orthographic level: It draws distinction among the homographic forms used in the same text or similar other texts to make distinctions in their semantic roles.
- Syntactic level: It allows identification of syntactico-grammatical functions of words to assign their POS entities accordingly.

The POS tagging is the commonest form of text annotation, which is considered to be the first stage of a more comprehensive process where multiword expressions, such as, compound words, reduplicated forms, idiomatic expressions, proverbial expressions, set phrases, and others used in a text are assigned with chunking markers leading to eventual assignment of phrase markers to each of the sentences used in a text. Although the use of POS tags on a text makes the text very difficult to read and comprehend for human beings, the text becomes maximally suitable for providing linguistic information needed by a system for differentiating between words used in different parts-of-speech. Moreover, from application point of view, POS tagging is a useful technique that increases specificity in data retrieval from corpora and provides basic grammatical information about words required in semantic annotation, discourse annotation, parsing, dictionary compilation, grammar development, language teaching, and language planning. In simple words, the process POS tagging on a piece of text, in a systematic manner, may be carried out through the following eight steps:

- Step 1: Identification of words within a piece of text.
- Step 2: Identification of their orthographic forms and appearances.
- Step 3: Analysis of their morphological structures and formation.
- Step 4: Identification of their syntactic (grammatical) functions in sentence.
- Step 5: Determination of their grammatical roles and parts-of-speech.
- Step 6: Identification of their semantic roles in the sentences.
- Step 7: Assignment of POS tags – either manually or automatically.
- Step 8: Final verification and validation of the tags assigned to words.

Stages of POS Tagging

Following the steps, the process of POS tagging may be carried out on a piece of text at three separate stages as the followings:

- Stage 1: Pre-editing of a corpus text.
- Stage 2: Tag assignment to words.
- Stage 3: Post-editing of the tagged text data.

Stage 1: Pre-Editing of a Corpus Text

At the pre-editing stage, a digital text is converted into a suitable format for carrying out the POS tagging programme. At this stage, the entire text is meticulously checked to verify if there is any typographical and/or orthographical error of any type within the text data, and if there is any, it is manually or automatically corrected in accordance with the physical source text before the text is put to POS tagging. Moreover, if needed, a selected text data has to pass through the stages of text normalization and word tokenization to make the database maximally suitable for POS tagging, both manually and automatically.

Stage 2: Tag Assignment to Words

The tag assignment stage begins with the assignment of just one and only one POS tag to each and every word used in a sentence after considering specific syntactico-grammatical function of the words in sentence. For achieving higher level of accuracy at this stage, we can also use a lexical database where words are previously assigned with possible parts-of-speech for reference purposes. Such a lexical database is open-ended in the sense that it can be updated time-to-time with addition of new words obtained from various sources of language use. Also to deal with the newly found words in the corpus which is not available in the previously made lexical database, we can adopt various methods such as the lists of common affixes and case markers with their possible parts-of-speech for achieving greater accuracy in POS tagging.

Stage 3: Post-Editing of the Tagged Text Data

At post-editing stage, the entire tagged text data is post-edited to verify if words are rightly tagged and if any error is made in POS tag assignment. In case of large corpora, where manual verification of the entire database appears to be highly time consuming, tedious and error-prone, a probability matrix may be devised from the tagged database to deal with the problems of ambiguous tagging and dubious tag assignment. The matrix will help to specify transition probabilities underlying between the adjacent tags. For example, if a given word is tagged as noun ($W_{\_N}$), the probability of its immediately preceding word to be an adjective ($W_{\_JJ}$) is very high.

Although this probability matrix gives us certain amount of assurance about the POS identity of a word by way of analysing the POS identify of its immediately preceding and succeeding words, it is not a full-proof strategy, since a noun can easily be preceded by another noun or an adjective can easily be succeeded by two or more adjectives before a noun occurs. That means a probability matrix needs to be constantly updated and revised with new data collected from the corpus if we really want to understand the nature of word order.

Usually a human, who is engaged in assigning POS tags to the words, can do the work quite successfully if she is well versed in morphology and grammar of a language. On the other hand, a computer can also do this task quite successfully if it is supplied with adequate amount of linguistic information and rules for POS tag assignment as well as it is properly trained to do the work with less percentage of errors. That means a system designer who is engaged in designing a tool for automatic POS tag assignment to words should be highly well-equipped with adequate linguistic and grammatical knowledge of the language so that she can develop a robust and accurate computer tool to assign correct POS to words, terms, and other lexical items used in the text.

Early POS Tagset

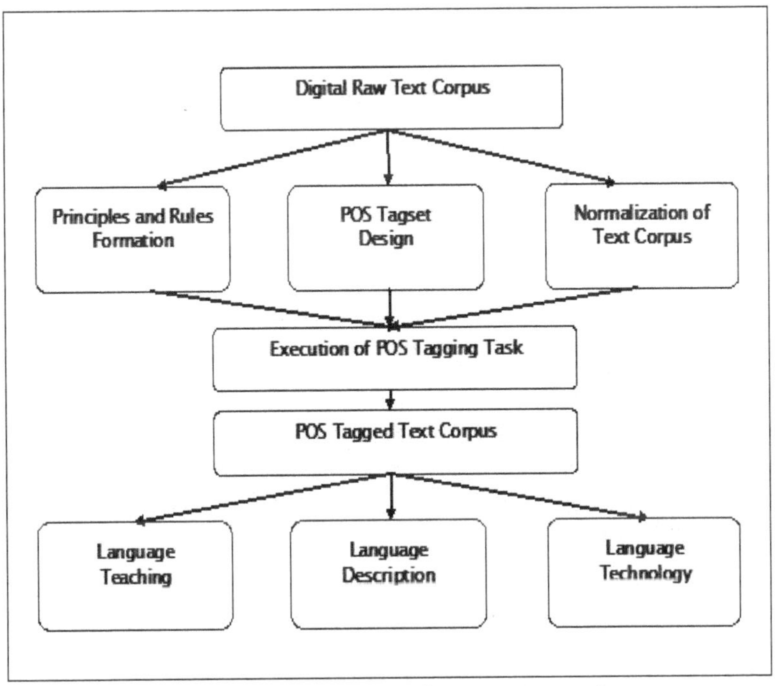

Architecture of POS Tagged Corpus Generation.

Although the techniques and tools for POS tagging are developed and used for English and many advanced languages in the early 1990s, these are yet to be developed and frozen for the most of the Indian languages. Even a decade ago people have either asked for a tagged corpora in Indian languages or have suggested for developing it at various platforms and forums, but none had taken serious initiative in this direction.

Rules for POS Tagging

Languages were taken to be sociological entities as clusters of properties shared by a group of speakers and lumped together as natural languages. These properties were lists of sounds, words, and morphemes. Any other properties were considered as universal logic or related to individual habits. Many linguistic works have dealt with the distribution of words and morphemes, syntax. However, nineteenth century syntax had no inherent structure or system unlike the twenty-first-century syntax. Thus, it is difficult to have a history of syntax unlike words, pronunciations, distributions, and semantics.

As sociological entities, natural languages are constantly changing either by figure of speech, context of words, or the human nature. Words can have one fixed meaning in the dictionary. However, when used in a sentence, its meaning might change based on its context or relation to other words. As a result, the determination of a word's context within a text is inherently difficult.

Formal language is a part of natural language. It only exists in well-formed sentences as specific rules can easily determine the structure of the formal sentence. However, it is unable to determine the semantics due to its reliance on fixed rules or when the structure is no longer formal.

The English language is considered as a Germanic language. Many factors influenced this language and converted it into the prevalently analytical language of modern time. In combination with scarcity of nominal forms and a verbal system, English outweighs the systems of many other European languages in terms of its segmentation of its verbal component. It has a rich vowel system along with an enormous set of vocabulary that is incomparable to other Germanic and non-Germanic languages. The modern English language reflects many centuries of development. The political and social events occurred in the past have profoundly affected how the language is structured. Similarly, other languages are subjected to the constant growth and decay. When a language ceases to change, it becomes a dead language. One good example is Latin. Currently, English has become native to many large populated countries. It has become a unique tool or even a bridge for mutual understanding between people of all parts of the world. Hence, as the English language becomes more prominent, its complexity will also increase.

English Structure

Human language consists of signs, which are defined as things that represent something else. There are three types of signs: iconic, indexical, and symbolic. Iconic signs resemble things they represent, i.e., photographs. Indexical signs point to a necessary connection with things they represent. i.e., a symptom to an illness. Symbolic signs are conventional representation of things. A good example is the indication of a wedding ring to marriage. These signs are often related to the context of a word in a sentence.

Certain aspects of word orders are considered as iconic. For example, the sentence, He cooks the food and became ill, has a different meaning when rearranged as He became ill and cooks the food. In addition, rules of the language or syntactic rules limit how words in the sentence are ordered. Thus, a sentence, like soap operas I, is inaccurate. Each word in a sentence is identified with a part of speech. A part of speech is consisted of verb (V), adjective (ADJ), pronoun (PN), noun (N), adverb (ADV), conjunction (CONJ), preposition (PREP), determiner (DET), transition (T) and modal (M). Each part can be decomposed into more sophisticated parts or be grouped with others to create another part. For example, modal (auxiliary verb) is a subpart of verb, and a determiner or an article when grouped with a noun creates the subject part. In combination to the arrangement of words, the tag of the word can change significantly. For example, the word round can be tagged differently.

- N: A round of drinks.
- A: A round table.
- V: Round off the numbers.
- Prep: Come round the corner.
- Adv: Come round with some fresh air.

There are two fundamental rules in generating the structure of a sentence: Phrase structure rules and transformation rules. These two rules are constitutive rules rather than regulatory rules (constraints). Phrase structure rules generate the deep underlying structure (D-struct) of the sentence through determining the linear order of words in a simple, positive and declarative sentence, the lexical and the tag to which the words belong and their hierarchical relationships with each other. The transformational rules either rearrange, add, or delete elements, but the semantic of the sentence remains. Transformation rules generate various sentence types of surface structure (S-struct):

- The dog uncovered the bone. (D-struct)
- The bone was uncovered by the dog. (S-struct)

Prior to the phrase structure rules, many linguists used immediate constituent analysis (IAC) which accounted for the linear order of words on the surface and the structure of the sentence. However, IAC was proven to be insufficient in dealing with an active and corresponding passive sentence as argued by Noam Chomsky. For example, the sentence, flying planes can be dangerous, has great ambiguity. Flying planes can either means an action or a noun. A phrase structure grammar consists of a set of ordered rules known as rewrite rules (Chomsky Normal Form). A simple sentence can be structured as:

$$S \Rightarrow NP + VP$$
$$NP \Rightarrow DET + N \mid N$$
$$VP \Rightarrow V \mid ADV\ V$$
$$O \Rightarrow N$$

The example S ⇒ NP + VP + O constitutes the grammar of a sentence that is composed of NP, VP and O. NP is composed of either DET and N or just N. Hence, S ⇒DET + N + VP + O | N + VP + O.

Sentences are composed of phrases, which are either sequence of words or a single word having syntactic significance where they form a constituent. A constituent is a word or a group of words that functions as a single unit in the hierarchical structure. A beautiful flower is a constituent where A (DET) beautiful (ADJ) flower (N) act as one subject. However, not all sequences of words function as constituents. It is the context that determines whether a sequence forms a constituent. To transform simple sentences into complex or compound sentences, phrases can be expanded :

$$S \Rightarrow NP\ VP$$
$$NP\,(\text{noun phrase}) \Rightarrow N$$
$$DET\ N$$
$$DET\ ADJ\ N$$
$$DET\ ADJ\ PREP\ N$$
$$DET\ N\ PREP\ N$$
$$DET\ ADJ\ N\ PREP$$
$$PN$$
$$\text{Proper Noun}\,(PrN)$$

$$AP\,(\text{adjective phrase}) \Rightarrow ADJ$$
$$ADV\ ADJ$$
$$ADV\ ADV\ ADJ$$
$$AdvP\,(\text{adverb phrase}) \Rightarrow ADV$$
$$ADV\ ADV$$
$$PP\,(\text{prepositional phrase}) \Rightarrow PREP\ NP$$
$$PREP\ PREP\ NP$$
$$PREP\ PP$$

$$\text{VP(verb phrase)} \Rightarrow \text{V NP}$$
$$\text{V NP PP}$$
$$\text{V NP NP}$$
$$\text{V AP}$$
$$\text{V NP AP}$$
$$\text{V PP}$$
$$\text{V PP PP}$$

$$\text{CONJ} \Rightarrow \text{PP} + \text{NP}$$
$$\text{P} + \text{P}$$
$$\text{NP} + \text{NP}$$
$$\text{AP} + \text{AP}$$
$$\text{A} + \text{A}$$
$$\text{AdvP} + \text{AdvP}$$

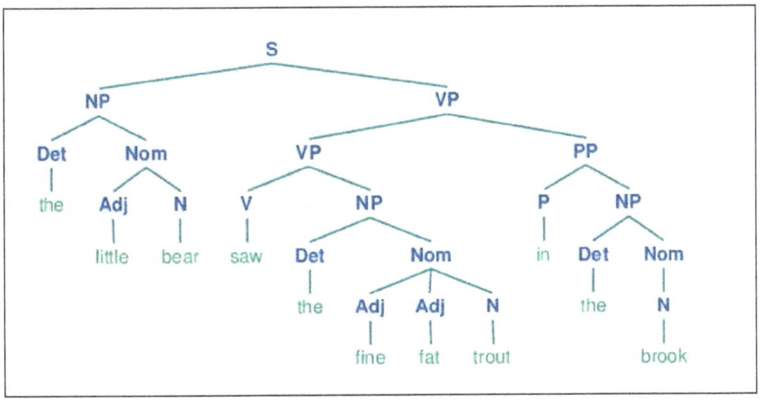

Phrase Structure Tree.

In addition, a sentence can be active or passive. It is induced through the usage of auxiliary verbs or modals (M). The structure of a sentence then becomes:

$$\text{S} \Rightarrow \text{NP Aux VP}$$

Passive sentences are derived from their active counterpart by the insertion of the passive auxiliary in the verb specifier position which causes thc NP to move to the by phrase.

- The art expert detects the forgery. (active)
- The forgery is detected by the art expert. (passive)

The most frequent kind of passive sentence in English is the agentless passive where the by phrase is not present. In addition, not all active sentences can be passivized. For a sentence to be passivized, the subject must be a performer of an action or an agent and the verb must have a direct or prepositional object that allows reorder of the subject position. Certain verbs like intransitive and copulative verbs cannot be passivized as they cannot have an object. Although many transitive verbs can be passivized, some may not be as the subject is not performing an action.

- Jack eats the chocolates. (can be passive)
- Jack hates the chocolates. (can't be passive)

Many D-struct sentences are active as opposed to passive, declarative, positive, and simple. These sentences serve as a base or a kernel sentence to produce passive, imperative, or negative sentences (S-struct) through the usage of transformation rules. Understanding the structure of a sentence allows the proper tagging or categorizing of its words.

Implementation

The rule-based POS tagger is written in C and implemented on top of Lex and Yacc. There are two main files, pos.l and pos.y. Lex uses the pos.l file for lexicon and scanner rules. It is essentially the tagger file. Meanwhile, Yacc uses the pos.y file to create tags and to build structure rules. Yacc is a parser developed for Unix systems. Lex is a lexical analyzer built in conjunction with it. The tagger is constructed utilizing a very small lexicon. The lexicon primarily contains words that are often used and usually have a fixed tag. For example, words belong in the tag, determiner, are a small set of words.

The tagger is rather reliance on linguistic rules to determine the tag of unknown words and ambiguity. When a word is parsed, it is checked with the lexicon first. If matched, it is passed onto the addword method, a set of linguistic rules are applied to determine the tag for the word, then the word is allocated within a doubly linked-list structure. The structure contains the word, its tag, its left neighbor, and its next neighbor.

If the word failed to match in the lexicon, it is passed onto the lookup method and the first round of rules is applied. The first-round checks to see if the word fits in a part of speech by checking its suffix and prefix. For example, if the word is end in ous or est, it is tagged as an adjective. In addition, if the word cannot be determined through its suffix or prefix, then linguistic rules are applied to determine its tagged. These rules check the location of the current word in comparison to the previous word. For example, he is fighting John, where the current word is John, it is checked with fighting and see that it is a verb. The tagger will tag it as a noun as it sees that John cannot be a conjunction nor a determiner since the word is unknown. The rules within the lookup method follows:

- If the word doesn't pass the suffix/prefix check, then it is checked using linguistic rules.
- If the previous word is not tagged as a DET, PN, DET-PN, or POSS-N, then it is tagged as NOUN.
- If the previous word is an ADV, then it is tagged as V.
- If the previous word is an AUX_BE, then it is tagged as ADJ.
- If the previous word is a PREP_BASIC, then it is tagged as V.
- If the previous word is the word be, then it is tagged as ADJ.
- If it is the first word and undetermined, then it is tagged as a noun.

If the word is matched with any of the rules, then the addword method is called. Before the word is allocated onto the structure, it goes through another round of rules like the first round with slight variations. This decreases the ambiguity within the sequence of tags. The addword method serves to overwrite the state of a word either unknown or known to the lexicon. For example, the word bear can be tagged as a verb initially after matching in the lexicon. After applying the rules, it is found that the previous word was an article or a modal, and then it is now tagged as a noun.

Once the word is tagged and added to structure, the lexical analyzer returns its tag. The Yacc parser uses the returned tag and the Backus Normal Form (BNF) to check for the sentence of the structure. The rules mentioned in section English Structure are applied. In addition, certain tags are broken down into more sophisticated tags to accommodate linguistic rules that deal with ambiguity. For example, noun was broken W, T Word, tag W, T down further into det-noun, pronoun, noun-day and many more. As a result, the rules are more sophisticated when it comes to checking the tag and reduces further ambiguity.

Evaluation

The rule-based POS tagger utilized many linguistic rules to determine the tag of a word. The set of rules are limited to a small set to prevent the occurrence of contradictions. As the set of linguistic rules grow, the chance of contradiction also increases. Through limitation of a small set of rules, the tagger is unable to properly tag a word in a complex sentence. Meanwhile, simple sentences and some complex sentences are properly tagged. Simple sentences are properly tagged as they follow formal language rules. Some sentences are properly tagged since no contradictions appeared when the linguistic rules are applied or when matched in the lexicon. For example, He is happily eating his sandwich today, and He is running with his aunt, are properly tagged.

However, due to contradictions within certain rules, the tagger can incorrectly tag the word. For example, the sentence, she is going to work today, is tagged as pronoun-modal-verb-prep-noun. The word today is an adverb in this case. This example is a common issue for both rule-based and stochastic approach. It is difficult to find good rules, or a set of training data to set what is after a preposition. In many cases, a noun is often after a preposition which requires a rule for such case. To implement a rule for a verb after a preposition is contradictory to that rule.

Handling unknown words is a main issue for both rule-based and stochastic tagging. Both have different approaches in handling such issue. In the stochastic approach, unknown words are tagged based on transition probability whereas affix analysis is used to tackle ambiguity. The rule-based tagger can determine the tag of unknown words through the usage of rules, which it does not require a large lexicon However, it is unable to pickup an unknown word if it is the first word in a sentence. This is due to the nature of the Lex scanner where it will discard an unknown word immediately.

In addition, when it comes to analyzing the structure of the input, the Yacc parser has troubles in checking the structure utilizing the BNF structure. In some random occurrences, it is unable to recognize the tag of an unknown word. This was subsequently fixed through returning the tag in both lookup and addword methods and during the lexicon matching phase. Furthermore, the tagger does not have the ability of error-correction. Spelling error-detection is not necessary as the rule-based approach only look at the structure of the words within the sentence to tag. However, it can be handy when matching words in the lexicon.

Computational Semantics

Computational semantics is a relatively new discipline that combines insights from formal semantics, computational linguistics, and automated reasoning. The aim of computational semantics is to find techniques for automatically constructing semantic representations for expressions of human language, representations that can be used to perform inference.

Semantic Representations

First-Order Representations

Traditional formal semantic analyses of human language typically presuppose formalisms with high-expressive power (for example, higher-order logic augmented with modalities) but in computational semantics some variant of first-order logic is generally preferred. This choice is sensible for at least two reasons. First, first-order theorem provers (and to a lesser extent, first-order model builders) now offer levels of performance which make them genuinely useful for certain reasoning tasks. Second, first-order logic is able to deal (at least to a good approximation) with a wide range of interesting phenomena. In short, first-order logic offers an attractive compromise between the conflicting demands of expressivity and inferential effectiveness.

Every first-order language has a vocabulary, telling us which symbols are used and how. Suppose we have a vocabulary consisting of the constants SUNSET-BOULEVARD, MULHOLLAND-DRIVE, the one-place relations WOMAN, AFRAID, and the two-place relations POLICE-REPORT, LOCATION, and CROSS. Such symbols are often called the non-logical symbols of the language. The remaining ingredients of a first-order language are a collection of variables (x, y, z and so on), the boolean connectives ($\wedge, \vee, \neg, \rightarrow$), the quantifiers ($\exists, \forall$), and the brackets plus the comma to group together symbols. The variables and constants are the terms of the language. The formulas of language are defined as follows:

- If R is a symbol of arity n, and $\tau_1,\ldots,\tau_n$ are terms, then $R(\tau_1,\ldots,\tau_n)$ is a formula.
- If τ_1 and τ_2 are terms, then $\tau_1=\tau_2$ is a formula.
- If φ and φ are formulas then so are $\neg\varphi$, $(\varphi\wedge\varphi)$, $(\varphi\vee\varphi)$ and $(\varphi\rightarrow\varphi)$.
- If φ is a formula, and x is a variable, then both $\exists x\varphi$ and $\forall x\varphi$ are formulas.
- Nothing else is a formula.

Here is an example of an English statement and its first-order translation:

- A woman crosses Sunset Boulevard.
- $\exists x(\text{WOMAN}(x)\wedge\exists y(y=\text{SUNSET-BOULEVARD}\wedge\text{CROSS}(x,y)))$

Interpreting First-Order Representations

First-order formulas are interpreted in models (these can be seen as abstract realizations of situations) with the aid of variable assignment functions (these can be seen as supplying extra contextual information). What do models look like? In set-theoretic terms, a model M is an ordered pair (D;F) consisting of a domain D and an interpretation function F specifying semantic values in D. Here's a simple example (it should be clear that this model is a situation in which the formula just given is true):

$$D=\{d1,d2,d3\}\ F(\text{WOMAN})=\{d1\}$$
$$F(\text{CROSS})=\{(d1,d2),(d3,d2)\}$$
$$F(\text{SUNSET-BOULEVARD})=d2.$$

The crucial link between descriptions (first-order formulas) and situations (models) is made precise in the satisfaction definition. Formally, the satisfaction definition specifies a three place relation between a model M = (D;F), a formula f, and a variable assignment g (a function which maps variables to elements of D). The satisfaction relation is defined as follows:

$$
\begin{array}{ll}
M, g \models R(\tau_1,\ldots,\tau_n) & \text{iff } \left(I_F^g(\tau_1),\ldots, I_F^g(\tau_n)\right) \in F(R), \\
M, g \models \neg\phi & \text{iff not } M, g \models f, \\
M, g \models \phi \wedge \psi & \text{iff } M, g \models f \text{ and } M, g \models \psi, \\
M, g \models \phi \vee \psi & \text{iff } M, g \models f \text{ or } M, g \models \psi, \\
M, g \models \phi \rightarrow \psi & \text{iff not } M, g \models f \text{ or } M, g \models \psi, \\
M, g \models \exists \times \phi & \text{iff } M, g' \models f, \text{ for some x-variant } g' \text{of } g, \\
M, g \models \forall \times \phi & \text{iff } M, g' \models f, \text{ for all x-variants } g' \text{ of } g.
\end{array}
$$

In the first clause, I_F^g is F (c) if the term t is a constant c, and g(x) if τ is a variable x. In the last two clauses, by an x-variant g' of an assignment g we simply mean an assignment g' such that g'(y) = g(y) for all variables y≠x. Intuitively, variant assignments allow us to 'try out' new values for the variable bound by the quantifier (here x). Once the satisfaction definition has been given, the way is open to defining some fundamental inferential concepts. For example, a set of first-order formulas φ is said to be consistent if and only if all of them can be satisfied together in some model with respect to the same variable assignment (that is, φ is consistent if it describes a realizable situation). And a set of first-order formulas φ is informative if and only if it is not satisfied in all models (that is, φ is informative if what it describes rules out some situations). We must first consider whether first-order logic offers us the kind of expressivity needed in computational semantics.

First-Order Semantic Representations

It is sometimes argued that first-order logic is too restrictive to model the semantics of human language in an interesting way. Such claims don't withstand scrutiny. To be sure, well-known results such as the Compactness Theorem and the Löwenheim-Skolem theorems show that first-order logic has expressivity limitations but the limitations they reveal (such as its inability to distinguish infinite cardinalities) are usually tangential to the central concerns of computational semantics. The kind of expressivity first-order logic offers opens the way to quite fine-grained analyses of semantic phenomena- if we are prepared to be flexible about the kinds of entities which inhabit our models.

Modalities

At first glance, intensional phenomena (such as constructions involving necessity and possibility, or knowledge and belief) seem to take us beyond the realm of first-order logic, and many formal semanticists use various kinds of modal logic to cover these aspects of human language. Here's an example. Extend first-order logic with the formula prefix operators € (to express necessity) and ◇ (to express possibilities). Thus we can now say things like:

Maybe Mulholland Drive is where the accident was.

$$\exists x\left(x = \text{MULHOLLAND-DRIVE} \wedge \exists y\left(\text{ACCIDENT}(y) \wedge \Diamond \text{LOCATION}(x,y)\right)\right)$$

There must be a police report of the accident.

$$\exists x\left(\text{ACCIDENT}(x) \wedge \Box \exists y\left(\text{POLICE-REPORT}(y,x)\right)\right)$$

At first blush, such examples may seem beyond the reach of first-order logic. But they're not. In fact, semantics for modal logic is interesting precisely because it explains these rather mysterious looking intensional operators in terms of ordinary (extensional) first-order quantification. And it's simple to exploit a first-order semantic representation language. Add a second sort of entity to our models (call them 'possible worlds' or 'situations'). Add an accessibility relation R across these worlds. Add a one-place predicate symbol ACTUAL-WORLD to pick out the actual world. Add an extra argument place to each relation on ordinary individuals to relativise its interpretation to a particular world. Then translate away modalities as follows:

$$(\Box \phi, w)^{m2f} = \forall v\left(R(w,v) \rightarrow (\phi, v)^{m2f}\right),$$

$$(\Diamond \phi, w)^{m2f} = \exists v\left(R(w,v) \wedge (\phi, v)^{m2f}\right).$$

For example, the modal representation of 'There must be a police report of the accident' becomes:

$$\exists w(\text{ACTUAL-WORLD}(w) \wedge \exists x(\text{ACCIDENT}(w,x) \wedge \forall v$$

$$\left(R(w,v) \rightarrow \exists y\left(\text{POLICE-REPORT}(V,Y,X)\right)\right).$$

In short, by letting models be mathematical pictures of richer ontologies (in this case, an ontology containing possible worlds) we have moved from modal logic back to ordinary first-order logic.

Tense and Aspect

Various temporal phenomena in human language (such as tense and aspect) can be analyzed using the modal apparatus of Prior-style tense logic, or various modal logics of intervals, but we are not forced to follow either route. For a start, both Prior-style tense logic and interval logics can be translated into first-order logic so the way is open for either point-based or interval-based first-order semantic analyses. But other options are possible. For example, we could take a Davidsonian route and enrich our models with primitive events and relations over them. This would allow us to take a sentence such as:

A woman crossed Sunset Boulevard and represent it as:

$$\exists x(\text{WOMAN}(x) \wedge \exists e(\text{CROSS}(e) \wedge \text{AGENT}(e,x) \wedge \text{THEME}(e,\text{SUNSETBOULEVARD}) \wedge \exists t(\text{TLOC}(e,t) \wedge e < s)).$$

As before, if we are willing to countenance a richer ontology (either one containing points of time, or intervals, or events) the way lies open to first-order analyses of the semantics of temporal constructions.

Plurals

How can we deal with the semantics of plurals in first-order logic? Here's one way: enrich our models with plural entities, add a one place predicate group to pick out such entities, and use a two-place relation member to indicate that an ordinary individual belongs to a group entity. Then we can represent the sentence:

Two well-dressed men are drinking coffee.

Using the first-order formula:

$$\exists u(\text{GROUP}(u) \wedge \text{TWO}(u) \wedge \forall x(\text{MEMBER}(x,u) \leftrightarrow (\text{MAN}(x) \wedge \text{WELL-DRESSED}(x) \wedge \text{DRINKS-COFFEE}(x)))).$$

We can further constrain the interpretation of the symbol two by formulating a meaning postulate:

$$\forall u\left(\text{TWO}(u) \leftrightarrow \exists x \exists y\left(\text{MEMBER}(x,u) \wedge \text{MEMBER}(y,u) \wedge x \neq y\right)\right).$$

This axiom states that a plural entity has the property two if and only if it has at least two distinct members.

Methodology of First-Order Modeling

First-order logic offers expressive power relevant to the semantics of human language. The key to realizing this power is to be flexible about the kinds of entities we include in our models. To put it another way, first-order approaches to the semantics of human language go hand-in-hand with rich ontologies. This may be unpalatable to some philosophers. Arguably, however, the most promising methodology for the semanticist is to try to get to grips with the unruly ontology that human language seems to presuppose; the semanticist should engage in "natural language metaphysics". Indeed, it is arguable that this project is an indispensable prelude to philosophical analysis.

Are there limitations to this style of first-order modeling? Yes. When we introduce new entities we have to introduce constraints governing how they behave. For example, we might want to constrain the accessibility relation on possible worlds to be reflexive, or constrain the precedence relation on events to be transitive, or insist that groups must have at least two ordinary individuals as members. When (as in these examples) the required constraints can be stated in first-order logic, nothing more needs to be said. However if some postulates can't be written in this way, then our first-order modeling is only an approximation. For example, if we developed the first-order approach to plurals, we would eventually find that we needed constraints that first-order logic couldn't handle.

But approximations are not to be despised, and many are remarkably good. Perhaps the best known approximation is the quasi-reduction of higher-order logic to first-order logic by introducing extra entities into models and constraining them to act like higher-order functions. Not all the required constraints can be written in a first-order way of course (if they could, there would be no distinction between first- and higher-order logic) but enough first-order postulates can given to yield an approximation to higher-order logic that in many respects is better behaved than standard higher-order logic.

All in all, viewed from the perspective of contemporary computational semantics, the expressivity offered by first-order logic seems a reasonable starting point for semantic modeling. Indeed, when computational semanticists express doubts about first-order logic, their doubts don't center on traditional issues of expressivity, but on its (lack of) dynamic potential. Here's an example. It's not easy to deal with discourse anaphora in first-order logic. Consider the discourse:

A woman crosses Sunset Boulevard. She is afraid.

Now, this clearly means the same as the following first-order formula:

$$\exists x\left(\mathrm{WOMAN}(x) \wedge \mathrm{CROSS}(x, \mathrm{SUNSET\text{-}BOULEVARD}) \wedge \mathrm{AFRAID}(x)\right).$$

So there is no expressivity problem: first-order logic captures the content of this discourse. But there is a trickier question how can we systematically construct such representations? If we use (either of) the approaches described we will probably end up with,

$$\exists x\left(\mathrm{WOMAN}(x) \wedge \mathrm{CROSS}(x, \mathrm{SUNSET\text{-}BOULEVARD})\right) \wedge \mathrm{AFRAID}(x).$$

This representation is incorrect the final occurrence of variable x is not bound by the quantifier, and thus is not linked with the variable x in WOMAN(x). Several approaches to such issues have been explored. In Dynamic Predicate Logic (DPL) the first-order satisfaction definition is changed so that the two representations just given mean exactly the same thing. In Discourse Representation Theory (DRT), on the other hand, we would represent the discourse using the following Discourse Representation Structure (DRS):

$$[\{x,y\},\{\text{WOMAN}(x), y = \text{SUNSET-BOULEVARD}, \text{CROSS}(x,y), \text{AFRAID}(x)\}].$$

Here the occurrence of x in AFRAID is linked to the x in {x, y}, and hence to the other occurrences of x. Now, for present purposes it's not important to know how DRT and DPL manage to get things right but it is important to realise that neither formalism increases the expressive power at our disposal. Neither DPL nor DRT is more expressive than ordinary first-order logic. All three formalisms can be freely inter-translated. To put it another way, they are notational variants.

But it would be highly misguided to conclude from this that the choice between them is merely a matter of convenience. It's not. For some purposes (notably, dealing with anaphora and presuppositions in a principled way) DRS notation (essentially a 'flat' form of first-order logic without explicit quantifiers) is pretty much essential. This is an instance of a lesson that comes up time and time again in computational semantics: we need to be flexible about the form our representations take. For example we sometimes need to think about representations in an abstract 'underspecified' way. So when we argue that first-order representations are useful in computational semantics, our claim should be interpreted in this spirit. We're not arguing for blind devotion to orthodox first-order syntax: in practice it may be useful to freely move between orthodox syntax and variants (such as DRSs) as the need arises.

Computing Semantic Representations

How do we automate the process of assigning semantic representations to sentences of human language? That is, once we have fixed on representation formalism (first-order logic, for example) how do we write programs which take human language sentences as input and return semantic representations as output? We will compare two standard approaches one making extensive use of unification, and one based on the lambda-calculus. Both approaches require a grammar describing the syntactic structure of the fragment of language of interest. We first consider the unification-based approach, probably the most popular method in contemporary computational semantics.

Unification-Based Approaches

To guide the process of constructing semantic representations for a fragment of English, a fully specified syntax for the fragment is required. We will assume a syntactic analysis based on a collection of syntactic categories, whose interrelationships are described in phrase structure rules, and whose contents are represented in lexical entries. The categories themselves are represented as feature structures (familiar from various linguistic formalisms, and sometimes referred to as signs). Variables used for unification are represented by numbers in boxes. Here are some sample lexical entries:

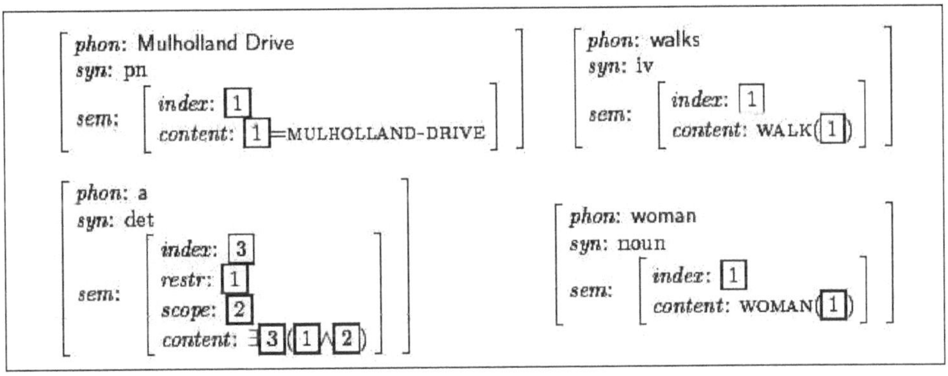

Complex structures are used to instantiate the feature sem (that is, the semantic feature). Most lexical entries have an index feature designating a variable that needs to be equated with some other piece of (still missing) information. Determiners (here ‘a’) have, in addition, features restr and scope whose task is to ensure correct placement of the two key components of the representation, namely the restriction and the nuclear scope (in the sentence ‘a woman walks’, for example, linguists would call ‘woman’ the restriction of the determiner ‘a’, and ‘walks’ its nuclear scope).

The phrase structure rules of the grammar direct the correct unification of all features in the semantic part of a sign. The rules have the form LHS → RHS, where LHS (left-hand side) is a non-lexical category, and RHS (right-hand side) a non-empty ordered set of lexical or non-lexical categories. The rules state how LHS categories can be expanded into a sequence of RHS categories. Here are some sample grammar rules.

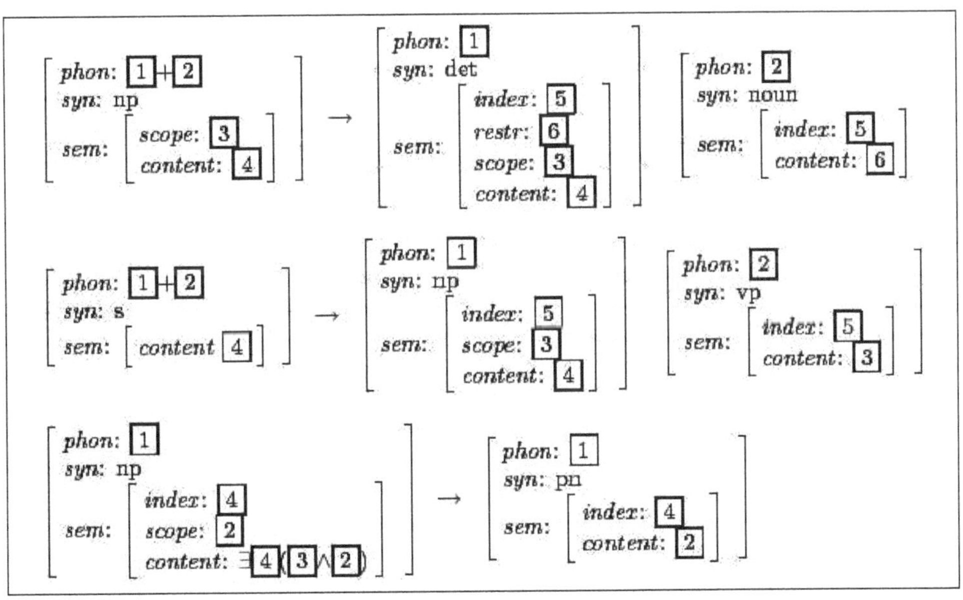

Note how variables are used to pass on semantic information from daughter to mother categories. You may find it instructive to work through the analysis of the sentence 'A woman walks.' If you do so you will obtain the feature structure,

$$\begin{bmatrix} \textit{phon}\text{: a woman walks} \\ \textit{syn}\text{: s} \\ \textit{sem}\text{: } \begin{bmatrix} \textit{content}\text{: } \exists \boxed{1}(\text{WOMAN}(\boxed{1}) \wedge \text{WALK}(\boxed{1})) \end{bmatrix} \end{bmatrix}$$

The value assigned to the content feature clearly amounts to $\exists x(\text{WOMAN}(x) \wedge \text{WALK}(x))$, as we would expect. The unification-based approach can be applied to deal with a wide range of semantic phenomena, and is very efficient. Many grammar formalisms which make use of feature structures build semantic representations in more-or-less the manner just sketched. Head-driven Phrase Structure Grammar (HPSG) is a case in point.

But despite its merits, the unification-based approach makes no principled distinction between variables used for unification and variables used in semantic representations. This gives rise to problems in cases where chunks of semantic representation need to be copied: a well-known case is coordination. Even such a simple sentence as 'Harry and Neal stare at the remains of the two cars' forces the value of the index feature of 'stare' to unify with the indexes of 'Harry' and 'Neal'. This fails when the values are represented by constants, and yields an incorrect representation when they are represented as variables, and so the correct representation cannot be constructed.

Grammar engineers generally find a way around the problems posed by coordination (and other grammatical phenomena where copying is involved) by ad-hoc techniques applied to the lexicon or grammar rules. But there is a more principled approach to such difficulties: make use of the machinery provided by the lambda calculus.

Lambda-Based Approaches

Let's use the lambda calculus as 'glue-language' to combine semantic representations systematically. This approach is attractive from a grammar engineering perspective: as it distinguishes between the variables used to drive semantic construction and the variables used in semantic representations, it bypasses the problems raised by copying constructions such as coordination, thus making it easier to add a semantic component to large-scale grammars.

We first need to add 'glue' to our representations: we will use the λ-operator to abstract over missing information, and the @-operator to express functional application. More precisely, all first-order formulas will be regarded as lambda expressions. Moreover, if x is a variable, and F is a lambda expression, then l´F is also a lambda expression. In this expression the variable x is bound; it is these lambda-bound variables that drive the semantic construction process. Finally, if F and A are lambda expressions, then so is (F@A). Linking two expressions with an @ is essentially an instruction that the two representations have to be combined in the manner described below (with F as the functor and A as the argument). We continue our practice of dropping brackets if no confusion arises. Secondly, we have to reorganize our lexicon. Typical entries will now look like this:

$$\begin{bmatrix} \textit{phon}: \text{Mulholland Drive} \\ \textit{syn}: \text{pn} \\ \textit{sem}: \lambda x.x{=}\text{MULHOLLAND-DRIVE} \end{bmatrix} \quad \begin{bmatrix} \textit{phon}: \text{woman} \\ \textit{syn}: \text{noun} \\ \textit{sem}: \lambda x.\text{WOMAN}(x) \end{bmatrix}$$

$$\begin{bmatrix} \textit{phon}: \text{a} \\ \textit{syn}: \text{det} \\ \textit{sem}: \lambda p.\lambda q.\exists x(p@x \wedge q@x) \end{bmatrix} \quad \begin{bmatrix} \textit{phon}: \text{every} \\ \textit{syn}: \text{det} \\ \textit{sem}: \lambda p.\lambda q.\forall x(p@x \rightarrow q@x) \end{bmatrix} \quad \begin{bmatrix} \textit{phon}: \text{walks} \\ \textit{syn}: \text{iv} \\ \textit{sem}: \lambda x.\text{WALK}(x) \end{bmatrix}$$

And thirdly, the grammar rules. We still make use of variable unification, but we won't use it to manipulate variables in the semantic representation (so we don't get any unwanted interactions, and coordination will pose no difficulties):

$$\begin{bmatrix} \textit{phon}: \boxed{1}+\boxed{2} \\ \textit{syn}: \text{np} \\ \textit{sem}: (\boxed{3}@\boxed{4}) \end{bmatrix} \rightarrow \begin{bmatrix} \textit{phon}: \boxed{1} \\ \textit{syn}: \text{det} \\ \textit{sem}: \boxed{3} \end{bmatrix} \begin{bmatrix} \textit{phon}: \boxed{2} \\ \textit{syn}: \text{noun} \\ \textit{sem}: \boxed{4} \end{bmatrix}$$

$$\begin{bmatrix} \textit{phon}: \boxed{1}+\boxed{2} \\ \textit{syn}: \text{s} \\ \textit{sem}: (\boxed{3}@\boxed{4}) \end{bmatrix} \rightarrow \begin{bmatrix} \textit{phon}: \boxed{1} \\ \textit{syn}: \text{np} \\ \textit{sem}: \boxed{3} \end{bmatrix} \begin{bmatrix} \textit{phon}: \boxed{2} \\ \textit{syn}: \text{vp} \\ \textit{sem}: \boxed{4} \end{bmatrix}$$

$$\begin{bmatrix} \textit{phon}: \boxed{1} \\ \textit{syn}: \text{np} \\ \textit{sem}: \lambda q.\exists x(\boxed{2}@x \wedge q@x) \end{bmatrix} \rightarrow \begin{bmatrix} \textit{phon}: \boxed{1} \\ \textit{syn}: \text{pn} \\ \textit{sem}: \boxed{2} \end{bmatrix}$$

Let's consider an example. Here's what the approach would yield for 'a woman walks':

$$\begin{bmatrix} \textit{phon}: \text{a woman walks} \\ \textit{syn}: \text{s} \\ \textit{sem}: ((\lambda p.\lambda q.\exists x(p@x \wedge q@x)@\lambda x.\text{WOMAN}(x))@\lambda x.\text{WALK}(x)) \end{bmatrix}$$

That is, as we combine the various syntactic units, a sequence of function applications (the @s) records how the semantic representations are to be combined. Let's now carry out the semantic combination (and in so doing get rid of all those @s). We do this using an operation called β-conversion (also known as β-reduction or lambda-conversion). β-conversion is the process of resolving all applications (expressions formed by the @-operator) by substituting the argument (the right-hand side of the @-operator) for the lambda-bound variables in the functor (the left-hand side of the @-operator). In the example just given this induces the following reduction steps:

$$((\lambda p.\ \lambda q \exists x(p@x \wedge q@x)@\ \lambda x.\text{WOMAN}(x))@\ \lambda x.\text{WALK}(x)) =$$
$$(\lambda q.\exists x(\lambda x.\text{WOMAN}(x)@x \wedge q@x)@\ \lambda x.\text{WALK}(x)) =$$
$$(\lambda q.\exists x(\text{WOMAN}(x) \wedge q@x)@\ \lambda x.\text{WALK}(x)) =$$
$$\exists x(\text{WOMAN}(x) \wedge \lambda x.\text{WALK}(x)@x) =$$
$$\exists x(\text{WOMAN}(x) \wedge \text{WALK}(x)).$$

The process of β-conversion can make use of a process called α-conversion (renaming of bound variables) to avoid accidental variable bindings. β-conversion can either be performed during syntactic processing or in a distinct post-processing phase. There are standard procedures available that implement both α-conversion and β-conversion. We now have two ways of computing semantic representations. Note that the choice of method is independent of our style of syntactic analysis.

References

- Morphology: ling.upenn.edu, Retrieved 08, March 2020
- Parts-of-Speech-Tagging-Rule-Based-339972799: researchgate.net, Retrieved 22, June 2020

2

Natural Language Processing

The area of study within computer science which seeks to provide computers with the ability to understand text and speech similar to the way humans understand them is known as natural language processing. This chapter closely examines the key concepts of natural language processing such as corpus linguistics, finite automata and natural language generation to provide an extensive understanding of the subject.

Maxims and Principles of Corpus Annotation

The basic purpose of corpus annotation or tagging is to add-up various interpretative (intralinguistic and extralinguistic) information to a written or spoken text database by some encoding attached to, or interspersed with the electronic version of the text. That means apart from pure language database, a language text may also be provided with additional intralinguistic and extralinguistic information, which may be divided broadly into following two types:

- Representational information.
- Interpretative information.

For a written text corpus database, representational information is the actual form of text that contains characters, words, terms, phrases, sentences, spellings, punctuations, and other visual information. Interpretative information, on the other hand, is something which is added to the basic text database, usually by expert linguists presumed to have insight into, or knowledge of, the linguistic features of the text as well as of the language. There are, at least, three basic criteria indispensable in any kind of text annotation. These include:

- Consistency,
- Accuracy,
- Speed.

While consistency demands for a kind of uniformity in the scheme of text annotation throughout the language database stored within a corpus; accuracy demands for freedom from any kind of error or mistake in the tagset or in the process of tagging. It also asks for adherence with definitions and guidelines of the strategy designed for annotation. Finally, speed directs towards automatic implementation of the scheme on a very large amount of corpus database within a short span of time.

Although a corpus annotated with various types of linguistic information is usually considered to be a highly precious resource for a language for several works of applied linguistics and language technology, the process of annotation invariably asks for long-time involvement of trained experts, money, and time. Moreover, it asks for pointed efforts for coming up with bench-mark standards which can be adopted in a uniformed manner across language types for creation of annotated corpora. However, anyone who wants to annotate a corpus will have to deal with the following two major issues:

- What kind of linguistic information should be annotated in the corpus?
- How should it be annotated?

For the first question, it is envisaged that one should come up with a well-defined scheme which will allow one to annotate various types of linguistic information. This linguistic information can be of part-of-speech, morphology, grammar, syntax, anaphora, semantics, discourse, pragmatics, and sociolinguistics. Although one may decide to annotate only one type of information initially, one should be able to augment, as and when required, other types of information to the already annotated corpus seamlessly. Therefore, it is taken for granted that annotation scheme of one type must support the other types. Moreover, the common consensus should be that there should be hardly any compromise with the amount of linguistic information to be annotated to the corpus.

Maxims of Annotation

Since the scheme of annotation of written text corpus is yet to standardise for most of the Indian languages and since the acceptance of annotation standards also depends on the corpus evaluation skill of the experts, there are a few practices and factors that should be considered while designing an annotation scheme or while annotating. Researchers have identifies the following seven maxims to be applied strictly in annotation of a text corpus:

- It should always be easy to dispense with annotation and revert to the raw corpus. The raw corpus should be recoverable.
- The annotations should, correspondingly, be extractable from the raw corpus to be stored independently or stored in an interlinear format.
- The scheme of analysis presupposed by the annotations the annotation scheme should be based on principles or guidelines accessible to the end-user. The annotation scheme should consist of the set of annotative symbols used, their definitions, and the rules and guidelines for their application.

- It should also be made clear beforehand about how and by whom all the annotations were applied.
- There can be no claim that the annotation scheme represents 'God's truth'. Rather, the annotated corpus is made available to a research community on a caveat emptor principle. It is offered as a matter of convenience only, on the assumption that many users will find it useful to use a corpus with annotations already built in, rather than to devise and apply their own annotation schemes from scratch (a task which could take them years to accomplish).
- Therefore, to avoid misapplication, annotation schemes should preferably be based as far as possible on 'consensual', and 'theory-neutral analyses' of the corpus data.
- No annotation scheme should claim authority as the standard, although de facto interchange of 'standards' may arise through widening availability of annotated corpora. And this approach should be encouraged.

Principles of Annotation

For all natural languages, it is necessary to have a set of well-defined principles that are required for assigning relevant tags to various linguistic elements (e.g., characters, morphemes, words, multi-word units, phrases, etc.) to settle their lexico-semantic entities as well as their syntactico-grammatical functions in texts. Since such principles have not yet been developed for Indian languages, there is an urgent need for defining some principles to be adopted and followed for designing standards for text annotation schemes for the Indian languages. This leads us to formulate the following principles for annotation of Indian languages corpora of all text types and genres.

Principle 1: Generic Tagsets for all Indian Languages

Annotation is to be done with a clear focus on a particular set of information (e.g., part-of-speech of words). However, the long term goals should not be ignored for developing a generic scheme, which will be useful for incorporating all kinds of linguistic information easily at the later stages. Tagsets designed for different types of annotation (e.g., orthographic, prosodic, grammatical, semantic, discourse, etc.) should not be bias towards any particular Indian language or a language group, but should be generic in form so that the tagsets can work fine for all major and minor Indian languages belonging to all language families (e.g., Indo-Aryan, Dravidian, Sino-Tibetan, and Astro-Asiatic).

In fact, the annotation tagsets should be developed in such a way that they work equally fine for all natural languages across the world. This however, does not imply that the uniqueness of each language should be ignored due to generic tagset. Rather, it implies that the generic tagset may be customised based on the unique linguistic features and properties of a language or a variety. For instance, if it is noted that a particular language does not possess a grammatical category, then invariably, that particular category may be skipped for that language.

Principle 2: Uniform Tagset to be Designed for all Text Types

The tagset should not be skewed towards any particular type of text of a language. It should work elegantly well for all the text types of a language. That means a tagset designed for written text should also be equally useful for spoken texts. Similarly, a tagset developed for informative text, should be equally applicable for imaginative texts, scientific text, commercial texts, legal texts, medical texts, media text, other text types available in the language. Also, the tagset used for prose texts should equally be applicable for poetic as well as dramatic texts. In fact the same tagset may be extended for the texts retrieved from dialogic interactions, informal conversations and other types of spoken discourse found in a language.

Principle 3: Spatio-Temporal Dimension Should be Present in the Tagset

A tagset should be compatible with the existing form and texture of present day texts as well as with the old and obsolete texts available in a language. That means tagset designed for modern texts should equally be applicable for old texts of the language. It implies that the tagsets used should allow for diachronic studies when working with comparable corpora, so that it is relevant for all kinds of text marked with temporal properties.

Similarly, a tagset designed for the texts of the standard variety should equally be useful for the texts produced in dialects or regional varieties of the language. That means, for instance, a tagset designed while considering Bengali should work consistently not only for texts produced in Berlin, Germany but also for the texts produced in other states of the country as well as for the texts produced in other countries like Bangladesh, UK, USA, or other parts of the globe.

Principle 4: Layered Approach Should be used for Annotation

It is always better to adopt layered approach for tagging various kinds of linguistic information within a text, since a piece of text is enriched with varieties of information (both intralinguistic and extralinguistic). After annotation, in the resultant text, linguistic information is made explicit for end users. Therefore, it is highly desirable to tag as much linguistic information as possible within a given text. However, the reality is that linguistic information encoded within a text is quite complex and diverse in form and nature. Since capturing all kinds of linguistic information in one pass makes the task highly complex in operation, it is not a good idea both from the point of view of annotation and machine learning. Therefore, it is better to break up the collective linguistic information into layers and annotate each layer separately in the text.

Table: Linguistic information annotated at different layers.

Layer	Annotation	Linguistic Information
Layer 01	Orthographic	Characters and other symbols used in text.
Layer 02	Prosodic	Tone, accent, intonation, juncture, etc. In spoken text.
Layer 03	Morphological	Morphological forms and information of words.
Layer 04	Part- of- speech	Morpho- syntactic roles of words in text.
Layer 05	Word group	Perking compounds, reduplications collocations, etc.
Layer 06	Chunking	Marking phrase, idioms, proverbs, and mwus.
Layer 07	Parsing	Syntactic analysis of sentences, thematic roles, arguments, etc.
Layer 08	Semantic	Identifying meaning of words and sense disambiguation.
Layer 09	Anaphoric	Identifying nominal and pronominal referential relations.
Layer 10	Discoursal	Identifying discourse and pragmatic elements in texts.
Layer 11	Sociolinguistic	Socio cultural, register and ethnic elements and cues.
Layer 12	Etymological	Marking original antiquity of words used in text.

It is obvious that these layers are bound to be inter-dependent to each other because one is not dealing with totally isolated linguistic elements, but with words which are used in a text to perform varied explicit and/or implicit functions for the text. Besides, the output information obtained from one layer becomes, in some cases, the input information for the other layers. However, the degree of interdependence may vary depending on the type of a text and the nature of linguistic information marked up in the respective layers.

Principle 5: Hierarchical Formation of Tagset is Desired

Annotation of a text may be done either manually or automatically. In both cases, it has to be done starting with the lowest level tagset of the hierarchy. Once the lower level tag is selected and assigned, the higher level tags should be identified and tagged automatically. It is always better to design a tagset keeping open the possibility of including more than one level of information to words at various tiers. This is possible only when the tagset has been designed in hierarchical format. For instance, within the POS tagset we may include 'Noun' (/N/) as the head category [Level_1] where different subtypes of noun (e.g., proper noun, common noun, collective noun, abstract noun, material noun, etc.) may be used as lower level categories [Level_2 and Level_3] under the head category "Noun", as the following table shows.

Table: A hierarchical tagset for Bengali nouns.

SN	Category			Label	Examples
	Level_1	Level_2	Level_3		
1	Noun			/N/	

1.1		Proper Noun		/N_NP/	India/N_NP/
1.2		Common Noun		/N_CM/	boy/N_CM/
1.3		Collective Noun		/N_CL/	army/N_CL/
1.4		Abstract Noun		/N_AB/	love /N_AB/
1.5		Material Noun		/N_MA/	iron/N_MA/
1.6		Verbal Noun		/N_NV/	Swimming/N_NV/

Similarly, we can tag 'Verb' (/V/) as the top-level category, while 'main verb' (/VM/), 'auxiliary verb' (/VAUX/), 'finite verb' (/VF/), and 'non-finite verb' (/VNF/) may be tagged as the lower level categories of the top-level 'Verb' (/V/).

Principle 6: Meta-data Format Should be used for Tagset

All kinds of linguistic and extralinguistic information encoded and used in the tagset should be stored in the form of meta-data (e.g., HTML, SGML, XML, etc.) so that these are understandable and accessible by a computer program designed and applied for annotation. Since a language corpus may consist of several kinds of text, it is important to maintain and preserve some meta-data about each text document included in the corpus. Thus, information regarding language, title, author, source, domain, text type, time, creator of digital text document, etc. should be marked on each text in a Header File as 'Metadata', manually or automatically. An example for meta-data annotation is given in table.

Table: Header File and its information annotated with metadata.

<Header Type>	Information	<Header Type>	Information
<Language>	Bangla	<Author>	Sudhanshu Patra
<Language Type>	Written Text	<Publisher>	Dey's Publishing
<Head Category>	Humanities	<Publication Place>	Kolkata, India
<Category>	Literature	<Publication Date>	1993
<Subcategory>	Fiction	<Index No.>	B0035
<Text Type>	Imaginative	<Date Creator Code>	61802
<Source Type>	Book	<Date of Creation>	12. 09. 2006
<Title of text>	Bhut ar Bhuto	<Data Collector>	Anami Sarkar
<Volume>	Single	<Proof Reader>	Aprakash Gupta
<Issue>	Not Applicable	<Text Normalization>	16. 08. 2007
<Edition>	First	<No. of Sentences>	130
<Headline>	Bhut ar Bhuto	<Total No. of Words>	5017

The information stored in the Header File actually contains varieties of extralinguistic information, which are necessary and useful for maintaining records of documents, dissolving copyright problems, and for carrying out research in sociolinguistics, language planning, stylistics, and discourse. Therefore, it is rational to adopt a judicious approach for annotating a text with information mentioned above in universally accepted norms and rules of marking the metadata within a text.

Principle 7: Tagset Should be at Par with Global Standard

The tagset designed for the Indian languages must comply with the global standard guidelines that are defined by various agencies, such as, ELRA (European Languages Resource Association), TEI (Text Encoding Initiative), CLAWS (Constituent Likelihood Automatic Word-tagging System), ACL (Association of Computational Linguistics), ISLE (international Standards for Language Engineering), EAGLES Corpus Encoding Standard, etc., wherever available. The global guidelines would be followed to the extent that if someone works for any Indian language the output annotated text must become globally accessible and operational.

Principle 8: Extensibility of Tagset is Required for Specific Languages

The tagset should be extensible enough to include language specific requirements as well as for addition of new tags, if required. To make a tagset maximally flexible and adjustable for a language means that the tagset should be such that if and when a new set of information is found, it can be incorporated in the existing annotation scheme at various levels of the hierarchy, as the case may be. It also implies that if a particular type of annotation is redundant for a language or a text type, it should be deprecated for that particular language.

Principle 9: Dispensability of Tagset from a Text is Mandatory

It should be easy to dispense with the tagged information in an annotated text and revert it quickly to the state of raw text. The raw corpus must be recoverable, as and when needed. This is an important pre-condition of text annotation, as recovering the original raw text is essential for many works where annotated text has little applicational relevance.

Principle 10: Standardization of Tagset is a Pre-Requisition

The annotation tagset should be designed in such a manner that it can handle a wide range of applications of language technology and applied linguistics. That means the tagset should support linguistic research activities independent of a particular text type or domain of application. Moreover, it should be applicable for various tasks of language description, grammar book writing, dictionary compilation, language teaching, and language planning, etc.

Principle 11: User Friendly Tagset Should be Designed

The annotation tagset should be maximally annotator-friendly and user-friendly. This is an important feature because the primary purpose of a tagset is to annotate a text a task that is normally carried out by human beings, at least, at the initial stage of tagged text development in a language.

Principle 12: Non-Ambiguity is must for a Tagset

The task of annotation involves decision making at every stage of the task. If a proposed tagset contains a number of tags, which can have multiple interpretations, this will lead to inconsistency and confusion in the subsequent stages of annotation work. Therefore, it is suggested that all kinds of ambiguities should be avoided at the time of tagset designing.

Corpus Linguistics

Corpus Linguistics is a multidimensional area. It is an area with a wide spectrum for encompassing all diversities of language use in all domains of linguistic interaction, communication, and comprehension. The introduction of corpus in language study and application has incorporated a new dimension to linguistics. In principle, Corpus Linguistics is an approach that aims at investigating language and all its properties by analysing large collections of text samples. This approach has been used in a number of research areas for ages: from descriptive study of a language, to language education, to lexicography, etc. It broadly refers to exhaustive analysis of any substantial amount of authentic, spoken and/or written text samples. In general, it covers large amount of machine-readable data of actual language use that includes the collections of literary and non-literary text samples to reflect on both the synchronic and diachronic aspects of a language. The uniqueness corpus linguistics lies in its way of using modern computer technology in collection of language data, methods used in processing language databases, techniques used in language data and information retrieval, and strategies used in application of these in all kinds language-related research and development activities.

Electronic (digital) language corpus is a new thing. It has a history of nearly half a century. Therefore, we are yet to come to a common consensus as to what counts as corpus, and how it should be designed, developed, classified, processed and utilised. The basic philosophy behind corpus linguistics has two wings:

- We have a cognitive drive to know how people use language in their daily communication activities.
- If it is possible to build up intelligent systems that can efficiently interact with human beings.

With this motivation both computer scientists and linguists have come together to develop language corpus that can be used for designing intelligent systems (e.g., machine translation system, language processing system, speech understanding system, text analysis and understanding system, computer aided instruction system, etc.) for the benefit of the language community at large. All branches of linguistics and language technology can benefit from insights obtained from analysis of corpora. Thus, description and analysis of linguistic properties collected from a corpus becomes of paramount importance in all many areas of human knowledge and application.

The term corpus is derived from Latin corpus "body". At present it means representative collection of texts of a given language, dialect or other subset of a language to be used for linguistic analysis. In finer definition, it refers to:

- Loosely anybody of text.
- Most commonly a body of machine readable text.
- More strictly a finite collection of machine-readable texts sampled to be representative of a language or variety.

Corpus contains a large collection of representative samples of texts covering different varieties of language used in various domains of linguistic interactions. Theoretically, corpus is (C)apable (O)f (R)epresenting (P)otentially (U)nlimited (S)elections of texts. It is compatible to computer, operational in research and application, representative of the source language, processable by man and machine, unlimited in data, and systematic in formation and representation.

Salient Features of Corpus

- Quantity: It should be big in size containing large amount of data either in spoken or written form. Size is virtually the sum of its components, which constitute its body.
- Quality (= authenticity): All texts should be obtained from actual examples of speech and writing. The role of a linguist is very important here. He has to verify if language data is collected from ordinary communication, and not from experimental conditions or artificial circumstances.
- Representation: It should include samples from a wide range of texts. It should be balanced to all areas of language use to represent maximum linguistic diversities, as future analysis devised on it needs verification and authentication of information from the corpus representing a language.
- Simplicity: It should contain plain texts in simple format. This means that we expect an unbroken string of characters (or words) without any additional linguistic information marked-up within texts. A simple plain text is opposed to any kind of annotation with various types of linguistic and non-linguistic information.
- Equality: Samples used in corpus should be of even size. However, this is a

controversial issue and will not be adopted everywhere. Sampling model may change considerably to make a corpus more representative and multi-dimensional.

- Retreavability: Data, information, examples, and references should be easily retrievable from corpus by the end-users. This pays attention to preserving techniques of language data in electronic format in computer. The present technology makes it possible to generate corpus in PC and preserve it in such way that we can easily retrieve data as and when required.
- Verifiability: Corpus should be open to any kind of empirical verification. We can use data form corpus for any kind of verification. This puts corpus linguistics steps ahead of intuitive approach to language study.
- Augmentation: It should be increased regularly. This will put corpus 'at par' to register linguistic changes occurring in a language in course of time. Over time, by addition of new linguistic data, a corpus achieves historical dimension for diachronic studies, and for displaying linguistic cues to arrest changes in life and society.
- Documentation: Full information of components should be kept separate from the text itself. It is always better to keep documentation information separate from the text, and include only a minimal header containing reference to documentation. In case of corpus management, this allows effective separation of plain texts from annotation with only a small amount of programming effort.

Conceptual Classification of Corpora

Since electronic corpus is a new thing, we are yet to reach to a common consensus to what counts as a corpus, and how it should be classified. The classification scheme here goes as far as it is prudent at the present moment. It offers a reasonable way to classify corpora, with clearly delimited categories wherever possible. Different criteria for classification are applied to corpora, sub-corpora, and their related components. Linguistic criteria may be external and internal. External criteria are largely mapped onto corpora from text typology concerned with participants, occasion, social setting, communicative function of language, etc. Internal criteria are concerned with recurrence of language patterns within the pieces of language. Taking all these issues under consideration we can classify corpora in a broad scheme in the following manner: Genre of text, Nature of data, Type of text, Purpose of design, and Nature of application.

Genre of Text

- Written Corpus: A written corpus (e.g., TDIL Corpus) by virtue of its genre contains only language data collected from various written, printed, published and electronic sources.

- Speech Corpus: A speech corpus (e.g., Wellington Corpus of Spoken New Zealand English) contains all formal and informal discussions, debates, previously made talks, impromptu analysis, casual and normal talks, dialogues, monologues, various types of conversation, on line dictations, instant public addressing, etc. There is no scope of media involvement in such texts.
- Spoken Corpus: Spoken corpus (e.g., London-Lund Corpus of Spoken English), a technical extension of speech corpus, contains texts of spoken language. In such corpus, speech is represented in written form without change except transcription. It is annotated using a form of phonetic transcription.

Nature of Data

- General Corpus: General corpus (e.g., British National Corpus) comprises general texts belonging to different disciplines, genres, subject fields, and registers. Considering the nature of its form and utility, it is finite in number of text collection. That means, number of text types and number of words and sentences in it are limited. It has an opportunity to grow over time, and to append new data with availability of new texts. It is very large in size, rich in variety, wide and representation, and vast in utilisation scope.
- Special Corpus: Special corpus (e.g., CHILDES Database) is designed from texts sampled in general corpus for specific variety of language, dialect and subject with emphasis on certain properties of the topic under investigation. It varies in size and composition according to purpose. It does not contribute to the description of a language because it contains a high proportion of unusual features. Its origin is not reliable as it records the data from people not behaving normally. Special corpus is not balanced (except within the scope of its given purpose) and, if used for other purposes, gives distorted and 'skewed' view of language segments. It is different in principle, since it features one or other variety of normal, authentic language. Corpus of language of children, non-native speakers, users of dialects, and special areas of communication (e.g., auction, medical talks, gambling, court proceeding, etc.) are designated as special corpus because of their non-representative nature of the language involved. Its main advantage is that texts are selected in such a way that the phenomena one is looking for occur more frequently in it than in balanced corpus. A corpus that is enriched in such a way is smaller than a balanced corpus providing same type of data.
- Sublanguage corpus: It consists of only one text variety of a particular language. It is at the other end of the linguistic spectrum of a Reference corpus. The homogeneity of its structure and specialised lexicon allows the quantity of data to be small to demonstrate typically good and closure properties.
- Sample corpus: Sample corpus (e.g., Zurich Corpus of English Newspapers) is

one of the categories of special corpus, which is made with samples containing finite collection of texts chosen with great care and studied in detail. Once a sample corpus is developed it is not added to or changed in any way because any kind of change will imbalance its constitution and distort research requirement. Samples are small in number in relation to texts, and of constant size. Therefore, they do not qualify as texts.

- Literary corpus: A special category of sample corpus is literary corpus, of which there are many kinds. Classification criteria considered for generation of such corpus include author, genre (e.g., odes, short stories, fictions, etc.), period (e.g., 15th century, 18th century, etc.), group (e.g., Romantic poets, Augustan prose writers, Victorian novelists, etc.), theme (e.g., revolutionary writings, family narration, industrialisation, etc.) and other issues as valued parameters.

- Monitor corpus: Monitor corpus (e.g., Bank of English) is a growing, non-finite collection of texts with scope for constant augmentation of data reflecting changes in language. Constant growth of corpus reflects change in language, leaving untouched the relative weight of its components as defined by parameters. The same composition schema is followed year by year. The basis of monitor corpus is of reference to texts spoken or written in one single year. From monitor corpus we find new words, track variation in usage, observe change in meaning, establish long-term norm of frequency distribution, and derive wide range of lexical information. Over time the balance of components of a monitor corpus changes because new sources of data become available and some new procedures enable scarce material to become plentiful. The rate of flow is adjusted from time to time.

Type of Text

- Monolingual corpus: It contains representative texts of a single language representing its use in a particular period or in multiple periods. It contains both written and spoken text samples so long their cohabitation and relational interface does not hamper proposed work of the investigators.

- Bilingual corpus: Bilingual corpus is formed when corpora of two related or non-related languages are put into one frame. If these languages are genetically or typologically related they become parallel corpus where texts are aligned following some predefined parameters. Size, content, and field may vary from corpus to corpus, which is not permitted in case of parallel corpus.

- Multilingual corpus: Multilingual corpus contains representative collections from more than two languages. Generally, here as well as in bilingual corpus, similar text categories and identical sampling procedures are followed although texts belong to different languages.

Purpose of Design

- Un-annotated corpus: It (e.g., TDIL Corpus) represents a simple raw state of plain texts without additional linguistic or non-linguistic information. It is of considerable use in language study, but utility of corpus is considerably increased by annotation.
- Annotated corpus: It (e.g., British National Corpus) contains tags and codes inserted from outside by designers to record some extra information (analytical marks, parts-of-speech marks, grammatical category information, etc.) into texts. In contrast to un-annotated corpus, annotated corpus is more suitable for providing relevant information useful in various tasks for language technology including morphological processing, sentence parsing, information retrieval, word sense disambiguation, machine translation, etc.

Nature of Application

- Translation Corpora: Translation corpora generally consist of original texts of source language and their translations taken from target language. These corpora usually keep meaning and function of words and phrases constant across languages, and as a consequence, offer an ideal basis for comparing realisation of particular meanings in two different languages under identical condition. Moreover, they make it possible to discover all cross-linguistic variants, i.e. alternative renderings of particular meanings and concepts. Thus, translation corpora provide more fruitful resources both for cross-linguistic data analysis and rule formulation necessary for translation.
- Aligned corpus: It is (e.g., The Canadian Hansard Corpus) a kind of bilingual corpus where texts in one language and their translations into other language are aligned, sentence by sentence, phrase by phrase, or even word by word.
- Parallel corpus: Parallel corpus (e.g., Chemnitz German-English Corpus) contains texts as and translations in each of the languages involved allowing double-checking translation equivalents. Texts in one language and their translations into another are aligned: sentence by sentence, phrase by phrase, or even word by word. Sometimes reciprocate parallel corpora are designed where corpora containing authentic texts and translations in each of the languages are involved.
- Reference corpus: It (e.g., Bank of English) is made to supply comprehensive information about a language. It is large enough to represent all relevant varieties of language and characteristic vocabulary, so that it can be used for writing grammars, dictionaries, thesauruses and other materials. It is composed on the basis of relevant parameters agreed upon by linguistic community. It includes spoken and written, formal and informal language representing various social

and situational registers. It is used as a 'benchmark' for lexicons, for performance of generic tools, and language technology applications. With growing influence of internal criteria, reference corpus is used to measure deviance of special corpus.

- Comparable corpus: It is (e.g., Corpus of European Union) a collection of 'similar' texts in more than one language or variety. It contains texts in different languages where texts are not same in content, genre, or register. These are used for comparison of different languages. It follows same composition pattern but there is no agreement on the nature of similarity, as there are few examples of comparable corpora. It is indispensable for comparison in different languages and in generation of bilingual and multilingual lexicons and dictionaries.
- Opportunistic corpus: An opportunistic corpus stands for inexpensive collection of electronic texts that can be obtained, converted, and used free or at a very modest price; but is often unfinished and incomplete. Therefore, users are left to fill in blank spots for themselves. Their place is in situations where size and corpus access do not pose a problem. The opportunistic corpus is a virtual corpus in the sense that selection of an actual corpus (from opportunistic corpus) is up to the needs of a particular project. Monitor corpus generally considered as opportunistic corpus. There can be some other types of specification such as closed corpus, synchronic corpus, historical corpus, dialect corpus, idiolect corpus, and sociolect corpus, etc. Therefore, the scheme of classification presented here is not absolute and final. It is open for re-categorisation as well as for sub-classification according to different parameters.

Text Corpus Generation

There are various issues related with corpus design, development, and management. The issues of corpus development and processing may vary depending on the type of corpus and the purpose of use. Issues related to speech corpus development differ from issues related to text corpus development. Developing a speech corpus involves issues like propose of use, selection of informants, choice of settings, manner of data-sampling, manner of data collection, size of corpus, problem of transcription, type of data encoding, management of data files, editing of input data, processing of texts, analysis of texts, etc. Developing a written text corpus involves issues like size of corpus, text representation, question of nativity, determination of target users, selection of time-span, selection of documents, collection of text documents (e.g., books, newspapers, magazines etc.), method of data sampling (e.g., sorting of collected materials according to one's need), manner of data input (e.g., random, regular, selective, etc.), corpus sanitation (e.g., error correction omission of foreign words, quotations, dialects etc.), corpus file management, problem of copy-right, etc.

Size of Corpus

How big a corpus will be? This implies that size is an important issue in corpus generation. It is concerned with total number of words (tokens) and different words (types) to be taken into a corpus. It also involves the decision of how many categories we like keep in the corpus, how many samples of texts we need put into each category, and how many words we shall keep in each sample. Although the question of size affects validity and reliability of a corpus, it is stressed that any corpus, however big, is nothing more than a minuscule sample of all speech and writing varieties produced by the users of a language. In early days of corpus generation, when computer technology for procuring language data was not much advanced, it was considered that a corpus containing one million words is large enough to represent a language or variety. But by the middle of 1980s, computer technology went through a vast change with unprecedented growth of its storage, processing, and accessing abilities that have been instrumental in changing the concept regarding the size of a corpus.

Now it is believed that the bigger the size of corpus the more it is faithful in representing the language under consideration. With advanced computer technology we can generate corpus of very large size containing hundreds of million of words. For instance, the Bank of English, British National Corpus, the COBUILD Corpus, the Longman/Lancaster Corpus, the International Corpus of English, the American National Corpus, etc. are indeed very large in size each one containing more than hundred million words.

Text Representation

In the long run, however, the question of size becomes irrelevant in the context of representation of text samples. Large corpus does not necessarily represent a language or a variety any better way than a small corpus which is properly balanced with texts of all language varieties. Any large collection of texts is not necessarily a corpus, until it is formed with proper text representation for any kind of generalisation. We can call a corpus 'truly representative' only when the findings obtained from its analysis can be generalised to language as a whole or to a specific part of it. Therefore, rather than focussing on quantity or amount of data in a corpus, it is always better to emphasise on the quality of data or text samples. That means data should be proportionately represented from all possible domains of language use within a corpus. In essence, the overall corpus size and balance need to be set against the diversity of source texts for achieving proper text representation.

Within any text category, the greater is the number of individual text samples, the greater is the reliability of analysis of linguistic variables of a corpus. For instance, the Brown and the LOB Corpus, as well as the Survey of English Usage are considered to be good representatives of English used in America and England because these are carefully designed with systematic representation of modern English texts. A simple comparison of these with the BNC (a corpus of 500 million words) will show that the

BNC is not only larger with regard to the amount of texts, but also far more diversified in structure and in text representation. This easily settles empirically the issue of size and representation of text samples in a corpus.

Question of Nativity

The question is whose texts (speech and writing) should be included in a corpus: the texts of the native users or that of the non-native users? The general argument is that if it is a monitor corpus, then texts produced by the native users should get priority over the texts produced by the non-native users. Because, the main aim of a monitor corpus is to represent the language or the variety, which can be considered as an 'ideal form' for all kinds of works in linguistics and language technology. It has been observed that the citation of 'made-up examples' and the listing of 'ungrammatical' sentences in a monitor corpus have fairly significant effect on the results of linguistic analysis of a corpus. In that case, we find large number of 'mention' rather than 'actual use' of words and phrases within a corpus.

If our main objective for building a corpus is to know the naturally occurring language, in order to see what does occur and what does not, then permitting 'made-up examples of sentences and phrases' will make a corpus less acceptable for proposed purposes. One way of avoiding this and many other potential problems, which may be found in a special corpus, is to apply a criterion for inclusion of texts in corpus that the texts should not be too technical in nature. In case of special corpus, texts produced by non-native users may be considered, since the aim of a special corpus is to highlight the peculiarities typical to the non-native users. Here the question of representation of texts in a corpus is not related with the language as a whole, but with the language used by a particular class of people who have learnt and used language as their second language.

The basic idea is to have a corpus that includes data from which we can gather information about how a language is commonly used in various mainstream activities of linguistic interaction. When we try to produce references that will provide faithful guidance to word use, spelling variations, syntactic constructions, meanings, usages, etc. most likely, we would like to acquire texts produced by the native users. In principle, the texts written and spoken by the native users will be far more directive, appropriate, and representative for enhancing the ability of language understanding and use for the non-native users. Perhaps, this goes rightly along with the desire of the non-native users, who while learning a second language, aim to achieving the efficiency of a native language user. However, the question of nativity becomes complicated and case-sensitive when we find that the same language is used by two different speech communities separated by geographical or political distance (e.g., British English and American English).

In this case, we need to tread on a different track. It is better to recognise and generate separate corpus with separate lexical items and syntactic constructions that are common in, or typical of, the native speakers especially those which differ from one another (e.g., words and sentences typical to British English vs. words and sentences typical to American English). We also need to get into the things that are correct by the 'rules' of grammar and usage of the American English, and perfectly understandable; but just not 'right' in rules of grammar and usage in the British English. This usually betrays the most proficient 'native' speaker of American English the opportunity for enlisting their languages in corpus of British English. In this context let us consider about the Indian English. When Indian people are exposed to lots of linguistic materials that show the marks of being non-Indian English (as Indians are often exposed to many texts of the British English and the American English), people who want to describe, recognise, understand, and generate Indian English will definitely go for the texts produced by native speakers of Indian English, which will highlight the linguistic traits typical to Indian English, and thus will defy the all-pervading influence of the British English or the American English over the Indian English.

Identification of Target Users

There are no fixed target users for a general corpus. Anybody and everybody can use it for any kind of linguistic or non-linguistic purpose. For a specialised corpus, however, the question of target user is important. Since, each investigator or researcher has specific requirement, a corpus has to be designed accordingly. For instance, a person who is working on developing tools for machine translation will require a parallel corpus rather than a general corpus. Similarly, a person who is working on the comparative studies between two or more languages will require a comparable corpus rather than a monitor corpus. In the following list, we have summed up the type of corpus users and their needs with regard to the type of corpus.

Table: Type of corpus users and their needs with regard to the type of corpus.

Target users	Corpus
Descriptive linguists	General, written, and speech corpus.
NLP and LT people	General, monitor, parallel, spoken, aligned corpus.
Speech technology people	Speech corpus and spoken corpus.
Lexicographers and terminologists	General, monitor, specialised, reference, opportunistic corpus.
Dialogue researchers	Speech, spoken, annotated, specialised corpus.
Sociolinguistics	General, written, speech, monitor corpus.
Psycholinguistics	Specialised, speech, written corpus.
Historians	Literary, diachronic corpus.
Social scientists	General, speech, written and special corpus.
Comparative linguists	Bilingual, multilingual, parallel, comparable corpus.
MT specialists	Bilingual, multilingual, parallel, comparable, annotated corpus.
Information retrieval specialists	General, monitor, and annotated corpus.

Tagging, processing and parsing specialists	Annotated, monitor, written, spoken, general corpus.
Core-grammar designer	Comparable, bilingual, and general corpus.
Word-Sense disambiguation worker	Annotated, monitor, written, spoken, general corpus.
Teachers and students	Learner, monitor, and general corpus.
Linguists	All types of corpus.

Selection of Time-span

Language changes with time. So determination of particular time-span is required to capture the features of a language or a variety reflected within a specific time span. A corpus should attempt to capture a particular period of time with a clear time indicator. For instance the text materials produced and published between the year 1981 and 1995 are included in the TDIL corpus with an assumption that the data will sufficiently represent the nature and character of use of the language as noted within this time-span.

Selection of Texts Type

An important issue in text corpus generation is to determine if it will contain written texts of all types. Most of the corpora incline towards written texts of standard writings. The aim of a general corpus is to identify what are the central (common) and typical (special) to a language. Therefore, it is sensible to build a corpus with all kinds of texts of contemporary writings where a measured and proportional representation will suffice. To be realistic we should include works of the mass of ordinary writers along with works of established and well-known writers. Thus, a corpus will contain a collection of texts taken from all possible branches of human knowledge. Here the writings of highly reputed authors as well as of little-known writers are of equal importance. The catalogues and lists of publications of different publishing houses need to be consulted for collection of source materials (e.g., books, newspapers, magazines, journals, etc.) for text selection and collection. A corpus which gathers texts from various sources and disciplines where individuality of particular source is made obscured is broadly heterogeneous in nature. In essence, diversity is the safeguard to corpus against any kind of skewed text representation.

Method of Data Sampling

Text data has to be sampled and selected from the collected source materials according to the need on an investigator. Sampling of data can be random, regular, or selective. There are various ways for data sampling to ensure maximum representativeness of texts in a corpus. We must clearly define the kind of language we want to study before we define the sampling procedures for the corpus. However, random sampling is a good technique that can save a corpus from being skewed and unrepresentative. This is a standard technique which is widely used in many areas of natural and social sciences. Another approach is to define a sampling frame based on the nature of study.

Designers of the Brown Corpus, for example, adopted this. They used all the books, periodicals, magazines, journals and other texts published in a particular year. This written corpus was made up with texts of different genres such as newspaper reports, romantic fictions, legal statutes, scientific writings, social sciences, technical reports, and so on. Another reliable way is to use the complete bibliographical index available in a language. For instance, the British National Bibliography, and the Willing's Press Guide are used for generation of the Lancaster-Oslo-Bergen corpus.

Methods of Data Input

- Data from electronic sources: In this process texts from newspapers, journals, magazines, books etc. are included if these are found in electronic form.
- Data from the websites: This includes texts from web pages, web sites, and home pages.
- Data from e-mails: Electronic typewriting, e-mails, etc. are also used as source of data.
- Machine reading of text: It converts printed texts into machine-readable form by way of optical character recognition (OCR) system. Using this method, printed materials are quickly entered into a corpus.
- Manual data input: It is done through typing texts in computer. This is the best means for data collection from hand-written materials, transcriptions of spoken texts, and old manuscripts.

The process of data input is indirectly based on the method of text sampling. We can use two pages after every ten pages from a book. This makes a corpus best representative of data stored in a physical text. For instance, if a book has several chapters, each chapter containing different subject matters written by different writers, then the text samples collected in this process from all chapters are properly represented.

Each text file should have a Header which contains metadata the physical information about the texts such as genre of the text (e.g., literature, science, commerce, technology, engineering, etc.), type of text (e.g., literature, story, travelogue, humour, etc), sub-type of text (e.g., fiction, historical, social, biographical, science fiction, etc.), name of book, name of the author(s), name of the editor(s), year of publication, edition number, name of the publisher, place of publication, number of pages taken for input, etc. This information is required for maintaining records and dissolving copyright problems. It is also advantageous to keep detailed records of the materials so that the texts are identified on grounds other than those, which are selected as formatives of corpus. Information whether the text is a piece of fiction or non-fiction, book, journal or newspaper, formal or informal etc. are useful for both linguistic and non-linguistic studies. At time of input of text, the original text of the physical source must be kept unchanged. After a paragraph is entered, one blank line should be given before a new paragraph starts. When texts are collected in a random sampling manner, a unique mark or flag is needed to be posted at the beginning of a new sample of text.

Management of Data Files

Corpus data management is indeed a tedious task. It involves various related tasks such as holding, storing, processing, screening, and retrieving information from the corpus, which require utmost care and sincerity on the part of the corpus creators. Once a corpus file is created and stored in computer, one needs schemes for its regular maintenance and augmentation. There are always some errors to be corrected, some modifications to be made, and some adjustment to be made, and some improvements to be implemented. The adaptation to new hardware and software technology and the change in requirements of the users are also to be taken care of. In addition to this, there has to be constant vigilance on the retrieval tasks as well as on the processing and analytic tools to be applied on the corpus. At present, the computer technology is developed to such an extent that executing these tasks with full satisfaction is no more a dream. But this solicits for more care in handling of the digital databases, since we know that the more powerful weapon we have in our hands, the more care is needed in their use and application to avoid unwanted damages on the resources.

Corpus Sanitation

The process of corpus sanitation begins (i.e., text editing) after the texts are produced in electronic form. Generally, five types of error may occur at the time of manual data entry:

- Omission of character,
- Addition of character,
- Repetition of character,
- Substitution of character,
- Transposition of character.

To remove spelling errors, we need to thoroughly check the corpus and compare it with the actual physical data source, and do manual corrections. Care has to be taken to ensure that the spelling of words used in the corpus must resemble with the spelling of words used in the source texts. Also, it has to be checked if words are changed, repeated or omitted, punctuation marks are properly used, lines are properly maintained, and separate paragraphs are made for each text.

Besides error correction, we have to verify the omission of foreign words, quotations, dialectal forms, etc. after generation of a corpus. The naturalised foreign words are, however, allowed to enter into the corpus. Others should be omitted. Dialectal variations are allowed. Punctuation marks and transliterated words are faithfully reproduced. Usually, books on natural and social sciences contain more foreign words, phrases and sentences than books of stories or fiction. Similarly, quotations from other languages, poems, songs, mathematical expressions, chemical formulae, geometric diagrams, images, tables, pictures, figures, flow-charts and similar symbolic representations of the source texts are not entered into corpus. All kinds of processing and reference works become easier and authentic if corpus is properly edited and errors are removed.

Problems of Copyright

To be in the safe side we need clearance of copyright from all the copyright holders (i.e., publishers and/or authors, and speakers for spoken texts). Copyright laws are quite complicated. There is very little which is obviously right or wrong, and legal or illegal. Moreover, copyright problems differ in various countries. If one uses the material only for personal use, then there is no problem. This is fine not only for a single individual but also for a group of scholars who are working together on some areas of research and investigation.

So long it is not directly used for commercial purpose there is no problem to get copy-right permission for the texts to be stored in a corpus. However, using materials one can generate new tools and systems to commercialise. In that case also the copyright is not violated. The reformed generation of output provides safeguards against possible attacks from the copyright holders. But in case of direct commercial work, we must have prior permission from the legal copyright holders.

Finite Automata

The alphabet of a formal language is the set of symbols, letters, or tokens from which the strings of the language may be formed; frequently it is required to be finite. The strings formed from this alphabet are called words, and the words that belong to a particular formal language are sometimes called well-formed words or well-formed formulas. A formal language is often defined by means of a formal grammar such as a regular grammar or context-free grammar, also called its formation rule. The field of formal language theory studies the purely syntactical aspects of such languages that is, their internal structural patterns. Formal language theory sprang out of linguistics, as a way of understanding the syntactic regularities of natural languages. In computer science, formal languages are often used as the basis for defining programming languages and other systems in which the words of the language are associated with particular meanings or semantics.

A formal language L over an alphabet Σ is a subset of Σ^*, that is, a set of words over that alphabet. In computer science and mathematics, which do not usually deal with natural languages, the adjective "formal" is often omitted as redundant. While formal language theory usually concerns itself with formal languages that are described by some syntactical rules, the actual definition of the concept "formal language" is only as above: a (possibly infinite) set of finite-length strings, no more nor less. In practice, there are many languages that can be described by rules, such as regular languages or context-free languages. The notion of a formal grammar may be closer to the intuitive concept of a "language," one described by syntactic rules.

Formal Language

A formal grammar (sometimes simply called a grammar) is a set of formation rules for strings in a formal language. The rules describe how to form strings from the language's alphabet that are valid according to the language's syntax. A grammar does not describe the meaning of the strings or what can be done with them in whatever context-only their form. A formal grammar is a set of rules for rewriting strings, along with a "start symbol" from which rewriting must start. Therefore, a grammar is usually thought of as a language generator. However, it can also sometimes be used as the basis for a "recognizer" a function in computing that determines whether a given string belongs to the language or is grammatically incorrect. To describe such recognizers, formal language theory uses separate formalisms, known as automata theory. One of the interesting results of automata theory is that it is not possible to design a recognizer for certain formal languages.

Alphabet

An alphabet, in the context of formal languages, can be any set, although it often makes sense to use an alphabet in the usual sense of the word, or more generally a character set such as ASCII. Alphabets can also be infinite; e.g. first-order logic is often expressed using an alphabet which, besides symbols such as ∧, ∨, ¬, € and parentheses, contains infinitely many elements xo, x1, x2, ... that play the role of variables. The elements of an alphabet are called its letters.

Word

A word over an alphabet can be any finite sequence, or string, of letters. The set of all words over an alphabet Σ is usually denoted by Σ^* (using the Kleene star). For any alphabet there is only one word of length o, the empty word, which is often denoted by e, ε or λ. By concatenation one can combine two words to form a new word, whose length is the sum of the lengths of the original words. The result of concatenating a word with the empty word is the original word.

Operations on Languages

Certain operations on languages are common. This includes the standard set operations, such as union, intersection, and complement. Another class of operation is the element-wise application of string operations. Examples: suppose L1 and L2 are languages over some common alphabet.

- The concatenation L1L2 consists of all strings of the form vw where v is a string from L1 and w is a string from L2.
- The intersection L1 ∩ L2 of L1 and L2 consists of all strings which are contained in both languages.
- The complement ¬L of a language with respect to a given alphabet consists of all strings over the alphabet that are not in the language.
- The Kleene star: The language consisting of all words that are concatenations of 0 or more words in the original language.
- Reversal:
    - Let e be the empty word, then eR = e.
    - For each non-empty word w = x1...xn over some alphabet, let wR = xn...x1.
    - Then for a formal language L, LR = {wR | w L}.
- String homomorphism.

Such string operations are used to investigate closure properties of classes of languages. A class of languages is closed under a particular operation when the operation, applied to languages in the class, always produces a language in the same class again. For instance, the context-free languages are known to be closed under union, concatenation, and intersection with regular languages, but not closed under intersection or complement. The theory of trios and abstract families of languages studies the most common closure properties of language families in their own right.

Language

"A language is a collection of sentences of finite length all constructed from a finite alphabet of symbols. In general, if ∑ is an alphabet and L is a subset of ∑*, then L is said to be a language over ∑, or simply a language if ∑ is understood. Each element of L is said to be a sentence or a word or a string of the language.

Example: {0, 11, 001}, {ε, 10}, and {0, 1}* are subsets of {0, 1}*, and so they are languages over the alphabet {0, 1}.

The empty set φ and the set { } are languages over every alphabet. φ is a language that contains no string. { } is a language that contains just the empty string. The union of two languages L1 and L2, denoted L1 L2, refers to the language that consists of all the strings that are either in L1 or in L2, that is, to { x | x is in L1 or x is in L2 }. The intersection of L1 and L2, denoted L1 L2, refers to the language that consists of all the strings that are both in L1 and L2, that is, to {x | x is in L1 and in L2}. The complementation of a language L over Σ , or just the complementation of L when Σ is understood, denoted $\overline{L}$, refers to the language that consists of all the strings over Σ that are not in L, that is, to { x | x is in Σ * but not in L }.

Grammar

It is often convenient to specify languages in terms of grammars. The advantage in doing so arises mainly from the usage of a small number of rules for describing a language with a large number of sentences. For instance, the possibility that an English sentence consists of a subject phrase followed by a predicate phrase can be expressed by a grammatical rule of the form <sentence>→<subject><predicate> (The names in angular brackets are assumed to belong to the grammar metalanguage.) Similarly, the possibility that the subject phrase consists of a noun phrase can be expressed by a grammatical rule of the form <subject>→<noun>.

G is defined as a mathematical system consisting of a quadruple <N, Σ , P, S> where:

- N is an alphabet, whose elements are called non-terminal symbols.
- Σ is an alphabet disjoint from N, whose elements are called terminal symbols.
- P is a relation of finite cardinality on $(N \cup \Sigma)^*$, whose elements are called production rules.

Moreover, each production rule (x, β) in P, denoted x→β , must have at least one nonterminal symbol in α. In each such production rule, α is said to be the left-hand side of the production rule, and β is said to be the right-hand side of the production rule. S is a symbol in N called the start, or sentence, symbol.

Types of Grammars

- Prescriptive: Prescribes authoritative norms for a language.
- Descriptive: Attempts to describe actual usage rather than enforce arbitrary rules.
- Formal: A precisely defined grammar, such as context.
- Generative: A Formal grammar that can generate natural language expressions.

Chomsky Hierarchy of Languages

The Chomsky hierarchy consists of the following levels:

- Type-0 grammars (unrestricted grammars) include all formal grammars. They generate exactly all languages that can be recognized by a Turing machine. These languages are also known as the recursively enumerable languages. Note that this is different from the recursive languages which can be decided by an always.

- Type-1 grammars (context-sensitive grammars) generate the context-sensitive languages. These grammars have rules of the form áAâ → áãâ with A non-terminal and α,β and γ strings of terminals and non-terminals. The strings α and β may be empty, but γ must be non-empty. The rule S→ε is allowed if S does not appear on the right side of any rule. The languages described by these grammars are exactly all languages that can be recognized by a linear bounded automaton (a nondeterministic Turing machine whose tape is bounded by a constant times the length of the input).

- Type-2 grammars (context-free grammars) generate the context-free languages. These are defined by rules of the form $A \to \gamma$ with A a non-terminal and γ is a string of terminals and non-terminals. These languages are exactly all languages that can be recognized by a non-deterministic pushdown automaton. Context-free languages are the theoretical basis for the syntax of most programming languages.

- Type-3 grammars (regular grammars) generate the regular languages. Such a grammar restricts its rules to a single non-terminal on the left-hand side consisting of a single terminal, possibly followed (or preceded, but not both in the same grammar) by a single nonterminal. The rule S → ε is also allowed here if S does not appear on the right-hand side of the rule. These languages are exactly all languages that can be decided by a finite state automaton. Additionally, this family of formal languages can be obtained by languages are commonly used to define search patterns and the lexical structure of programming languages.

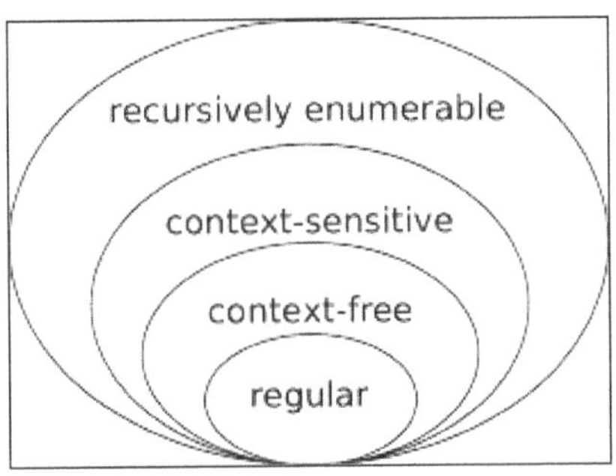

Examples:

1. The language consists of all strings begin with 0.

   {0}{0, 1}*

2. The language consists of all strings begin with 0, and end.

   {0}{0, 1}*{1}

3. The language consists of all strings with odd lengths.

   {0, 1}2n−1, n = 1, 2, . . .

4. The language consists of all strings with substring of three consecutive.

   0. {0, 1}*000{0, 1}*

5. The language consists of all strings without substring of three consecutive 0.

   {001, 01, 1}*

Regular Grammar

A regular grammar is any right-linear or left-linear grammar. A right regular grammar (also called right linear grammar) is a formal grammar (N, ∑, P, S) such that all the production rules in P are of one of the following forms:

- $B \rightarrow a$ where B is a non-terminal in N and a is a terminal in ∑.
- $B \rightarrow aC$ where B and C are in N and a is in ∑.
- $B \rightarrow \varepsilon$ where B is in N and ε denotes the empty string, i.e. the string of length 0.

In a left regular grammar (also called left linear grammar), all rules obey the forms:

- $A \rightarrow a$ where A is a non-terminal in N and a is a terminal in ∑.
- $A \rightarrow Ba$ where A and B are in N and a is in ∑.
- $A \rightarrow \varepsilon$ where A is in N and ε is the empty string.

An example of a right regular grammar G with N = {S, A}, ∑ = {a, b, c}, P consists of the following rules:

- $S \rightarrow aS$
- $S \rightarrow bA$
- $A \rightarrow \varepsilon$
- $A \rightarrow cA$

And S is the start symbol. This grammar describes the same language as the regular expression a*bc*.

Extended Regular Grammars

An extended right regular grammar is one in which all rules obey one of these:

- $B \rightarrow a$ where B is a non-terminal in N and a is a terminal in ∑.

- $A \rightarrow wB$ where A and B are in N and w is in Σ^*.
- $A \rightarrow \varepsilon$ where A is in N and ε is the empty string.

Some authors call this type of grammar a right regular grammar (or right linear grammar) and the type above a strictly right regular grammar (or strictly right linear grammar). An extended left regular grammar is one in which all rules obey one of:

- $A \rightarrow a$ where A is a non-terminal in N and a is a terminal in Σ.
- $A \rightarrow Bw$ where A and B are in N and w is in Σ^*.
- $A \rightarrow \varepsilon$ where A is in N and ε is the empty string.

Regular Expression

A regular expression (or regexp, or pattern, or RE) is a text string that describes some (mathematical) set of strings. A RE r matches a string s if s is in the set of strings described by r. Regular Expressions have their own notation. Characters are single letters for example 'a', ' '(single blank space), '1' and '-' (hyphen). Operators are entries in a RE that match one or more characters.

Regular expressions consist of constants and operator symbols that denote sets of strings and operations over these sets, respectively. The following definition is standard, and found as such in most textbooks on formal language theory. Given a finite alphabet Σ, the following constants are defined as regular expressions:

- (Empty set)φ denoting the set φ.
- (Empty string) ε denoting the set containing only the "empty" string, which has no characters at all.
- (Literal character) a in Σ denoting the set containing only the character a.

Given regular expressions R and S, the following operations over them are defined to produce regular expressions:

- (Concatenation) RS denoting the set { αβ | α in set described by expression R and β in set described by S }. For example {"ab", "c"} {"d", "ef"} = {"abd", "abef", "cd", "cef"}.
- (Alternation) R | S denoting the set union of sets described by R and S. For example, if R describes {"ab", "c"} and S describes {"ab", "d", "ef"}, expression R | S describes {"ab", "c", "d", "ef"}.
- (Kleene star) R* denoting the smallest superset of set described by R that contains ε and is closed under string concatenation. This is the set of all strings that can be made by concatenating any finite number (including zero) of strings from set described by R. For example, {"0","1"}* is the set of all finite binary

strings (including the empty string), and {"ab", "c"}* = {ε, "ab", "c", "abab", "abc", "cab", "cc", "ababab", "abcab", ... }.

To avoid parentheses it is assumed that the Kleene star has the highest priority, then concatenation and then alternation. If there is no ambiguity then parentheses may be omitted. For example, (ab)c can be written as abc, and a|(b(c*)) can be written as a|bc*. Examples:

- a|b* denotes {ε, "a", "b", "bb", "bbb", ...}.
- (a|b)* denotes the set of all strings with no symbols other than "a" and "b", including the empty string: {ε, "a", "b", "aa", "ab", "ba", "bb", "aaa", ...}.
- ab*(c|ε) denotes the set of strings starting with "a", then zero or more "b"s and finally optionally a "c": {"a", "ac", "ab", "abc", "abb", "abbc", ...}.

Deterministic Finite Automaton

- In the automata theory, a branch of theoretical computer science, a deterministic finite automaton (DFA) also known as deterministic finite state machine is a finite state machine that accepts/rejects finite strings of symbols and only produces a unique computation (or run) of the automaton for each input string. 'Deterministic' refers to the uniqueness of the computation.
- A DFA has a start state (denoted graphically by an arrow coming in from nowhere) where computations begin, and a set of accept states (denoted graphically by a double circle) which help define when a computation is successful.
- A DFA is defined as an abstract mathematical concept, but due to the deterministic nature of a DFA, it is implementable in hardware and software for solving various specific problems. For example, a DFA can model software that decides whether or not online user-input such as email addresses are valid.
- DFAs recognize exactly the set of regular languages which are, among other things, useful for doing lexical analysis and pattern matching. DFAs can be built from nondeterministic finite automata through the power set construction.

Formal Definition of DFA

A deterministic finite automaton M is a 5-tuple, $(Q, \Sigma, \delta, q_0, F)$ consisting of:

- A finite set of states (Q).
- A finite set of input symbols called the alphabet (Σ).
- A transition function ($\delta : Q \times \Sigma \rightarrow Q$).
- A start state ($q_0 \in Q$).
- A set of accept states ($F \in Q$).

Let w = a1 a2 ... an be a string over the alphabet Σ. The automaton M accepts the string w if a sequence of states, $r_o, r_1, \ldots, r_n$, exists in Q with the following conditions:

- $r_o = q_o$.
- $r_{i+1} = \delta(r_i, a_{i+1})$, for i = 0, ..., n-1.
- $r_n \in F$.

In words, the first condition says that the machine starts in the start state q_o. The second condition says that given each character of string state to state according to the transition function δ. The last condition says that the machine accepts w if the last input of w causes the machine to halt in one of the accepting states. Otherwise, it is said that the automaton rejects the string. The set of strings M accepts is the language recognized by M and this language is denoted by L(M).

Transition Function of DFA

A deterministic finite automaton without accept states and without a starting state is known as a transition system or semi automaton Given an input symbol $a \in \Sigma$, one may write the transition function as $\delta_a : Q \to Q$, using the simple trick of currying, that is, writing $\delta(q,a) = \delta_a(q)$ for all $q \in Q$. This way, the transition function can be seen in simpler terms: it's just something that "acts" on a state in Q, yielding another state. One may then consider the result of applied to the various functions δ_a, δ_b and so on. Using this notion we define $\hat{\delta}: Q \times \Sigma^* \to Q$. Given the pair of letters $a,b \in \Sigma$, one may define a new function $\hat{\delta}$, by insisting that $\hat{\delta}_{ab} = \delta_a \circ \delta_b$ where o denotes function composition. Clearly, this process can be recursively continued. So, we have following recursive definition:

$\hat{\delta}(q,\in) = q$, where $\in$ is empty string and

$\hat{\delta}(q,wa) = \hat{\delta}_a(\hat{\delta}(q,w))$, where $w \in \Sigma^*, a \in \Sigma$ and Σ and $q \in Q$.

$\hat{\delta}$ is defined for all words $w \in \Sigma^*$.

Advantages and Disadvantages of DFA

- DFAs were invented to model of a Turing machine, which was too general to study properties of real world machines.
- DFAs are one of the most practical models of computation, since there is a trivial linear time, constant-space, online algorithm there are efficient algorithms to find a DFA recognizing:
    - The complement of the language.
    - The union/intersection of the languages recognized by two given DFAs.

- Because DFAs can be reduced to a efficient algorithms to determine:
    - Whether a DFA accepts any strings.
    - Whether a DFA accepts all strings.
    - Whether two DFAs recognize the same language.
- The DFA with a minimum number of states for a particular regular language.
- DFAs are equivalent in computing power of non-deterministic finite automata (NFAs).This is because, firstly any DFA is also an NFA, so an NFA can do what a DFA can do one can build a DFA that recognizes the same language as the NFA, although the DFA could have exponentially larger number of states than the NFA.
- On the other hand, finite state automata are of strictly limited power in the languages they can recognize; many simple languages, including any problem that requires more than constant space to solve, cannot be recognized by a DFA.
- The classical example of a simply described language that no DFA can recognize is bracket language, i.e., language that consists of properly paired brackets such as word "(( )( ))".
- No DFA can recognize the bracket language because there is no limit to recursion, i.e., one can always embedded another pair of brackets inside.
- It would require an infinite amount of states to recognize. Another simpler example is the language consisting of strings of the form $a_n b_n$ some finite number of a's, followed by an equal number of b's.

Nondeterministic Finite Automaton

- In the automata theory, a nondeterministic finite automaton (NFA) or nondeterministic finite state machine is a finite state machine where from each state and a given input symbol the automaton may jump into several possible next states.
- This distinguishes it from the deterministic finite automaton (DFA), where the next possible state is uniquely determined.
- Although the DFA and NFA have distinct definitions, a NFA can be translated to equivalent DFA using power set construction, i.e., the constructed DFA and the NFA recognize the same formal language. Both types of automata recognize only regular languages.
- A NFA is represented formally by a 5-tuple, $(Q, \Sigma, \Delta, q_0, F)$, consisting of:
    - A finite set of states Q.
    - A finite set of input symbols Σ.

- A transition relation $\Delta : Q \times \Sigma \rightarrow P(Q)$.
- An initial (or start) state q_0.
- A set of states F distinguished as accepting (or final) states F.

- Here, P(Q) denotes the power set of Q. Let $w = a_1a_2... an$ be a word over the alphabet Σ. The automaton M accepts the word w if a sequence of states, $r_0, r_1, ..., r_n$, exists in Q with the following conditions:
  - $r_0 = q_0$.
  - $r_{i+1} \in \Delta(r_i, a_{i+1})$, for $i = 0, ..., n$.
  - $r_n \in F$.

Implementation of NFA

There are many ways to implement a NFA:

- Convert to the equivalent DFA. In som size of the automaton and thus auxiliary space proportional to the number of states in the NFA (as storage of the state value requires at most one bit for every state in the NFA).
- Keep a set data structure consumption of the last input symbol, if one of these states is a final state, the machine accepts the string.
- In the worst case, this may require auxiliary space proportional to the number of the NFA; if the set structure uses one bit per NFA state, then this solution is exactly equivalent to the above.
- Create multiple copies. For each n way decision, the NFA creates up to n-1 copies of the machine. Each will enter a separate state.
- If, upon consuming the last input symbol, at least one copy of the NFA is in the accepting state, the NFA will accept. (This, too, requires linear storage with respect to the number of NFA states, as there can be one machine for every NFA state.)
- Explicitly propagate tokens through the transition structure of the NFA and match whenever a token reaches the final state. This is sometimes useful when the NFA should encode additional context about the events that triggered the transition.

Natural Language Generation

NLG is a sub-field of Natural Language Processing (NLP). NLG often works closely with Natural Language Understanding (NLU), another sub-field of NLP. Where input is unstructured text, NLU helps in producing a structured representation that can be consumed by NLG. Generating language uses more of our brain than understanding it. Likewise, computers might find NLG a more difficult task than NLU. A mature NLG system can free humans from mundane writing, create narratives quickly, enable almost real-time reporting, and streamline operations.

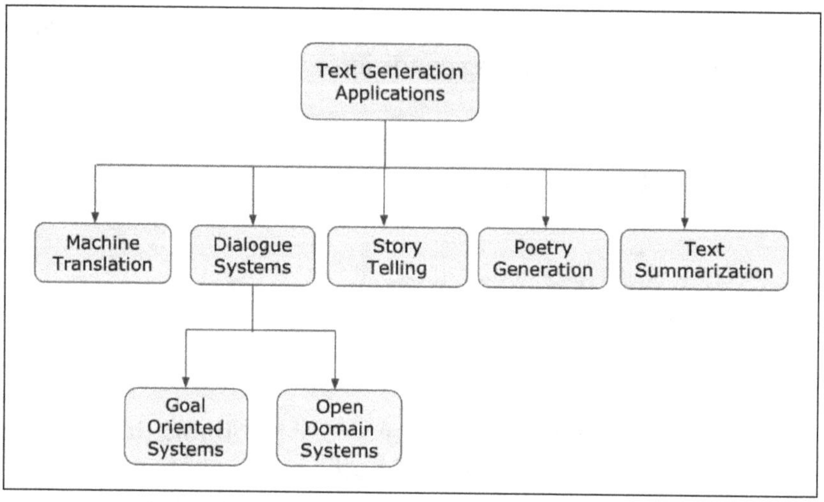

Features of a NLG System

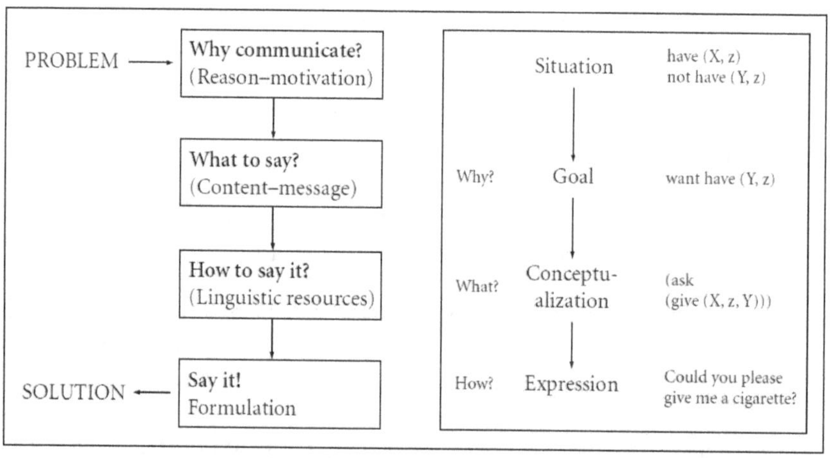

Overview of an NLG system.

NLG must include in its response information that's most relevant to the user in the current context. This includes the level of detail that's to be included. For effective communication, information must be presented in a sensible order. Thus, organization and structure are important. One sentence must follow logically from another. Likewise, NLG must know when to group them into paragraphs or even sections. NLG must conform to the syntax of the language. In addition, it's a good idea to use common expressions. A sophisticated system could be trainable, domain-independent, and even capable of sarcasms and idiomatic expressions. Style matters. If the intent is to present high-level financial summary to top management, the writing style must be formal, concise and fact-based. If the intent is to convince readers of a certain point of view, the style could be argumentative with references to supporting evidence. On the whole, NLG is about making choices and pursuing specific communicative goals.

NLG Application Pipeline

A typical NLG pipeline has these basic steps:

- Content Determination and Text Planning: Determine the information to be communicated. Structure the information. It's also called Macro Planning or Document Planning. Information could come from a knowledge base. Selection of information must consider goals and preferences of both writer and reader.
- Sentence Planning: Decide how information must be split into sentences and paragraphs. Plan for a flowing narrative. Also called Micro Planning, this involves techniques such as referring expressions, aggregation, lexicalization and grammaticalization.
- Surface Realization: Generate individual sentences in a grammatically correct manner. This involves syntax selection and inflection.
- Physical Presentation: The output could be written or spoken text. Either way, this step does articulation, punctuation and layout.

Important Tasks in NLG

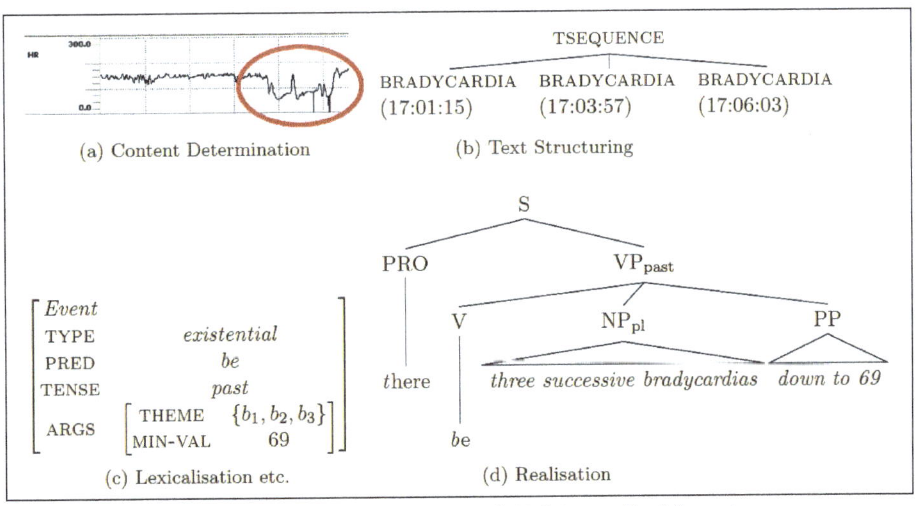

Illustrating a few components of NLG in medical domain.

We describe a few NLG components:

- Aggregation: Combining two sentences into one using a conjunction, such as

"Sam has high blood pressure and low blood sugar." Aggregation could also be applied to paragraphs and higher-order structures.

- Lexicalization: This is about word choice. Between 'depart' and 'leave', "the train departed" is more formal than "the train left".
- Referring Expression Generation: Using preceding context, select words or phrases to identify domain entities. An example is the use of pronouns, such as "I just saw Mrs. Black. She has a high temperature."
- Using Discourse Markers: The inclusion of the word 'also', makes this sentence more fluent: "If Sam goes to the hospital, he should also go to the store."
- Linguistic Realization: Consider the sentence "There are 20 trains each day from Aberdeen to Glasgow." Following syntactic rules, NLG has added function words 'from' and 'to'. Due to morphology, the plural form of 'train' has been used. Due to orthography, the first word is capitalized and full stop added at the end.

NLG System Approaches

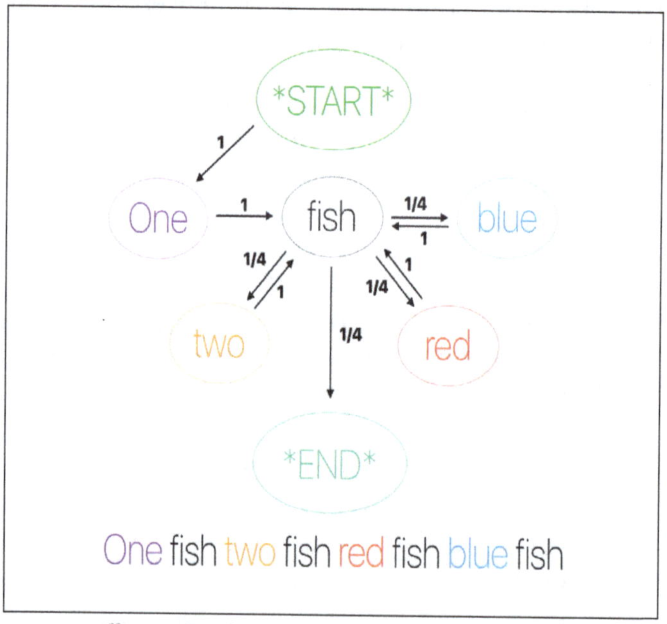

Illustrating the use of Markov Chain in NLG.

We've two approaches to NLG:

- Template-based: Texts have pre-defined structure with gaps. Gaps are filled with data. These systems evolved to allow greater control via scripts and business rules. These developed further to include linguistic capability to generate grammatically correct text.

- Dynamic Creation: At a micro level, sentences are created dynamically from semantic representations and a desired linguistic structure. At a macro level, sentences are organized into a logical narrative as suited for the audience and the purpose of communication.

For dynamic creation of text, a Markov Chain model was initially applied. Given the current word and its relationships with other words, this model predicts or generates the next word. However, such models often lacked structure and context. More recently, Language Modelling has been applied to NLG. Given recent words, the model predicts the next word. An n-gram model is a specific way to build a language model. Later, neural networks were successfully applied to language modelling. Some classify NLG into Basic NLG, Templated NLG and Advanced NLG.

Application of Neural Networks to Build NLG Models

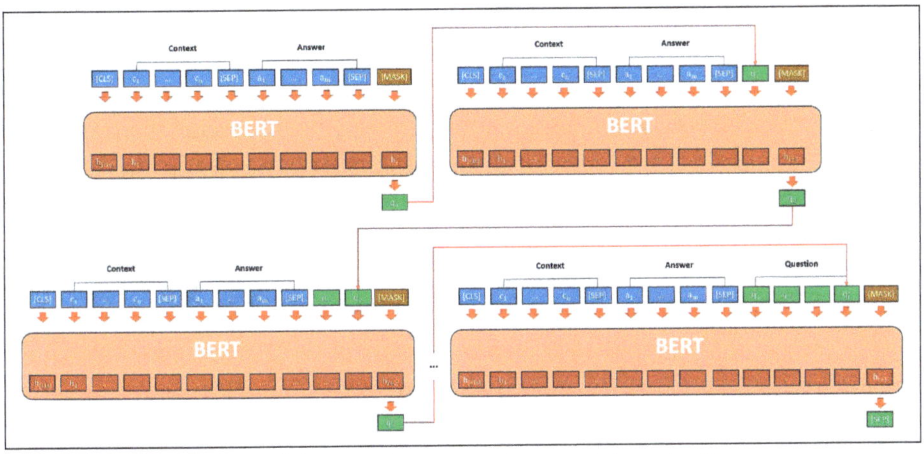

BERT used for question generation, one token at a time.

RNNs, LTSMs and transformer networks have been used for NLG models. RNNs exploit the sequential nature of text and "remember" previous words to predict the next word. LSTMs are better than RNNs at remembering longer word sequences. They also have a mechanism to selectively forget when context changes. Transformers have become popular due to their state-of-the-art performance. They look at the relationships among words in context. All words are represented individually in the vector space instead of reducing them to a single fixed-length vector. Transformers have been used to build language models and thereby enable NLG. Two popular ones are BERT and GPT-2. However, it's been remarked that GPT-2 lacks language understanding.

Neural networks typically take an end-to-end approach to NLG. We could use an encoder-decoder architecture along with an attention layer. The encoder produces a hidden representation of the input text. The decoder generates the text. Compared to template-based systems, neural network models give less control but are more flexible and expressive.

Evaluating NLG Models

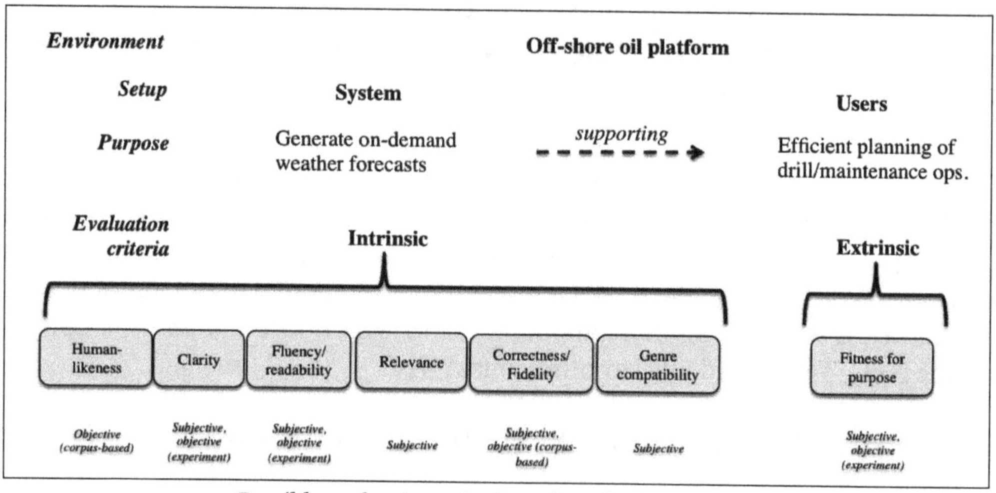

Possible evaluation criteria and methods for NLG.

Evaluating NLG systems is a challenge in itself and this has been addressed since the mid-1990s. Evaluations are useful to assess the underlying theory of an NLG system, compare two NLG systems, or determine if a particular is showing improvements. In black box evaluation, we evaluate the entire system. In glass box evaluation, we evaluate the system's component parts such as document structuring or aggregation. Evaluations should look at accuracy (conveying the desired meaning) and fluency (text flows and is readable). These two factors are not necessarily correlated. Evaluations can be by humans or automated. Multiple methods and metrics are preferred.

Evaluation metrics can be word-based (TER, BLEU, ROUGE), grammar-based (readability, spelling errors, characters per word, etc.) or measure semantic similarity. Another way to categorize the metrics is n-gram overlap (BLEU, GTM, CIDEr), content overlap (MASI, SPICE) and string distance (Levenshtein, TER). BLEU has been criticized by researchers. The E2E NLG Challenge used five metrics: BLEU, NIST, METEOR, ROUGE-L, and CIDEr; plus RankME. Rank-based Magnitude Estimation (RankME) enables reliable and consistent human evaluation.

Milestones

1950

During the 1950s and 1960s, NLG is not seen as a dedicated field of study but as a component of machine translation systems. It's only in the 1970s that researchers look into NLG for the purpose of communication. In the 1980s, NLG becomes a dedicated field of research. Also in the 1950s, the approach is template-based and therefore NLG produces the same output to all listeners in all situations.

Nov 1970

CONDITION	RULE	RESULT: V STRING FIRST	RESULT: V STRING REMAINDER	REGISTERS
START	Put verb on FIRST Set SUBJ & OBJ values	BUILD		SUBJ John OBJ house
VOICE-PASSIVE	Add -en to FIRST Put BE on FIRST EXCHANGE SUBJ & OBJ Add BE to OBJ	BUILD + EN BE	 built	SUBJ house OBJ by John
FORM-PROGRESSIVE	Add -ing to FIRST Put BE on FIRST	BE + ING BE	built being built	
ASPECT-PERFECT	Add -en to FIRST Put HAVE on FIRST	BE + EN HAVE	being built been being built	
TENSE-FUTURE	Put WILL on FIRST	Will	have been being built	
MOOD-INTERROGATIVE	FIRST + SUBJ + VSTRING REMAINDER + OBJ will + the house + have been being built + by John			

Example of sentence form determination.

Simmons and Slocum adapt semantic networks to the task of NLG. Nodes are word senses. Connecting paths are relations. Essentially, the network defines the grammar as ordered sets of syntactic transformations. The grammar includes voice, form, aspect, tense, mood, and so on. This is used by the algorithm when generating text. They implement this in LISP.

1974

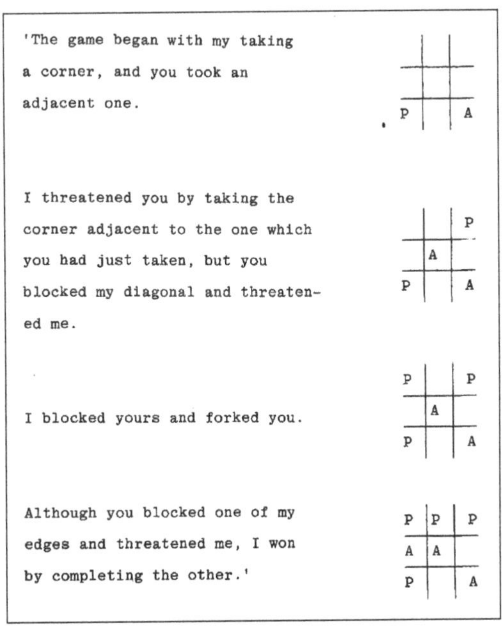

Discource production: game commentary on a sequence of moves.

Davey makes the case that production (NLG) is not a reverse process of comprehension (NLU). While language syntax may benefit comprehension, it's not sufficient for discourse-based production. From a given semantic representation, the form that the sentence would take is unpredictable.

1992

As one of the earliest commercial applications of NLG, Goldberg et al. describe a system that generates bilingual weather reports from graphical weather predictions.

Mar 1997

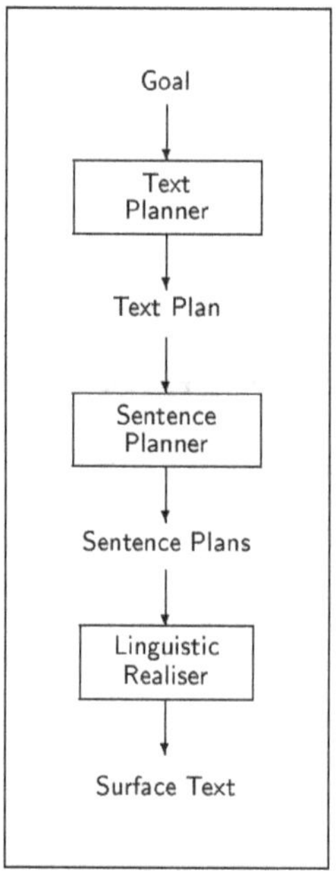

Architecture of an NLG system.

Reiter and Dale note that the most common architecture for NLG is a three-stage pipeline. They describe each stage along with essential tasks that belong to each stage. They give guidelines to developers to build practical NLG systems. They also note that NLG may not be the right approach for some use cases. Instead, present information graphically, use mail-merge systems or employ human authors.

Sep 1989

Hovy notes that beyond the literal meaning of words, we often tune our communication in relation to the listener, the situation, or interpersonal goals. Hovy therefore studies the importance of pragmatics. NLG has often asked two questions: "what shall I say?" and "how shall I say it?" NLG should also concern itself with "why should I say it?" Hovy also implements a program called PAULINE, which he acknowledges being primitive and much more research needs to be done.

Protester	University
On April 4,	On April 4,
concerned Yale students	*a small group of* students
	took over
constructed a shantytown	
on *Boesak Plaza*	*Beinecke Plaza*
	and built some shanties;
as a *reminder* to	they wanted to *force*
those in Woodbridge Hall	*Yale*
that Yale is complicit...	to sell its stocks...

The same event is described differently by different stakeholders.

1993

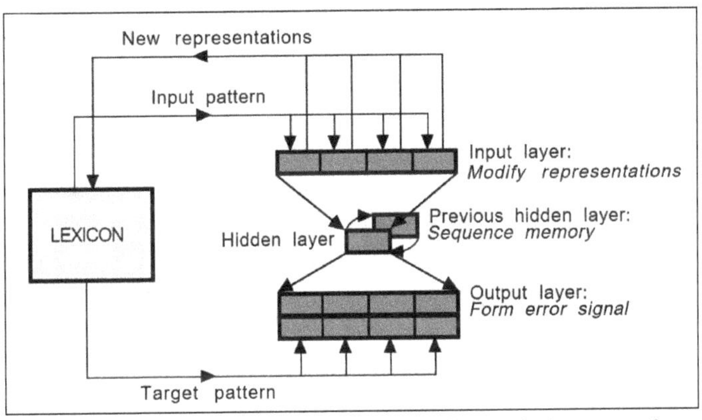

Word representations stored in the lexicon are learned via a neural network.

Miikkulainen proposes DISCERN as a sub-symbolic neural network model for NLG. It can create summaries or answer questions. The system includes parsers, at sentence level and story level. For generation, there's a story generator and a sentence generator. These are helped by a memory block and a lexicon. Distributed real-valued vectors represent words both at lexical and semantic levels. Representations are based on thematic case roles. Other early neural networks for NLG from the 1990s include ANA and FIG.

Jun 2000

The first International Natural Language Generation Conference (INLG) is held, as a continuation of international workshops on NLG held regularly during 1982-1998. INLG becomes an almost biennial event. Full papers of these conferences are available online.

2007

For college basketball in the US, StatSheet is launched to provide game previews, injury reports, and recaps. Much of this is generated automatically. Soon it becomes the top website for college basketball statistics. In 2011, StatSheet changes its name to Automated Insights and partners with NFL for automated content production.

2013

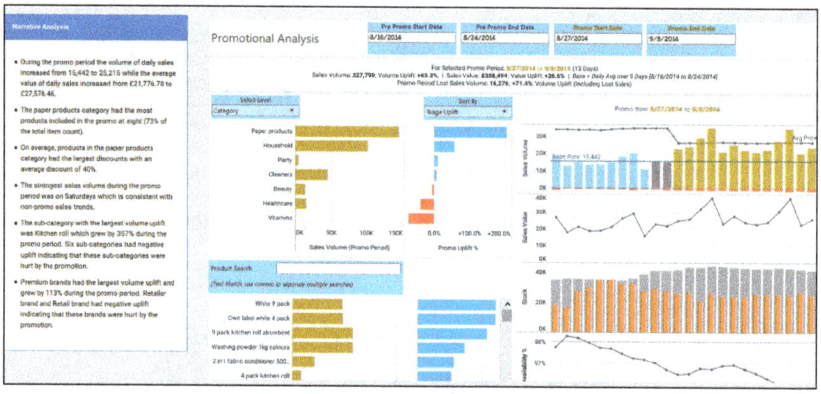

Screenshot of a demo showing generated text (left panel) in retail promotional analysis.

NLG enters the fields of data analysis and business intelligence. A particular example is Allstate Industries adopting NLG. In 2015, Gartner names NLG as an official technology space. It predicts that by 2020, NLG will be a standard feature in 90% on these platforms. By 2016, NLG gets integrated into many BI and data visualization platforms such as Tableau, MicroStrategy and Power BI.

Jun 2016

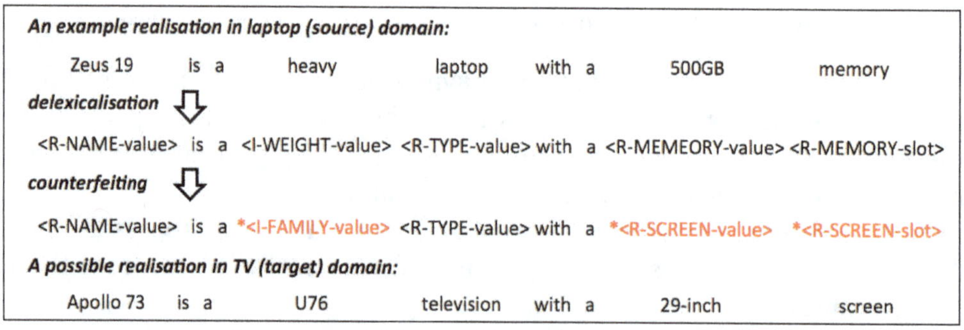

Data counterfeiting used for multi-domain NLG.

By exploiting similarities across domains, Wen et al. propose a method to train models for multi-domain NLG. Synthesized out-of-domain training data is created by data counterfeiting. Then the model is fine-tuned using a much smaller dataset of in-domain utterances. Semantically Conditioned Long Short-Term Memory (SC-LSTM) network is used. Reading gates control semantic input features presented to the network.

Aug 2016

Researchers show that when users are presented with uncertain data, NLG improves decision making. They use graphs of weather forecasts with likelihoods. Decisions are better by 24% with NLG, and by 44% when NLG is combined with graphs. The improvement is as high a 87% for women.

Mar 2017

MR	name[The Wrestlers], priceRange[cheap], customerRating[low]
Reference	The wrestlers offers competitive prices, but isn't highly rated by customers.

Attribute	Data Type	Example value
name	verbatim string	*The Eagle, ...*
eatType	dictionary	*restaurant, pub, ...*
familyFriendly	boolean	*Yes / No*
priceRange	dictionary	*cheap, expensive, ...*
food	dictionary	*French, Italian, ...*
near	verbatim string	*Zizzi, Cafe Adriatic, ...*
area	dictionary	*riverside, city center, ...*
customerRating	dictionary	*1 of 5 (low), 4 of 5 (high), ...*

MR-Reference example and restaurant domain ontology.

Researchers initiate the E2E NLG Challenge. Whereas there are many distinct steps in traditional text generation method, end-to-end generation attempts to combine all steps into a single model. Such a model would be trained on vast amounts of annotated text. For the Challenge, a crowd-sourced dataset of 50k instances in the restaurant domain is used. Training data consists of meaning representations (MRs) and corresponding reference texts. In 2018, from 62 submissions, a seq2seq-based ensemble model with re-ranker is judged the overall winner.

Text Generation using Statistical Language Models

First of all let's see how we can generate text with the help of a statistical model, like an N-Gram model. Suppose we have to generate the next word for the below sentence:

"There she built a?"

Let's say that our N-Gram model considers a context of 3 previous only to predict the next word. So, the model will try to maximize the probability P (w | "she built a"), where 'w' represents each and every word in the text dataset. Whichever word that maximizes that probability will be generated as the next word for the sentence "There she built a...". However, there are certain drawbacks of using such statistical models that use the immediate previous words as context to predict the next word. Let us give you some extra context.

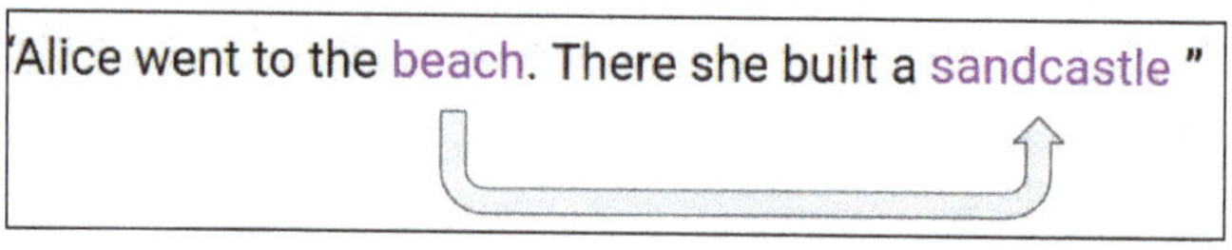

Now we have some more information about what's going on. The term "sandcastle" is very likely as the next word because it has a strong dependency on the term "beach" because people build sandcastles on beaches mostly right. So, the point is that "sandcastle" does not depend on the immediate context ("she built a") as much as it depends on "beach".

Text Generation using Neural Language Models

To capture such unbounded dependencies among the tokens of a sequence we can use an RNN/LSTM based language model. The following is a minimalistic representation of the language model that we will use for NLG.

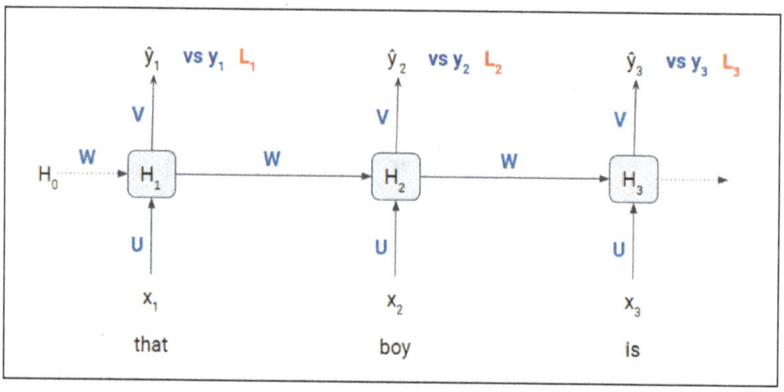

- x_1, x_2, and x_3 are the inputs word embeddings at timestep 1, timestep 2, and timestep 3 respectively.
- $\hat{y}_1$, $\hat{y}_2$, and $\hat{y}_3$ are the probability distribution of all the distinct tokens in the training dataset.
- y_1, y_2, and y_3 are the ground truth values.
- U, V, and W are the weight matrices.
- H_0, H_1, H_2, and H_3 are the hidden states.

Understanding the Functioning of Neural Language Models

We will try to understand the functioning of a neural language model in three phases:

- Data Preparation,

- Model Training,
- Text Generation.

Data Preparation

Let's assume that we will use the sentences below as our training data.

['alright that is perfect',

'that sounds great',

'what is the price difference']

The first sentence has 4 tokens, the second has 3 and the third has 5 tokens. So, all these sentences have varying lengths in terms of tokens. An LSTM model accepts sequences of the same length only as inputs. Therefore, we have to make the sequences in the training data have the same length. There are multiple techniques to make sequences of equal length. One technique is padding. We can pad the sequences with padding tokens wherever required. However, if we use this technique then we will have to deal with the padding tokens during loss calculation and text generation.

So, we will use another technique that involves splitting a sequence into multiple sequences of equal length without using any padding token. This technique also increases the size of the training data. Let me apply it to our training data. Let's say we want our sequences to have exactly three tokens. Then the first sequence will be split into the following sequences:

['alright that is',

'that is perfect']

The second sequence is of length three only so it will not be split. However, the third sequence of the training data has five tokens and it will be broken down into multiple sequences of tokens:

['what is the',

'is the price',

'the price difference']

Now the new dataset will look something like this:

['alright that is',

'that is perfect',

'that sounds great',

'what is the',

'is the price',

'the price difference']

Model Training

Since we want to solve the next word generation problem, the target should be the next word to the input word. For example, consider the first text sequence "alright that is".

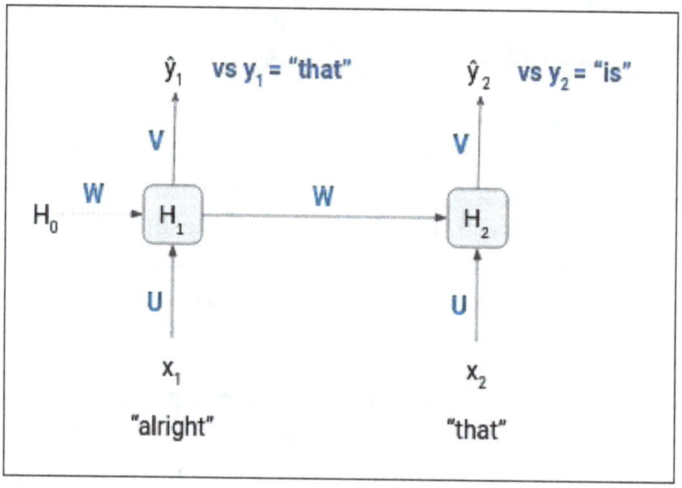

With respect to the first sequence of our training data, the inputs to the model are "alright" and that", and the corresponding target tokens are "that" and "is". Hence, before starting the training process, we will have to split all the sequences in the dataset to inputs and targets.

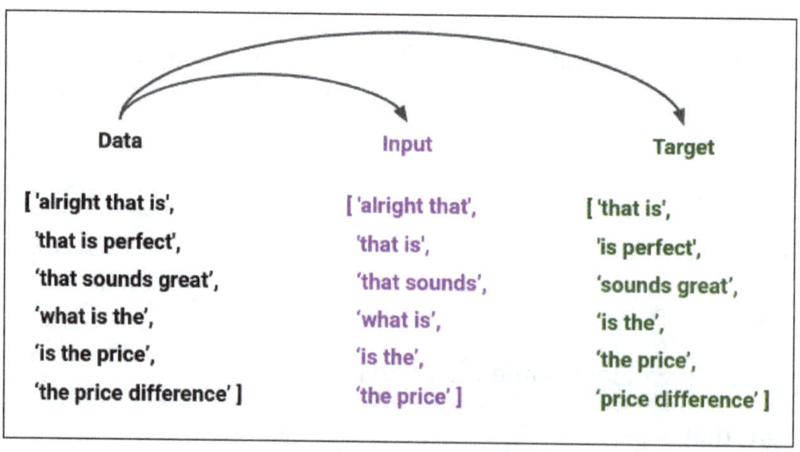

So, these pairs of sequences under Input and Target are the training examples that will be passed to the model, and the loss for a training example will be the mean of losses at each timestep.

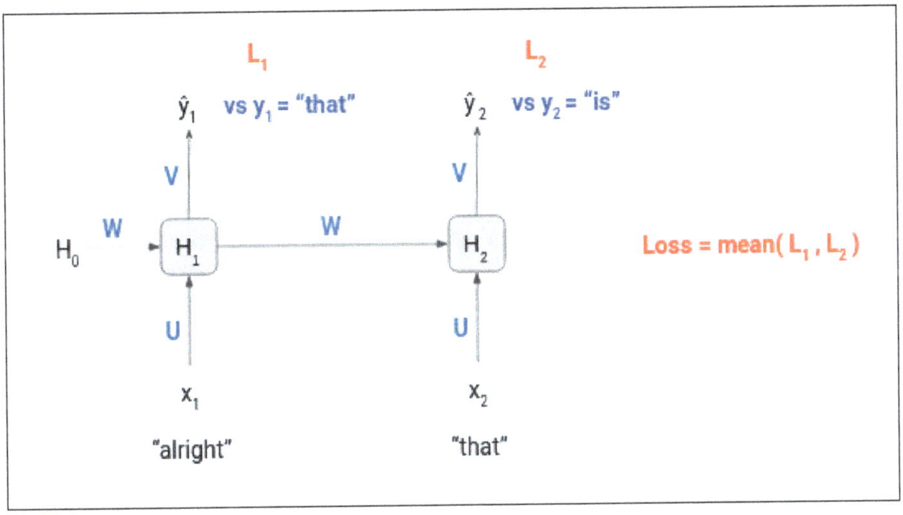

Text Generation

Once our language model is trained, we can then use it for NLG. The idea is to pass a text string as input along with a number of tokens you the model to generate after the input text string. For example, if the user passes "what is" as the input text and specifies that the model should generate 2 tokens, then the model might generate "what is going on" or "what is your name" or any other sequence.

input text = "what is"

n = 2

Step 1: The first token ("what") of the input text is passed to the trained LSTM model. It generates an output ŷ1 which we will ignore because we already know the second token ("is"). The model also generates the hidden state H1 that will be passed to the next timestep.

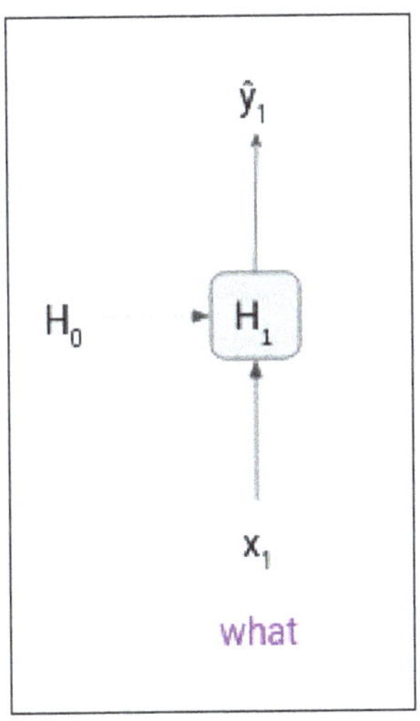

Step 2: Then the second token ("is") is passed to the model at timestep 2 along with H1. The output at this timestep is a probability distribution in which the token "going" has the maximum value. So, we will consider it as the first generated or predicted token by our model. Now we have one more token left to generate.

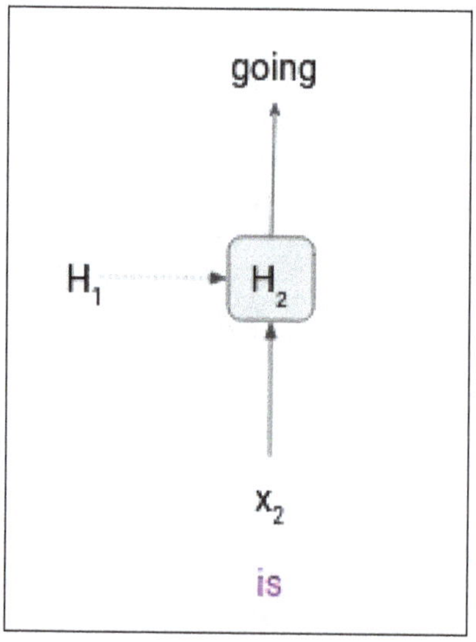

Step 3: In order to generate the next token we need to pass an input token to the model at timestep 3. However, we have run out of the input tokens, "is" was the last token that generated "going". So, what do we pass next as input? In such a case we will pass the previously generated token as the input token.

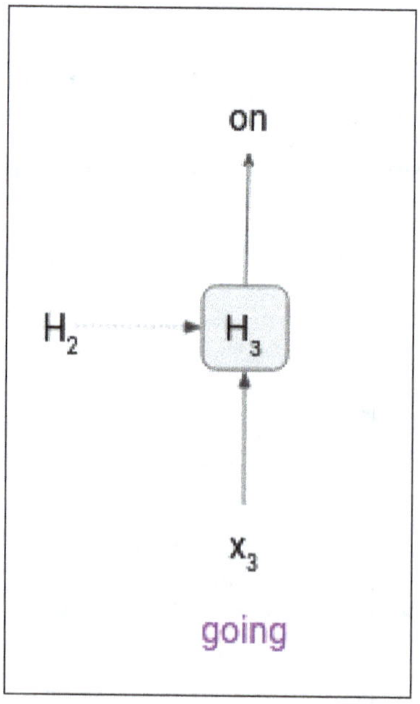

The final output of the model would be "what is going on". That is the text generation strategy that we will use to perform NLG.

References

- Corpus-Linguistics: ldcil.org, Retrieved 12, August 2020
- Natural-language-generation: devopedia.org, Retrieved 08, April 2020
- Build-a-natural-language generation-nlg-system-using-pytorch: analyticsvidhya.com, Retrieved 13, January 2020

3

Language Theory and Parsing

The analysis of string of symbols in computer languages, data structures or natural language, which conform to the rules of formal grammar, is known as parsing. The topics elaborated in this chapter will help in gaining a better perspective about language theory and parsing as well as context-free languages and top-down parsing.

Regular Languages

Lexical analysis, also called scanning, is the phase of the compilation process which deals with the actual program being compiled, character by character. The higher level parts of the compiler will call the lexical analyzer with the command "get the next word from the input", and it is the scanner's job to sort through the input characters and find this word. The types of "words" commonly found in a program are:

- Programming language keywords, such as if, while, struct, int etc.
- Operator symbols like =, +, -, &&, !, <= etc.
- Other special symbols like: ( ), { }, [ ], ;, & etc.
- Constants like 1, 2, 3, 'a', 'b', 'c', "any quoted string" etc.
- Variable and function names (called identifers) such as x, i, t1 etc.

Some languages (such as C) are case sensitive, in that they differentiate between e.g. if and IF; thus the former would be a keyword, the latter a variable name. Also, most languages would insist that identifiers cannot be any of the keywords, or contain operator symbols (versions of Fortran don't, making lexical analysis quite difficult). In addition to the basic grouping process, lexical analysis usually performs the following tasks:

- Since there are only a finite number of types of words, instead of passing the actual word to the next phase we can save space by passing a suitable representation. This representation is known as a token.
- If the language isn't case sensitive, we can eliminate differences between case at this point by using just one token per keyword, irrespective of case; e.g.

```
#define IF - TOKEN 1
#define WHILE - TOKEN 2
.....
.....
if we meet "IF", "If", "iF", "if" then return IF_TOKEN
if we meet "WHILE, "While", "WHile", ... then return WHILE - TOKEN
```

- We can pick out mistakes in the lexical syntax of the program such as using a character which is not valid in the language. (we do not worry about the combination of patterns; e.g. the pattern of characters "+*" would be returned as PLUS-TOKEN, MULT-TOKEN, and it would be up to the next phase to see that these should not follow in sequence.)
- We can eliminate pieces of the program that are no longer relevant, such as spaces, tabs, carriage-returns (in most languages), and comments.

In order to specify the lexical analysis process, what we need is some method of describing which patterns of characters correspond to which words.

Regular Expressions

Regular expressions are used to define patterns of characters; they are used in UNIX tools such as awk, grep, vi and, of course, lex. A regular expression is just a form of notation, used for describing sets of words. For any given set of characters ∑, a regular expression over ∑ is defined by:

- The empty string, ε, which denotes a string of length zero, and means "take nothing from the input". It is most commonly used in conjunction with other regular expressions e.g. to denote optionality.
- Any character in ∑ may be used in a regular expression. For instance, if we write a as a regular expression, this means "take the letter a from the input"; i.e. it denotes the (singleton) set of words {"a"}.
- The union operator, "|", which denotes the union of two sets of words. Thus the regular expression a|b denotes the set {"a", "b"}, and means "take either the letter a or the letter b from the input".
- Writing two regular expressions side-by-side is known as concatenation; thus the regular expression ab denotes the set {"ab"} and means "take the character a followed by the character b from the input".
- The Kleene closure of a regular expression, denoted by "*", indicates zero or more occurrences of that expression. Thus a* is the (infinite) set {ε, "a", "aa", "aaa", . . . } and means "take zero or more as from the input".

Brackets may be used in a regular expression to enforce precedence or increase clarity.

Non-Deterministic Finite-State Automata

In order to try and understand how lex builds a scanner, we will construct a formal model of the scanning process. This model should take characters one-by-one from the input, and identify them with particular patterns which match up with a regular expression. The standard model used is the finite-state automaton. We can convert any definition involving regular expressions into an implementable finite automaton in two steps:

Regular expression ↔ NFA ↔ DFA

A non-deterministic finite-state automaton (NFA) consists of:

- An alphabet Σ of input symbols.
- A set of states, of which we distinguish:
    - A unique start state, usually numbered "0".
    - A set of final states.
- A transition relation which, for any given state and symbol gives the (possibly empty) set of next states.

We can represent a NFA diagrammatically using a (labelled, directed) graph, where states are represented by nodes (circles) and transitions are represented by edges (arrows). The purpose of an NFA is to model the process of reading in characters until we have formed one of the words that we are looking for.

How an NFA Operates

- We begin in the start state (usually labelled 0) and read the first character on the input.
- Each time we are in a state, reading a character from the input, we examine the outgoing transitions for this state, and look for one labelled with the current character. We then use this to move to a new state.
    - There may be more than one possible transition, in which case we choose one at random.
    - If at any stage there is an output transition labelled with the empty string, ε, we may take it without consuming any input.
- We keep going like this until we have no more input, or until we have reached one of the final states.

- If we are in a final state, with no input left, then we have succeeded in recognising a pattern.
- Otherwise we must backtrack to the last state in which we had to choose between two or more transitions, and try selecting a different one.

Basically, in order to match a pattern, we are trying to find a sequence of transitions that will take us from the start state to one of the finish states, consuming all of the input. The key concept here is that: every NFA corresponds to a regular expression. Moreover, it is fairly easy to convert a regular expression to a corresponding NFA. To see how NFAs correspond to regular expressions, let us describe a conversion algorithm.

Converting a Regular Expression to a NFA-Thompson's Algorithm

We will use the rules which defined a regular expression as a basis for the construction:

1. The NFA representing the empty string is:

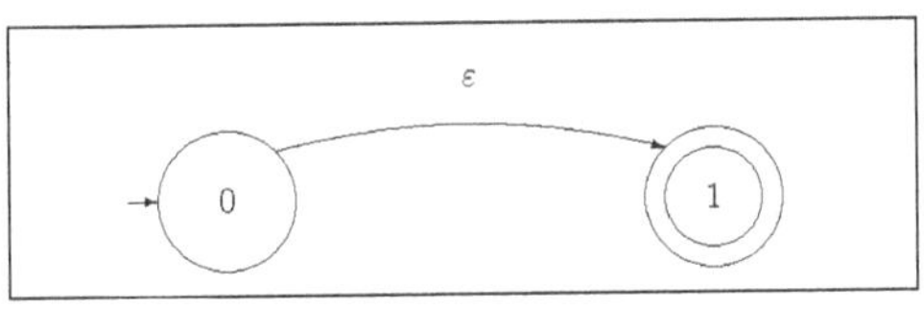

2. If the regular expression is just a character, e.g. a, then the corresponding NFA is:

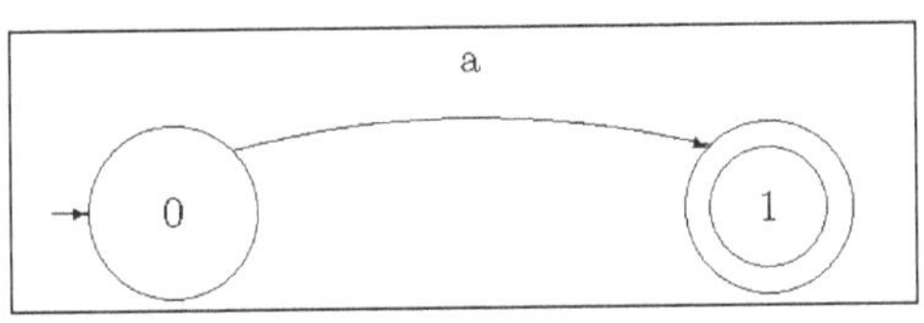

3. The union operator is represented by a choice of transitions from a node; thus a|b can be represented as:

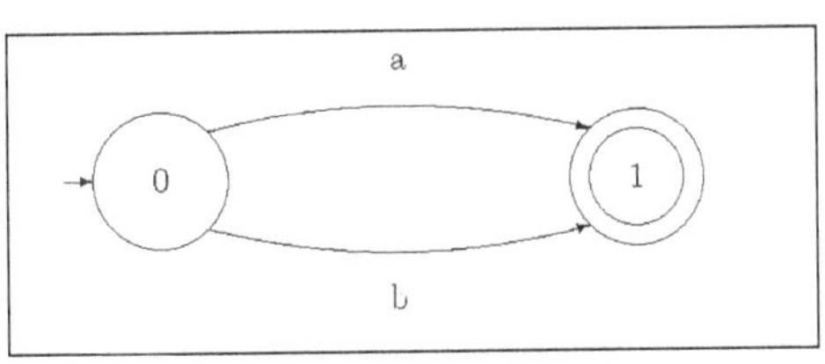

4. Concatenation simply involves connecting one NFA to the other; e.g. ab is:

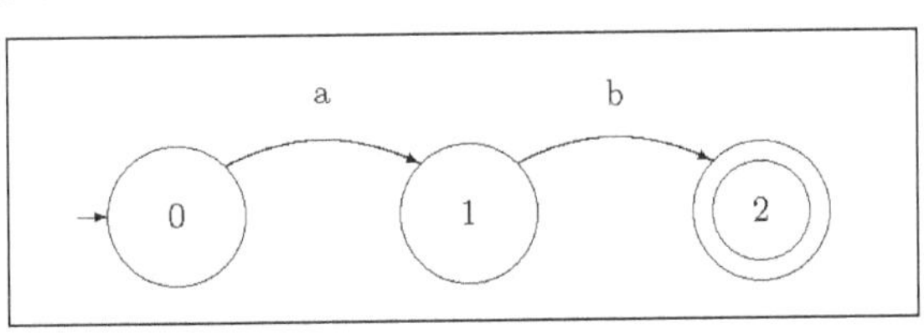

5. The Kleene closure must allow for taking zero or more instances of the letter from the input; thus a* looks like:

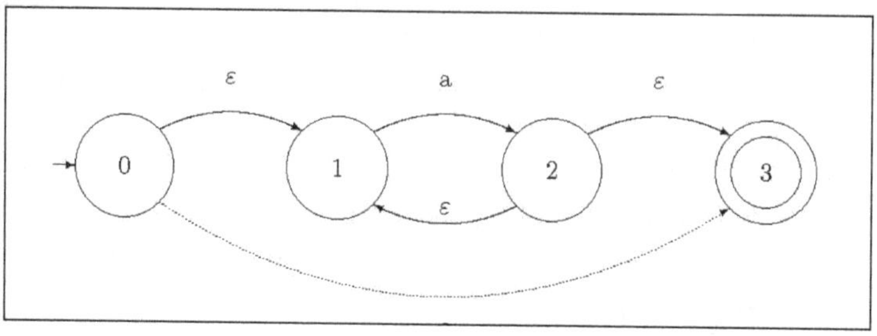

Kleene's Theorem

We have shown how to convert a regular expression to an NFA; the proof that these represent the same language is straightforward (by induction). However, we have asserted that there is a correspondence in both directions; this is formalised in Kleene's Theorem:

1. Kleene's Theorem, part 1: To each regular expression there corresponds a NFA.

Strategy: The corresponding NFA is the one constructed by Thompson's Algorithm; proof that it is equivalent is by induction over regular expressions.

2. Kleene's Theorem, part 2: To each NFA there corresponds a regular expression.

Strategy: Proof by induction over the states of the NFA (sort of).

The language represented by a NFA can be partitioned into the union of a number of smaller languages, each defined as follows:

Let the states of the NFA be numbered from 1 to N.

Let p and q be states, and let J be a number such that $0 \le J \le N$.

Then:

$$L(p,q,J) = \left\{ \begin{array}{r} x \in \Sigma^* \mid x \text{ corresponds to a path in the NFA between p and q} \\ \text{that passes through no state numbered as high as J} \end{array} \right\}$$

If S is the start state, then the union of all L(S, F, N + 1) for all finish states F is the language accepted by the NFA. Equally, if we can show that L(p, q, J) has a corresponding regular expression for all p, q and J, we will have proved the theorem. The proof of this will proceed by induction over J.

Proof:

- Base Case: J = 1

We must be able to get from p to q without passing through any states; therefore either p=q, or we go directly in one transition from p to q. The only strings that can be recognised in this case are ε and single characters from ∑. The rules R_1 and R_2 give us a regular expression corresponding to these situations.

- Inductive Step: J = K + 1

The induction hypothesis is that for some K such that 1 ≤ K ≤ N, the language L(p, q, K) has a corresponding regular expression. Now we must prove that, based on this assumption, L(p, q, K +1) has a corresponding regular expression.

Suppose the machine L(p, q, K + 1) consumes some string x; we must find a regular expression corresponding to x. Now suppose also that it passes through state K on its way (if it doesn't, then x is in L(p, q, K), which has a corresponding regular expression by the induction hypothesis). Since the machine can "loop" on K arbitrarily many times, we can split x up into three substrings:

- a which moves the machine from state p to state K.
- b which causes the machine to "loop" on state K.
- c which moves the machine from state K to state q.

While any of the above strings may cause us to start or finish at state K, none of them actually cause us to move through K. Thus we have:

$$
\begin{aligned}
&a \in L(p,K,K)\\
&b \in L(K,K,K)\\
&c \in L(K,q,K)
\end{aligned}
$$

By the induction hypothesis each of these have corresponding regular expressions, say A, B and C respectively, and thus the regular expression for x is A(B*)C. Since our choice of x was arbitrary, we have proved the theorem.

Converting a NFA to a Regular Expression

The last theorem actually yields an algorithm for converting a NFA to a regular expression. The proof was by induction; we can transform this into a recursive function where the recursion is based on an integer argument. The induction step tells us that to calculate the language L(p, q, K + 1) for any K > 1, it will either be:

- The language L(p, q, K).
- The language (L(p, K, K).L(K, K, K) ∗ .L(K, q, K)).

If we represent this "or" by the union operation, we then have a recursive definition of L(p, q, K + 1) in terms of languages of the form L(_,_, K). The base case is where K = 1. These machine components correspond to one-step transitions in the FSA, and the equivalent regular expressions are thus just the symbols which cause those transitions.

Based on this we can define function L, which takes three numbers as arguments and returns a regular expression, as follows:

```
regular-expression L(int I, int J, int K)
{
if (K == 1)
    return {a | there is an 'a' transition between states I and J}
else
    return L(p,q,K-1)|(L(p,K-1,K-1).L(K-1,K-1,K-1)*.L(K-1,q,K-1));
}
```

Given any FSA with N states altogether, where S is the start state and F is the final state, we convert it to a regular expression by calling the function L(S, F, N+1).

Deterministic Finite-State Automata

NFAs are useful, in that they are easily constructed from regular expressions, and give us some kind of computational idea of how a scanner might work. However, since they involve making decisions, and backtracking if that decision was wrong, they are not really suitable for implementation using conventional programming languages. Instead, we use a Deterministic Finite-State Automaton (DFA) which is a special case of a NFA with the additional requirements that:

- There are no transitions involving ε.
- No state has two outgoing transitions based on the same symbol.

Thus, when we are in some state in a DFA, there is no choice to be made; the operation of a DFA can very easily be converted into a program. Every NFA can be converted to an equivalent DFA. The basic idea here is that sets of states in the NFA will correspond to just one state in the DFA.

Constructing a DFA from an NFA

We merge together NFA states by looking at them from the point of view of the input characters:

- From the point of view of the input, any two states that are connected by an ε-transition may as well be the same, since we can move from one to the other without consuming any character. Thus states which are connected by an ε-transition will be represented by the same states in the DFA.

- If it is possible to have multiple transitions based on the same symbol, then we can regard a transition on a symbol as moving from a state to a set of states (i.e. the union of all those states reachable by a transition on the current symbol). Thus these states will be combined into a single DFA state.

To perform this operation, let us define two functions:

- The ε-closure function takes a state and returns the set of states reachable from it based on (one or more) ε-transitions. This will always include the state itself. We should be able to get from a state to any state in its ε-closure without consuming any input.
- The function move takes a state and a character, and returns the set of states reachable by one transition on this character.

We can generalise both these functions to apply to sets of states by taking the union of the application to individual states. E.g. If A, B and C are states, move ({A,B,C},'a') = move(A,'a') ∪ move(B,'a') ∪ move(C,'a').

Subset Construction Algorithm

- Create the start state of the DFA by taking the ε-closure of the start state of the NFA.
- Perform the following for the new DFA state (for each possible input symbol):
    - Apply move to the newly-created state and the input symbol; this will return a set of states.
    - Apply the ε-closure to this set of states, possibly resulting in a new set.
- This set of NFA states will be a single state in the DFA.
- Each time we generate a new DFA state, we must apply above step to it. The process is complete when applying above step does not yield any new states.
- The finish states of the DFA are those which contain any of the finish states of the NFA.

DFA Minimisation

Since we are interested in translating a DFA into a program, we will want to ensure that this program is as efficient as possible. In automata terms, one aspect of this will be to ensure that the constructed DFA has as few states as possible. This is achieved by an algorithm known as DFA minimisation. We take the "optimistic" approach: we start by assuming that all states are actually the same, and only distinguish those which we can prove are different. As for subset construction, the states of the minimised DFA will be sets of states from the original DFA. Two states are different if:

- One is a final state and the other isn't.
- The transition function maps them to different states, based on the same input character.

We base our algorithm on partitioning the states using this criterion.

- Initially start with two sets of states: the final, and the non-final states.
- For each state-set created by the previous iteration, examine the transitions for each state and each input symbol. If they go to a different state-set for any two states, then these should be put into different state-sets for the next iteration.
- We are finished when an iteration creates no new state-sets.

Further Properties of Regular Languages

We can prove facts about language membership by describing constructions on their corresponding automata. It is possible to prove facts other than language membership using a FSA.

Total DFA

The last type of FSA that we need to look at is the total DFA this has properties which we will need in the next section. A total FSA is one where each state has exactly one transition to some other state for every input symbol. Thus there are no "gaps" in the transition table for the machine: given any state and any input symbol, it will always be possible to make a transition.

We can convert any ordinary DFA to a total DFA as follows:

- Create some new state S, which we will use for "stuck" computations.
- For each input symbol, make a transition from state S to itself: thus it is never possible to leave this state.
- For each other state S', and for every possible input symbol a, check to see if S' has an outgoing transition on a; if it doesn't, then make a new transition from S' to S on a.

It can be easily seen that this DFA is total.

Closure of Regular Languages

By the definition of regular expressions (and by Thompson's algorithm), we know that the union, concatenation and Kleene closure of regular languages must also be a regular language. It is reasonable to ask: does this hold for other "set-theoretic" operations, such as intersection, difference and complement? These languages are regular by constructing the appropriate automata. Let L_1 and L_2 be regular languages over the alphabet Σ, and let M_1 and M_2 be their corresponding total DFAs. Let us define the components of M_1 and M_2 as follows:

- Let the set of states of M_1 be P, from which we distinguish:
  - p_0, the start state of M_1.
  - P_f, the set of final states of M_1.
- Let D_1 be the transition function for M_1; that is, the (partial) function:

  $D_1 : P \times \Sigma \rightarrow P$
- Let the set of states of M_2 be Q, from which we distinguish:
  - q_0, the start state of M_2.
  - Q_f, the set of final states of M_2.
- Let D_2 be the transition function for M_2; that is, the (partial) function:

  $D_2 : Q \times \Sigma \rightarrow Q$

Now we can define:

1. The intersection of L_1 and L_2 is the machine $M_1 \cap M_2$ defined by:
   - The set of states is $P \times Q$, the Cartesian product of P and Q. Thus for any $p \in P$ and $q \in Q$, the pair (p, q) is a state. We distinguish:
     - (p_0, q_0), the start state of $M_1 \cap M_2$.
     - $\{(p, q) \mid p \in P_f \text{ and } q \in Q_f\}$, the set of final states of $M_1 \cap M_2$.
   - The transition function: $D_{P \times Q} : (P \times Q) \times \Sigma \rightarrow (P \times Q)$ is defined, for any character 'a', by:

     $D_{P \times Q}((p, q), a) = (D_1(p, a), D_2(q, a))$

2. The difference of L_1 and L_2 is the machine $M_1 - M_2$, defined as for intersection, except that the set of final states is now: $\{(p, q) \mid p \in P_f \text{ and } q \notin Q_f\}$.

3. The complement of the language L_1 is the machine M_1', which is simply M_1 with the final and non-final states swapped; i.e. the set of final states is: $P - P_f$.

Other Decision Problems for FSAs

We use a FSA to answer a question of the form: "is x in the language L?" This is known as a decision problem, since the answer will be "yes" or "no". We can pose other decision problems for regular languages:

DP1 For any regular language L, is $L = \emptyset$?

DP2 For any two regular languages L_1 and L_2, is $L_1 \subset L_2$?

DP3 For any two regular languages L_1 and L_2, is $L_1 = L_2$?

Once again, we approach these problems by examining the corresponding FSAs. The corresponding FSA decision problem, and the decision algorithm, for the above are:

- DP1 Given a FSA M, does M accept any strings?

  A FSA accepts no strings if either there are no final states, or if there is no path from the start state to a final state. To see if this is so, we need to work out which states are "reachable" from the start state. Construct the following sets of states:

  - R_0 just contains the start state.
  - R_i is all the states in R_{i-1}, along with any states reachable in one transition from a state in R_{i-1}.

  We stop the construction when $R_i = R_{i-1}$ (this has to happen, as there are only a finite number of states altogether). When this happens, just examine the states in R_i; if this set doesn't contain any final states, then M accepts no strings.

- DP2 Given two FSAs M_1 and M_2, is the language accepted by M_1 a subset of that accepted by M_2.

  $L_1 \subset L_2$ if and only if $L_1 - L_2 = \emptyset$. Thus our algorithm is: construct the machine $M_1 - M_2$ (as in the last section), and apply the algorithm for [DP1].

- DP3 Given two FSAs M_1 and M_2, is the language accepted by L_1 equal to that accepted by M_2?

  $L_1 = L_2$ if and only if they are subsets of each other. Thus we simply apply [DP2] twice.

Grammars

Basically, a grammar consists of a set of production rules of the form:

$$A \rightarrow \alpha$$

Where A is a symbol known as a non-terminal, and α is a sequence of symbols. Each production rule can be seen as giving the definition of the non-terminal on the left-hand-side; the above rule states that "whenever we see an A, we can replace it with α".

A non-terminal may have more than one definition, in which case we use "|", the union operator; e.g.

$A \rightarrow \alpha$

$| \beta$

Means that "whenever we see an A, we can replace it with α or with β". We distinguish one special non-terminal in the grammar called the start symbol, usually written S. The production rules for this symbol are usually written first in a grammar. Any symbol used in the grammar which does not appear on the left-hand-side of some rule (i.e. has no definition) is called a terminal symbol. The following is an example of a grammar:

$S \rightarrow Xc$

$X \rightarrow Y X$

$| \varepsilon$

$Y \rightarrow a$

$| b$

The non-terminals of the grammar are S, X and Y; the terminals are a, b, c. A grammar works by starting with the start symbol, and successively applying the production rules (replacing the L.H.S. with the R.H.S.) until we get a word which contains no non-terminals; this is known as a derivation. Anything which we can derive from the start symbol by applying the production rules is called a sentential form. The last sentential form which contains no non-terminals is called a sentence. Any grammar may have an infinite number of sentences which can be derived; the set of all these sentences is the language defined by the grammar.

Some experimentation with the above grammar will show that it can derive all words which start with arbitrarily many 'a's or 'b's and finish with a 'c', this is the language defined by the regular expression (a|b)*c. In fact, every regular expression can be converted to a grammar. However, not every grammar can be converted back to a regular expression; any grammar which can is called a regular grammar; the language it defines is a regular language.

Regular Expression → Grammar

Regular Expression ← Regular Grammar

Regular Grammars

A regular grammar is a grammar where all of the production rules are of one of the following forms:

$A \rightarrow aB$

or $A \rightarrow a$

Where A and B represent any single non-terminal, and a represents any single terminal, or the empty string. If a grammar can only derive regular languages, but is not of the above form, then (we claim) it can be converted to this form. In order to justify our assertion that we can represent all regular expressions in this manner, we give an algorithm for converting from an FSA to a regular grammar.

Converting an FSA to a Regular Grammar

We will let each state in the NFA correspond to a non-terminal in the grammar. Each symbol used on the transitions corresponds to a terminal symbol. Let S_i denote the non-terminal corresponding to state i of the NFA. Then:

- The start symbol of the grammar is S_o, the non-terminal corresponding to the start state of the NFA.
- For each transition from state i to state j on some symbol 'a', create a production rule of the form: $S_i \rightarrow aS_j$.
- For each state i of the NFA which is a finish state, create a production rule of the form: $S_i \rightarrow \varepsilon$.

ε-transitions between states would generate production rules of the form $S_i \rightarrow S_j$, which says that "wherever we see S_i we can replace it with S_j" another indication that ε-transitions denote equivalence. This process will work equally well with a DFA, and can be applied in reverse to a regular grammar to produce the corresponding NFA.

Regular Expression ↔ NFA or DFA ↔ Regular Grammar

Limitations of Regular Languages

Since regular grammars are a special type of grammar, it is reasonable to assume that the set of regular languages is a subset of all possible languages. So what type of languages aren't regular? First of all, we note one very important point that 'Every finite language is regular'.

Any language is just a set of strings; a finite language is a set which contains a finite number of strings. We know this is regular, since if we have a finite language $\{w_1, w_2, ..., w_n\}$, we can rewrite it as the regular expression: $w_1 \mid w_2 \mid ... \mid w_n$.

How do we form an infinite regular language? The union or concatenation of two finite languages will still be a finite language; thus, any infinite regular language must be formed from a regular expression which uses Kleene closure. That means the regular expression which represents it must be of the form X(Y*)Z, where X, Y and Z are all regular expressions (possibly involving the use of Kleene-closure themselves). One implication of this is that every infinite regular language must have as a subset some set of words of the form xy^iz, for all $i \geq 0$, where x, y and z are strings which correspond to X, Y and Z respectively.

This conclusion is known as the Pumping Lemma for regular languages; i.c: if an infinite language L is regular, then there exist three strings x, y and z such that:

$$y \neq \varepsilon \text{ and } \{xy^iz \mid i \geq 0\} \subseteq L$$

The Pumping Lemma: Examples

Consider the following three languages:

$$L_1 = \{a^n b^n \mid 0 \leq n \leq 100\}$$
$$L_2 = \{a^n b^n \mid n \geq 0\}$$
$$L_3 = \{a^n b^m \mid n, m \geq 0\}$$

The first language is regular, since it contains only a finite number of strings. The third language is also regular, since it is equivalent to the regular expression (a*)(b*). The second language consists of all strings which contain a number of 'a's followed by an equal number of 'b's.

Lemma: L_2 is not regular.

Strategy: Proof by contradiction.

Proof: Let us assume that it is regular; then we must have some set of strings of the form $\{xy^iz \mid i \geq 0\} \subseteq L$. Suppose such a subset did exist.

- Obviously, y could not contain a mixture of 'a's and 'b's, since this would mean that xy^iz would have 'b's before 'a's. Thus, y must consist solely of 'a's or solely of 'b's.
- Let us assume then that y consists solely of 'a's. Then if, for some n we have that xynz is in the language, there is no way that $xy^{n+1}z$ can be in the language, since this will contain extra 'a's without any extra 'b's. Thus there will be no way for xy^iz to be in the language for every $i \geq 0$.
- We can use exactly the same argument to refute the supposition that y can consist entirely of 'b's.

Thus we have shown that y cannot consists of 'a's 'b's or their mixture; i.e no such y exists, and so the Pumping Lemma is not satisfied. Thus L_2 is not regular.

Context-Free Languages

Intuitively, a language is regular if it can be built from individual strings by concatenation, union, and repetition. In this note, we consider a wider class of context-free languages, which are languages that can be built from individual strings by concatenation, union, and recursion. Formally, a language is context-free if and only if it has a certain type of recursive description known as a context-free grammar, which is a structure with the following components:

- A finite set Σ, whose elements are called symbols or terminals.
- A finite set Γ disjoint from Σ, whose elements are called non-terminals.
- A finite set R of production rules of the form $A \rightarrow w$, where $A \in \Gamma$ is a non-terminal and $w \in (\Sigma \cup \Gamma)*$ is a string of symbols and variables.
- A starting non-terminal, typically denoted S.

For example, the following eight production rules describe a context free grammar with terminals $\Sigma = \{0,1\}$ and non-terminals $\Gamma = \{S, A, B, C\}$:

$S \rightarrow A$	$A \rightarrow 0A$	$B \rightarrow B1$	$C \rightarrow \varepsilon$
$S \rightarrow B$	$A \rightarrow 0C$	$B \rightarrow C1$	$C \rightarrow 0C1$

Normally we write grammars more compactly by combining the right sides of all rules for each non-terminal into one list, with alternatives separated by vertical bars. For example, the previous grammar can be written more compactly as follows:

$$S \rightarrow A \mid B$$
$$A \rightarrow 0A \mid 0C$$
$$B \rightarrow B1 \mid C1$$
$$C \rightarrow \varepsilon \mid 0C1$$

We will use the following notational conventions:

- Monospaced digits (0, 1, 2, . . .), and symbols (◇, \$, #, •, . . .) are explicit terminals.
- Early lower-case Latin letters (a, b,c, . . .) represent unknown or arbitrary terminals in Σ.
- Upper-case Latin letters (A, B, C, . . .) and the letter S represent non-terminals in Γ.
- Late lower-case Latin letters (. . . , w, x, y, z) represent strings in $(\Sigma \cup \Gamma)^*$, whose characters could be either terminals or non-terminals.

We can apply a production rule to a string in $(\Sigma \cup \Gamma)^*$ by replacing any instance of the non-terminal on the left of the rule with the string on the right. More formally, for any strings x, y, z $\in (\Sigma \cup \Gamma)^*$ and any non-terminal A $\in \Gamma$, applying the production rule A $\rightarrow$ y to the string xAz yields the string x yz. We use the notation x Az $\rightsquigarrow$ x y z to describe this application. For example, we can apply the rule C $\rightarrow$ 0C1 to the string 00C1BAC0 in two different ways:

$$00\underbrace{C}1BAC0 \rightsquigarrow 00\underbrace{0C1}1BAC0 \qquad 00C1BA\underbrace{C}0 \rightsquigarrow 00C1BA\underbrace{0C1}0$$

More generally, for any strings x, z $\in (\Sigma \cup \Gamma)^*$, we say that z derives from x, written x $\rightsquigarrow^*$ z, if we can transform x into z by applying a finite sequence of production rules, or more formally, if either:

- x = z, or
- x$\rightsquigarrow$y and y$\rightsquigarrow^*$z for some string y $\in (\Sigma \cup \Gamma)^*$.

Straightforward definition-chasing implies that, for any strings w, x, y, z $\in (\Sigma \cup \Gamma)^*$, if x$\rightsquigarrow^*$y, then wxz$\rightsquigarrow^*$ w yz. The language L(w) of any string w $\in (\Sigma \cup \Gamma)^*$ is the set of all strings in Σ^* that derive from w:

$L(w) := \{x \in \Sigma * \mid w \rightsquigarrow^* x\}$.

The language generated by a context-free grammar G, denoted L(G), is the language of its starting non-terminal. Finally, a language is context-free if it is generated by some context-free grammar. Context-free grammars are sometimes used to model natural languages. In this context, the symbols are words, and the strings in the languages are sentences. For example, the following grammar describes a simple subset of English sentences.

⟨sentence⟩ → ⟨noun phrase⟩⟨verb phrase⟩⟨noun phrase⟩

⟨noun phrase⟩ → ⟨adjective phrase⟩⟨noun⟩

⟨adj. phrase⟩ → ⟨article⟩ | ⟨possessive⟩ | ⟨adjective phrase⟩⟨adjective⟩

⟨verb phrase⟩ → ⟨verb⟩ | ⟨adverb⟩⟨verb phrase⟩

⟨noun⟩ → dog | trousers | daughter | nose | homework | time lord | pony| ···

⟨article⟩ → the | a | some | every | that | ···

⟨possessive⟩ → ⟨noun phrase⟩'s | my | your | his | her | ···

⟨adjective⟩ → friendly | furious | moist | green | severed | timey-wimey | little | ···

⟨verb⟩ → ate | found | wrote | killed | mangled | saved | invented | broke | ···

⟨adverb⟩ → squarely | incompetently | barely | sort of | awkwardly | totally | ···

Parse Trees

It is often useful to visualize derivations of strings in L(G) using a parse tree. The parse tree for a string w ∈ L(G) is a rooted ordered tree where:

- Each leaf is labeled with a terminal or the empty string ε. Concatenating these in order from left to right yields the string w.
- Each internal node is labeled with a non-terminal. In particular, the root is labeled with the start non-terminal S.
- For each internal node v, there is a production rule A → ω where A is the label of v and the symbols in ω are the labels of the children of v in order from left to right.

In other words, the production rules of the grammar describe template trees that can be assembled into larger parse trees. For example, the simple grammar on the previous page has the following templates, one for each production rule.

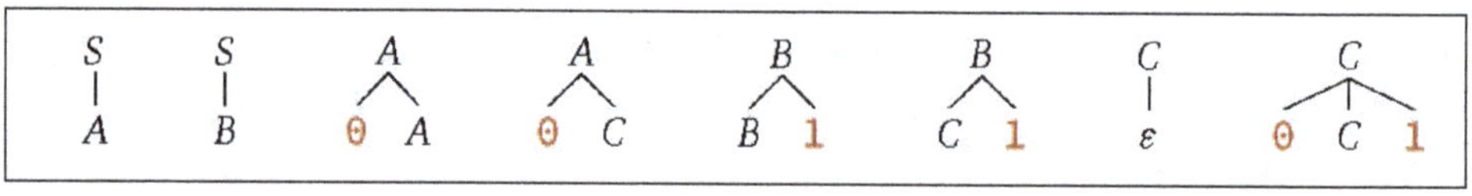

The same grammar gives us the following parse tree for the string 000011.

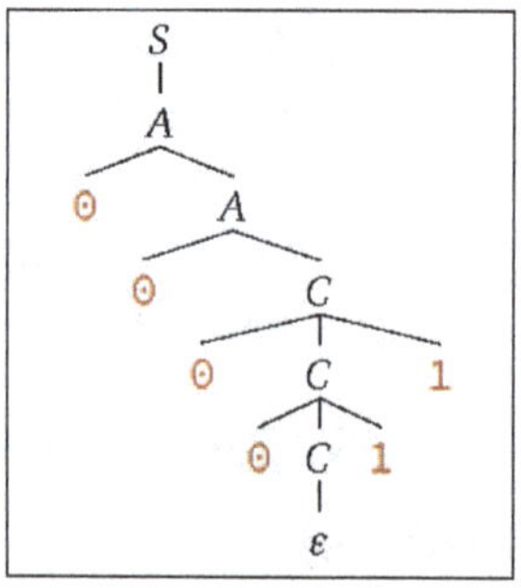

Our more complicated "English" grammar gives us parse trees like the following.

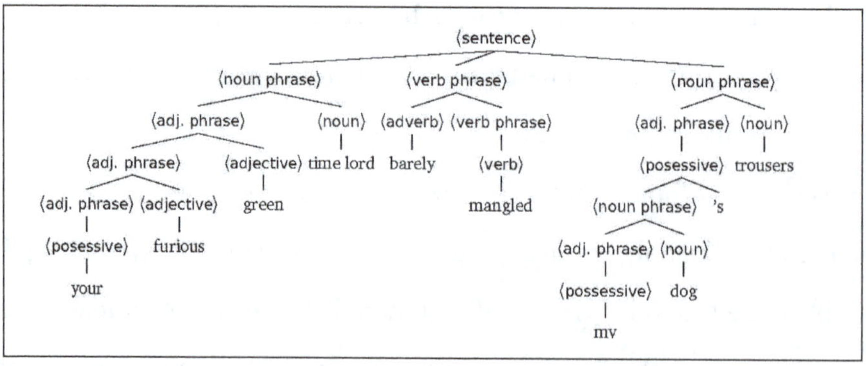

Any parse tree that contains at least one node with more than one non-terminal child corresponds to several different derivations. For example, when deriving an "English" sentence, we have a choice of whether to expand the first ⟨noun phrase⟩ ("your furious green time lord") before or after the second ("my dog's trousers").

A string w is ambiguous with respect to a grammar if there is more than one parse tree for w, and a grammar G is ambiguous is some string is ambiguous with respect to G. Neither of the previous example grammars is ambiguous. However, the grammar $S \rightarrow 1 \mid S{+}S$ is ambiguous, because the string 1+1+1+1 has five different parse trees.

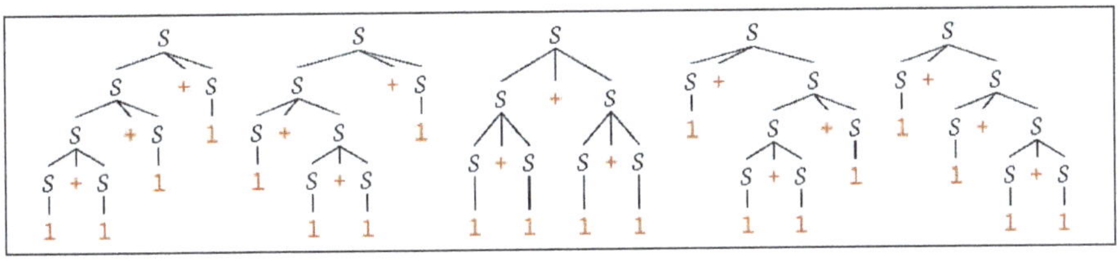

A context-free language L is inherently ambiguous if every context-free grammar that generates L is ambiguous. The language generated by the previous grammar (the regular language (1+)*1) is not inherently ambiguous, because the unambiguous grammar $S \rightarrow 1 \mid 1{+}S$ generates the same language.

From Grammar to Language

Let's figure out the language generated by our first example grammar:

$$S \rightarrow A \mid B \quad A \rightarrow 0A \mid 0C \quad B \rightarrow B1 \mid C1 \quad C \rightarrow \varepsilon \mid 0C1.$$

Since the production rules for non-terminal C do not refer to any other non-terminal, let's begin by figuring out L(C). After playing around with the smaller grammar $C \rightarrow \varepsilon \mid 0C1$ for a few seconds, you can probably guess that its language is {ε,01,0011,000111, . . .}, that is, the set all of strings of the form 0^n1^n for some integer n. For example, we can derive the string 00001111 from the start non-terminal S using the following derivation:

$$C \rightsquigarrow 0C1 \rightsquigarrow 00C11 \rightsquigarrow 000C111 \rightsquigarrow 0000C1111 \rightsquigarrow 0000\varepsilon1111 = 00001111$$

The same derivation can be viewed as the following parse tree.

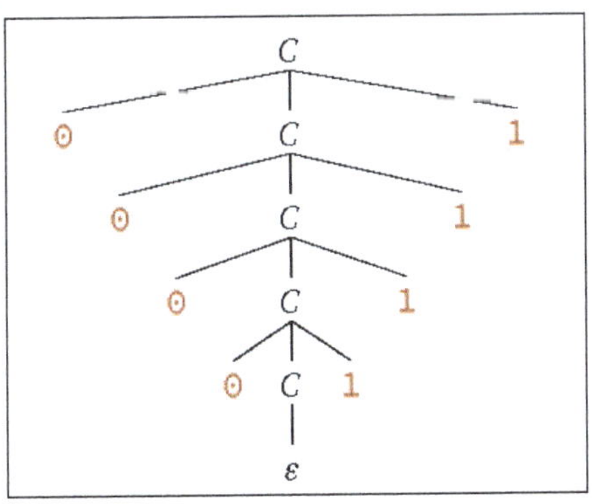

In fact, it is not hard to prove by induction that $L(C) = \{0^n1^n \mid n \geq 0\}$. As usual when we prove that two sets X and Y are equal, the proof has two stages: one stage to prove $X \subseteq Y$, the other to prove $Y \subseteq X$.

Lemma: $C \rightsquigarrow^* 0^n1^n$ for every non-negative integer n.

Proof: Fix an arbitrary non-negative integer n. Assume that $C \rightsquigarrow^* 0^k1^k$ for every non-negative integer $k < n$. There are two cases to consider.

- If $n = 0$, then $0^n1^n = \varepsilon$. The rule $C \rightarrow \varepsilon$ implies that $C \rightsquigarrow \varepsilon$ and therefore $C \rightsquigarrow^* \varepsilon$.
- Suppose $n > 0$. The inductive hypothesis implies that $C \rightsquigarrow^* 0^{n-1}1^{n-1}$. Thus, the rule $C \rightarrow 0C1$ implies that $C \rightsquigarrow 0C1 \rightsquigarrow^* 0(0^{n-1}1^{n-1})1 = 0^n1^n$.

In both cases, we conclude that that $C \rightsquigarrow^* 0^n1^n$, as claimed.

Lemma: For every string $w \in L(C)$, we have $w = 0^n1^n$ for some non-negative integer n.

Proof: Fix an arbitrary string $w \in L(C)$. Assume that for any string $x \in L(C)$ such that $|x| < |w|$, we have $x = 0^k1^k$ for some non-negative integer k. There are two cases to consider, one for each production rule.

- If $w = \varepsilon$, then $w = 0^01^0$.
- Otherwise, $w = 0x1$ for some string $x \in L(C)$. Because $|x| = |w| - 2 < |w|$, the inductive hypothesis implies that $x = 0^k1^k$ for some integer k. Then we have $w = 0^{k+1}1^{k+1}$.

In both cases, we conclude that $w = 0^n1^n$ for some non-negative integer n, as claimed.

The first proof uses induction on strings. The second proof uses structural induction on the parse tree of the string 0^n1^n. In both proofs, as in every proof by induction, the inductive hypothesis is "Assume there is no smaller counterexample." Similar analysis implies that $L(A) = \{0^m1^n \mid m > n\}$ and $L(B) = \{0^m1^n \mid m < n\}$, and therefore $L(S) = \{0^m1^n \mid m \neq n\}$.

Careful with those Epsilons

There is an important subtlety in the proof of lemma. The proof is written as induction on the length of the string w; unfortunately, this induction pattern does not work for all context-free grammars. Consider the following ambiguous grammar $S \rightarrow \varepsilon \mid SS \mid 0S1 \mid 1S0$. L(S) is the language of all binary strings with the same number of 0s and 1s. We cannot use the string-induction boilerplate for this grammar, because there are arbitrarily long derivations of the form:

$$S \rightsquigarrow SS \rightsquigarrow S \rightsquigarrow SS \rightsquigarrow S \rightsquigarrow SS \rightsquigarrow SS \rightsquigarrow \cdots \rightsquigarrow w,$$

Which alternately apply the productions $S \rightarrow SS$ and $S \rightarrow \varepsilon$. Specifically, even if we knew that our arbitrary string w can be written as x y for some strings x, y ∈ L(S), we cannot guarantee that |x| < |w| and | y| < |w|, to we cannot apply the standard string-induction hypothesis. However, we can still argue inductively about this grammar, by considering a minimum-length derivation of w, and basing the case analysis on the first production in this derivation. Here's an example of this induction boilerplate in action, with the modified boilerplate language highlighted.

Lemma: For every string w ∈ L(S), we have #(0, w) = #(1, w).

Proof: Let w be an arbitrary string in L(S). Fix an minimum-length derivation of w. Assume that for any string x ∈ L(S) that is shorter than w, we have x = 0^k1^k for some non-negative integer k. There are four cases to consider, depending on the first production in our fixed derivation.

- Suppose the first production is S → ε. Then w = ε and therefore #(0, w) = #(1, w) = 0 by definition.
- Suppose the first production is S → SS. Then w = x y for some strings x, y ∈ L(S). Both x and y must be non-empty; otherwise, we could shorten our derivation of w. Thus, both x and y are shorter than w. The inductive hypothesis implies #(0, x) = #(1, x) and #(0, y) = #(1, y), so #(0, w) = #(0, x) + #(0, y) = #(1, x) + #(1, y) = #(1, w).
- Suppose the first production is S → 0S1. Then w = 0x1 for some string x ∈ L(S). The inductive hypothesis implies #(0, x) = #(1, x) so #(0, w) = #(0, x) + 1 = #(1, x) + 1 = #(1, w).
- Finally, suppose the first production is S → 1S0. Then w = 1x0 for some string x ∈ L(S). The inductive hypothesis implies #(0, x) = #(1, x) so #(0, w) = #(0, x) + 1 = #(1, w) + 1 = #(1, w).

In all cases, we conclude that # (0, w) = # (1, w), as claimed. Another (more traditional) way to handle this issue is to fix an arbitrary derivation, and then induct on the length of the derivation, rather than the length of the string itself. The case analysis is still based on the first production in the chosen derivation. In fact, this subtlety only matters for grammars that either contain a nullable non-terminal A such that A $\rightsquigarrow^*$ ε or equivalent non-terminals A and B such that A $\rightsquigarrow^*$ B and B $\rightsquigarrow^*$ A. We describe algorithms to identify these pathologies and remove them from the grammar (without changing its language).

Mutual Induction

Another pitfall in induction proofs for context-free languages is that non-terminals may invoke each other. Consider, for example, the grammar:

$$S \to 0A1 \mid \varepsilon \qquad A \to 1S0 \mid \varepsilon$$

Because each non-terminal appears on the right side of a production rule for the other, we must argue about L(S) and L(A) simultaneously.

Lemma: $L(S) = (01)^*$.

Proof: We actually prove simultaneously that $L(S) = (01)^*$and $L(A) = (10)^*$.

First, we claim that for any non-negative integer n, we have $(01)^n \in L(S)$ and $(10)^n \in L(A)$.

Let n be an arbitrary non-negative integer, and assume, for all non-negative integers m < n, that $(01)^m \in L(S)$ and $(10)^m \in L(A)$. There are two cases to consider:

- If n = 0, the production rules $S \rightarrow \varepsilon$ and $A \rightarrow \varepsilon$ immediately imply $S \rightsquigarrow \varepsilon = (01)^n$ and $A \rightsquigarrow \varepsilon = (10)^n$.

- Suppose n > 0. We easily observe that $(01)^n = 0(10)^{n-1}1$, so the production rule $S \rightarrow 0A1$ and inductive hypothesis imply $S \rightsquigarrow 0A1 \rightsquigarrow^* (01)^n$. Symmetrically, $(10)^n = 1(01)^{n-1}0$, so the production rule $A \rightarrow 1S0$ and the inductive hypothesis implies $A \rightsquigarrow 1S0 \rightsquigarrow^* (10)^n$.

For every string $w \in L(S)$, we have $w = (01)^n$ for some non-negative integer n, and for every string $w \in L(A)$, we have $w = (10)^n$ for some non-negative integer n. The proof requires two stages:

- Let w be an arbitrary string in L(S), and assume for all $x \in L(A)$ such that $|x| < |w|$ that $x = (10)^n$ for some non-negative integer n. There are two cases to consider:
  - If $w = \varepsilon$, then $w = (01)^0$.
  - Suppose $w = 0x1$ for some string $x \in L(A)$. The inductive hypothesis implies $x = (10)^n$ for some non-negative integer n. It follows that $w = 0(10)^n1 = (01)^{n+1}$.
- Let w be an arbitrary string in L(A), and assume for all $x \in L(S)$ such that $|x| < |w|$ that $x = (01)^n$ for some non-negative integer n. There are two cases to consider:
  - If $w = \varepsilon$, then $w = (10)^0$.
  - Suppose $w = 1x0$ for some string $x \in L(S)$. The inductive hypothesis implies $x = (01)^n$ for some non-negative integer n. It follows that $w = 1(01)^n0 = (10)^{n+1}$.

Together these two claims imply $L(S) = (01)^*$ and $L(A) = (10)^*$, as required.

Parsing Schemata

A parsing system is a deduction system for a given grammar and string. A parsing schema is a more abstract object that defines a parsing system for arbitrary grammars and strings. First, we will consider a deduction system for a given grammar G = (N;Σ; P; S) and a given string $a_1...a_n$. The domain of such a deduction system is a subset of Trees(G). The set of deduction steps D encodes how new trees can be obtained from trees. The initial set of trees is given by the set of hypotheses H. A system is complete if all marked parse trees for the string are deduced. A system is sound if no marked parse tree for a different string of the same length can be deduced. It is conceivable, however, that a marked parse tree for a string of shorter length is deduced by a sound tree-based parsing system. Consider, for example, the case that $S \Rightarrow^* a_1 \dots a_k$ and $S \Rightarrow^*_{Sak+1} \dots a_n$. Then a marked parse tree $<S \rightarrow \underline{a}_1 \dots \underline{a}_k>$ could be found while parsing $a_1 \dots a_n$.

Instantiated Tree-Based Parsing System

Let G be a context-free grammar and $a_1 \dots a_n \in \Sigma^*$ and arbitrary string. A deduction system <$\mathcal{T}$, H, D> is called an instantiated tree-based parsing system for G and $a_1 \dots a_n$ when the following conditions are satisfied:

$\mathcal{T} \subseteq$ Trees(G).

$P_G^{(n)} \subset T$.

$<a \rightarrow a_i> \in H$ for each a_i, $1 \leq i \leq n$.

Usually we will drop the adjective "instantiated" and talk about a tree-based parsing system for G and $a_1 \dots a_n$. An instantiated tree-based parsing system <$\mathcal{T}$, H, D> for a grammar G and a string $a_1 \dots a_n$ is correct if the enhanced deduction system: $<\mathcal{T}, H, P_G^{(n)}, P_G(\dot{a}_1 \dots a_n), D>$ is correct.

The set of hypotheses H will be different for different input strings, obviously. It provides the initial trees from which everything else is derived. It would make sense that the set of deduction steps D is not dependent on a particular input string. This will be a consequence of the next definition, in which we consider parsing systems for arbitrary strings. The fact that the domain of a parsing system should be independent of the string that is to be parsed has been anticipated. It would suffice to demand that $P_G(a_1 \dots a_n) \subset \mathcal{T}$, rather than $P_G^{(n)} \subset \mathcal{T}$, so as to make sure that <$\mathcal{T}$, H, D> is a valid parsing system for $a_1 \dots a_n$. (The set of final entities would then be $P_G^{(n)} \cap \mathcal{T}$, which does not necessarily equal $P_G^{(n)}$). Marked parse trees of strings that are not to be parsed need not necessarily be contained in the domain of the system. But, obviously, all marked parses of any string must be in T if it is to serve as a domain of a parsing system for arbitrary strings.

Uninstantiated Tree-Based Parsing System

Let G be a context-free grammar. An uninstantiated tree-based parsing system for G is a triple <$\mathcal{T}$, $\mathcal{K}$, D> with K: $\Sigma^* \rightarrow \wp$(Trees(G)) a function such that <$\mathcal{T}$, $\mathcal{K}(a_1 \ldots a_n)$, D> is a tree-based parsing system for each $a_1 \ldots a_n \in \Sigma^*$. An uninstantiated tree-based parsing system <$\mathcal{T}$, $\mathcal{K}$, D> is correct if <$\mathcal{T}$, $\mathcal{K}(a_1 \ldots a_n)$, D> is correct for each $a_1 \ldots a_n \in \Sigma^*$.

We will blur the distinction between instantiated and uninstantiated systems somewhat; as a practical notation we write $\mathcal{T}(a_1 \ldots a_n)$ or simply $\mathcal{T}$ to denote both. In an instantiated system, $a_1 \ldots a_n$ denotes a particular string and in an uninstantiated system $a_1 \ldots a_n$ denotes a formal parameter for a string. This won't cause any confusion.

Tree-Based Parsing Schema

A tree-based parsing schema T for a class of grammars $\mathcal{CG}$ is a function that assigns an uninstantiated tree-based parsing system to every grammar G $\in \mathcal{CG}$. T is correct if, for each G $\in \mathcal{CG}$, the uninstantiated tree-based parsing system T(G) is correct.

The Function K

In all examples of tree-based parsing systems and schemata we will use the same function $\mathcal{K}$, defined by:

$$\mathcal{K}(a_1 \ldots a_n) = \left\{ \left\langle a \rightarrow \underline{a_i} \right\rangle \mid a = a_i \right\} \cup \left\{ \left\langle \# \rightarrow \underline{\#_0} \right\rangle, \left\langle \$ \rightarrow \underline{\$_{n+1}} \right\rangle \right\}.$$

The end-of-sentence marker $ and beginning-of-sentence marker # are added for convenience. In some parsing schemata it is rather more easy to dene D(G) when every word in the sentence has a left and right neighbour, also the first and the last word. It is always possible to convert a parsing system using the beginning-of-sentence marker into a system without it. One simply has to adapt the deduction steps for the special case that one of its arguments would extend to the left of position 0. The situation at the end of the sentence is different, however. It might be essential to know that a tree of a certain kind (c.q. the next word of the string) does not exist. As negative information can't be handled in our formalism, the nonexistence of a (n+1)-st word is stated in a positive way by the end-of-sentence marker. As we always use the same function $\mathcal{K}$, a parsing schema T is fully specified by a defining a pair <$\mathcal{T}$(G), D (G)> for an arbitrary grammar G $\in \mathcal{CG}$. For each grammar G $\in \mathcal{CG}$ and string $a_1 \ldots a_n \in \Sigma^*$ the schema materializes to a deduction system:

$$\hat{O}(G)(a_1 \ldots a_n) = \left\langle \mathcal{T}(G), \mathcal{K}(a_1 \ldots a_n), D(G) \right\rangle$$

It is possible, although somewhat cumbersome, to give a characterization of a universal class of parsing schemata. Let (X $\rightarrow$ Y) denote the class of functions from X to Y. Let CG be a class of context-free grammars, Sym be a universal set of symbols from which N, Σ, and $\underline{\acute{O}}$ are drawn, $\mathfrak{u}$ the universal set of labelled trees. Then $\mathcal{T} \subset \mathfrak{u}$, or $\mathcal{T} \in \wp(\mathfrak{u})$.

Furthermore, $\mathcal{K} \in (\text{Sym}^* \to \wp(\mathcal{U}))$ and $D \in \wp(\wp_{\text{fin}}(\mathcal{U}) \times \mathcal{U})$. Hence the universal class of parse schemata is a subclass of

$$\left(\mathcal{CG} \to \left(\wp(\mathcal{U}) \times \left(\text{Sym}^* \to \wp(\mathcal{U})\right) \times \wp\left(\wp_{\text{fin}}(\mathcal{U}) \times \mathcal{U}\right)\right)\right)$$

One could add constraints to this huge class of objects such that that only "meaningful" elements remain, but that is not very interesting. The more important fact is that we have a formally defined a "universe of parsing schemata", in which we can reason about schemata, define relations between them and invent substitutions that transform a parsing schema into a different parsing schema. Example: (PS, a schema for the Primordial Soup algorithm).

A Primordial Soup parsing schema PS is defined as follows. For an arbitrary $G \in \mathcal{CFG}$ and $a_1 \ldots a_n \in \Sigma^*$ we define a tree-based parsing system $\mathbb{T}_{PS} = \langle \mathcal{T}, \mathcal{K}(a_1 \ldots a_n), D \rangle$ with $\mathcal{K}(a_1 \ldots a_n)$. We make use of a predicate allowed that is true for a tree if both the word order constraint and the width constraint are obeyed. Different definitions for these constraints are possible; which one is chosen doesn't matter for the general idea of the Primordial Soup schema:

$$\mathcal{T} = \{\tau \in \mathit{Trees}(G) \mid \text{allowed}(\tau)\};$$

$$D^{(1)} = \{\vdash \langle A \to \alpha \rangle \mid A \to \alpha \in P\};$$

$$D^{(2)} = \{\sigma, \tau \vdash \sigma \triangleleft \tau \mid \sigma \triangleleft \tau \in \mathcal{T}\};$$

$$D = D^{(1)} \cup D^{(2)}.$$

We make a distinction here between elementary trees that constitute marked terminals (the hypotheses) and elementary trees that represent the productions of the grammar. These last ones are included in the deduction steps, but do not need an antecedent. Productions are always valid, irrespective of the sentence. The second set of deduction steps denotes all possible instances of valid composition. The description of production trees as (antecedentless) derivation steps, rather than hypotheses, is a consequence of the general principle that the sentence is coded by $\mathcal{K}$, while the grammar is covered by D. Example: (TCYK, a tree-based parsing schema for CYK) A tree-based parsing schema TCYK can be given for $\mathcal{CNF}$, the class of grammars in Chomsky Normal Form. For an arbitrary grammar $G \in \mathcal{CNF}$ we define $\mathcal{T}_{\text{CYK}} = \langle \mathcal{T}, \mathcal{K}(a_1 \ldots a_n), D \rangle$ by:

$$\mathcal{T} = \{\tau \in \mathit{Trees}(G) \mid \text{yield}(\tau) \in \underline{\Sigma}^*\};$$

$$D^{(1)} = \left\{\langle a \to \underline{a_j} \rangle \vdash \langle A \to \langle a \to \underline{a_j} \rangle \rangle \mid A \to a \in P\right\}$$

$$D^{(2)} = \left\{\langle B \leadsto \underline{a_{j+1} \ldots a_j} \rangle, \langle C \leadsto \underline{a_{j+1} \ldots a_k} \rangle \vdash \langle A \leadsto \underline{a_{j+1} \ldots a_k} \rangle \mid A \to BC \in P\right\}.$$

$$D = D^{(1)} \cup D^{(2)}.$$

The first set of deduction steps is to derive the non-terminals we usually start with, because for the sake of standardization the hypotheses cover the terminals in the sentence. We will now proceed to define item-based parsing schemata (in the sequel simply called parsing schemata) in much the same way as tree-based parsing schemata. For the domain of a system we do not take a subset of Trees(G) but a subset of a partition of Trees(G).

A partition $\prod(X) \subset \wp(X)$ is a collection of pairwise disjunctive non-empty subsets of X such that every $x \in X$ is contained in some 2 (X). Every partition defines an equivalence relation by:

$$x \sim y \text{ if there is a } \pi \in \prod(X) \text{ such that } \{x, y\} \subseteq \pi.$$

And reversed, if ~ is an equivalence relation on X then X/~ is a partition of X.

Item Set

Let Trees(G) be the set of trees for some context-free grammar G. A set $\mathcal{I} \in \wp(\text{Trees}(G))$ is called an item set if there is a partition $\prod$ of Trees(G) such that $\mathcal{I} \subseteq \Pi(\mathcal{T}\text{rees}(G)) \cup \{\phi\}$.

Types of Items

Let $\mathcal{I}$ be an item set.

- An item $\iota \in \mathcal{I}$ is called empty if $\iota = \varphi$.
- A non-empty item $\iota \in \mathcal{I}$ is called completed if, for each $\tau \in$, τ is a marked parse tree for some sentence.
- A non-empty item $\iota \in \mathcal{I}$ is called intermediate if, for each $\tau \in \iota$, τ is a not a marked parse tree for any sentence.
- An item $\iota \in \mathcal{I}$ is called mixed if there are $\sigma, \tau \in \iota$ such that σ is a marked parse tree and τ is not a marked parse tree.

Regular and Semiregular Item Set

An item set $\mathcal{I}$ is called regular if it contains neither mixed items nor the empty item. An item set $\mathcal{I}$ is called semiregular if it does not contain mixed items.

Final Items

Let $\prod$ be a partition of Trees(G) for some context-free grammar G, $a_1 \ldots a_n \in \Sigma^*$ a string. The set of final items $_{G,}^{(n)}$ for a string of length n is defined by,

$$\mathcal{F}_{G,\Pi}^{(n)} = \left\{\iota \in \prod(\mathcal{T}\text{rees}(G)) \mid \exists \tau \in \mathcal{P}_G^{(n)}\right\}.$$

The set of correct final items $\mathcal{C}_{G,\Pi}$ for a string $a_1 \ldots a_n$ is defined by

$$\mathcal{C}_{G,\Pi}(a_1 \ldots a_n) = \{\iota \in \Pi(\mathcal{T}rees(G)) \mid \exists \tau \in \iota : \tau \in \mathcal{P}_G(a_1 \ldots a_n)\}.$$

An item-based parser will be correct if all correct final items can be deduced from H and no other final items. After these preliminaries, the following definitions will not come as a surprise.

Instantiated Parsing System

Let G be a context-free grammar and $a_1 \ldots a_n \in \Sigma^*$ an arbitrary string. A deduction system $\langle \mathcal{I}, H, D \rangle$ is called an instantiated parsing system for G and $a_1 \ldots a_n$ when the following conditions are satisfied:

- $\mathcal{I} = \mathcal{I}(G, \Pi)$ is an item set.
- $\mathcal{F}^{(n)}_{G,\Pi} \subset \mathcal{I}$.
- $[a \rightarrow \underline{a_i}] \in H$ for each $a_i, 1 \leq i \leq n$.

Correct Parsing System

An instantiated parsing system $\langle \mathcal{I}, H, D \rangle$ for a grammar G and a string $a_1 \ldots a_n$ is correct if the enhanced deduction system $\langle \mathcal{I}, H, \mathcal{F}^{(n)}_{G,\Pi}, \mathcal{C}_{G,\Pi}(a_1 \ldots a_n), D \rangle$ is correct.

Uninstantiated Parsing System

Let G be a context-free grammar. An uninstantiated parsing system for G is a triple $\langle \mathcal{I}, \mathcal{K}, D \rangle$ where $\mathcal{K} : \Sigma^* \rightarrow \wp(\wp(\mathcal{T}rees(G)))$ is a function such that $\langle \mathcal{I}, \mathcal{K}(a_1 \ldots a_n), D \rangle$ is a parsing system for each $a_1 \ldots a_n \in \Sigma^*$. An uninstantiated parsing system $\langle \mathcal{I}, \mathcal{K}, D \rangle$ is correct if $\langle \mathcal{I}, \mathcal{K}(a_1 \ldots a_n), D \rangle$ is correct for each $a_1 \ldots a_n \in \Sigma^*$.

We will not make a clear distinction between instantiated and uninstantiated parsing systems and write $\mathbb{P}(a_1 \ldots a_n)$ or simply $\mathbb{P}$ to denote both.

Parsing Schema

A parsing schema P for a class of grammars $\mathcal{CG}$ is a function that assigns an uninstantiated parsing system to every grammar $G \in \mathcal{CG}$. P is correct if, for each $G \in \mathcal{CG}$, the uninstantiated parsing system P(G) is correct.

Regular Parsing Schemata

A parsing system $\langle \mathcal{I}, H, D \rangle$ is regular if $\mathcal{I}$ is a regular item set. A parsing schema P for a class of grammars $\mathcal{CG}$ is regular if, for each G ∈ $\mathcal{CG}$ and each $a_1 \ldots a_n \in \Sigma^*$, the parsing system P(G)($a_1 \ldots a_n$) is regular.

The Function K

In all examples of parsing systems and schemata we will use the the same function $\mathcal{K}$, defined by $\mathcal{K}(a_1 \ldots a_n) = \{[a \to \underline{a_i}] \mid a = a_i\} \cup \{[\# \to \underline{\#_0}]\}, \{[\$ \to \underline{\$_{n+1}}]\}$.

As a more conventional notation for hypothesis items we will write [a, i -1, i] rather than $[a \to \underline{a_i}]$. The end-of-sentence marker is denoted by [\$, n, n + 1], the beginning-of-sentence marker by [#; -1, 0]. As we have fixed the function $\mathcal{K}$, as usual, one only needs to specify $\mathcal{I}$(G, ∏) and D(G) for an arbitrary grammar G and a partition ∏(G) of Trees(G) in order to give a full specification of a parsing schema. For each grammar G ∈ $\mathcal{CG}$ and string $a_1 \ldots a_n \in \Sigma^*$ the schema materializes to a deduction system:

$$P(G)(a_1 \ldots a_n) = \langle \mathcal{I}(G, \Pi), \mathcal{K}(a_1 \ldots a_n), D(G) \rangle.$$

For the reader who really wants to know what kind of object a recognition schema is, in terms of set theory, it is remarked that the universal class of parsing schemata can be characterized as a sub-class of:

$$\left(\mathcal{CG} \to \left(\wp(\wp(\mathcal{U})) \times \left(\mathrm{Sym}^* \to \wp(\wp(\mathcal{U}))\right) \times \wp\left(\wp_{\mathrm{fin}}(\wp(\mathcal{U}))\right)\right)\right)$$

Again, the fact that the universal class of parsing schemata can be formally defined is rather more important than the particular structure of this type.

Example of the CYK parsing schema: At last, we define an item-based parsing schema CYK by giving an item-based parsing system $\mathbb{P}_{CYK}$ for arbitrary grammars G ∈ $\mathcal{CNF}$. Let [A, i, j] be an abbreviated notation for an item $[A \rightsquigarrow \underline{a_{i+1}} \ldots \underline{a_j}]$. Then $\mathbb{P}_{CYK}$ is defined by:

$$\mathcal{I} = \{[A, i, j] \mid A \in N \wedge 0 \le i \le j\};$$

$$D^{(1)} = \{[a, i-1, i] \vdash [A, i-1, i] \mid A \to a \in P\},$$

$$D^{(2)} = \{[B, i, j], [C, j, k] \vdash [A, i, k] \mid A \to BC \in P\},$$

$$D = D^{(1)} \cup D^{(2)}.$$

Note the difference with Example, where the domain contained only those items such that there is a tree that fits the item. Here we do allow items for which such a tree does not exist, hence CYK is not a regular parsing schema. But in the sequel we will show that CYK is semi regular, which is good enough for all practical purposes.

References

- Parsing: cs.may.ie, Retrieved 02, May 2020
- Algorithms, models: cs.illinois.edu, Retrieved 20, February 2020
- Parsing-Schemata- 11467942: ac.uk, Retrieved 29, July 2020

4

Machine Translation

Machine translation deals with the usage of software for the purpose of translating text or speech from one language to another. The method of machine translation which uses various machine translation approaches within a single machine translation system is known as hybrid machine translation. This chapter discusses in detail the different aspects of machine translation such as hybrid machine translation and dialogue systems.

Information plays a vital role in the growth of science and technology. Similarly the growth and development of a language, its culture and literature depends very much on sharing or spreading information. Hence, acquiring, transferring, disseminating and diffusing information is crucial to the development of a human society. Many of the decision-making processes and the research programs are based on the most valuable information concerning the respective areas. Translation is one of the strategies that plays an important role in disseminating information contents from one language to another. Since the last century this role has been given to Machine translation.

Machine translation, sometimes referred to by the abbreviation MT, is a sub-field of Computational Linguistics that investigates the use of computer software to translate text or speech from one natural language to another. At its basic level, MT performs simple substitution of words in one natural language for words in another. Using corpus techniques, more complex translations maybe attempted, allowing for better handling of differences in linguistic typology, phrase recognition, and translation of idioms, as well as the isolation of anomalies. A machine translation can be classified into several types:

- Human-Assisted Machine Translation (HAMT) is a style of translation, in which computer system does most of translation, appealing in case of difficulty to a human for help. It involves the help of a human to pre-edit the source language text before being fed to the computer for translating into a target language. Due to the information explosion and the necessity of faster and cheaper translation, HAMT is very suitable for translating texts in science and technology, weather reports, equipment manuals, military records, laboratory procedures, articles, research monographs, etc. Since human intervention is required in some form either pre-editing a SL text or feeding the input or specifying certain grammatical rules, most of the currently available MT systems belong to HAMT.
- Machine-Assisted Human Translation (MAHT) is a style of translation, in which a human does most of the work, but uses one or more computer systems, mainly as resources such as dictionaries and spelling checkers, as translation tools.

The translation is aided by the computer, providing suitable word equivalents from the already stored glossary of words. In certain technical and scientific area conveying the basic meaning is considered to be sufficient through word-to-word translation by MAHT.

- In recent times, the HAMT and MAT are grouped together under one term Computer-Aided Translation (CAT), which cover both of the meanings.
- Fully Automated Machine Translation (FAMT) is performed without the intervention of a human being during the translation process. Such a completely automated translation perhaps will become a reality one day when the entire domain knowledge with complete and appropriate translation rules are modeled to resolve the syntactic and semantic ambiguities of a natural language (NL). The extensive research in the area of Natural Language Processing (NLP) and the various tools of Artificial Intelligence (AI) would certainly lead the way to achieve this goal in the future at least in the field of science and technology.

There are several goals MT is used for:

- Dissemination: The production of translations of 'publishable' quality; not necessarily texts that are actually published but texts that are of that quality. Such texts are required usually by organizations and usually involve professional translators. The 'raw' untreated output from MT systems is inadequate, and publishable quality means human assistance; e.g. post-editing (revision) of the output text, pre-editing of the input, using a controlled language, or restricting the system to a specific subject domain. In general it has been found (through the experience of using MT) that the more the subject domain of an application can be restricted the more successful the system is, in terms of quality.
- Assimilation: The translation of texts for monitoring (or 'filtering') or skimming information, or the translation of texts for occasional users (e.g. non-specialist general public), where the 'raw' output from the system doesn't need to be edited; in other words, where recipients can accept poor quality as long as they can get an idea of what the text conveys. (In fact, we find that many MT systems are useful only in this function their outputs are unsatisfactory as drafts for dissemination tasks).
- Interchange: The communication between different languages by individuals, by correspondence, by email or by telephone. Here again the quality of the translation (and/or closeness to the original) is not so important, as long as people get the information they want, understand the message they receive, or manage to convey their intentions.
- Database access: The use of translation to assist in getting information from a database in a foreign language, one that the user does not well understand i.e., these days this means mainly the use of translation aids for searching the

Internet, for accessing web pages. While dissemination and assimilation have been traditional uses of MT and translation tools from the beginning, their uses for interchange and databases access are recent applications which are growing rapidly, primarily with the growth of the Internet itself.

Architectures and Paradigms of Machine Translation Systems

The success of a MT partly depends on inner architecture of a system the process of handling language in synthesis and generation to give final output. Systems can be built by different axis: architectures and paradigms. Architectures refer to the actual processing design (i.e., direct, transfer, interlingua), whereas the paradigm refers to informational components that aid the processing design (knowledge-based, example-based, statistics-based, etc.). Let us see what type of architectures and paradigms of MT systems have been developed by computational linguists. In general, an MT system involves feeding the program with a text in source language (SL), the text is undergoing translation process and, then, the machine gives out output in the target language. It looks like the following:

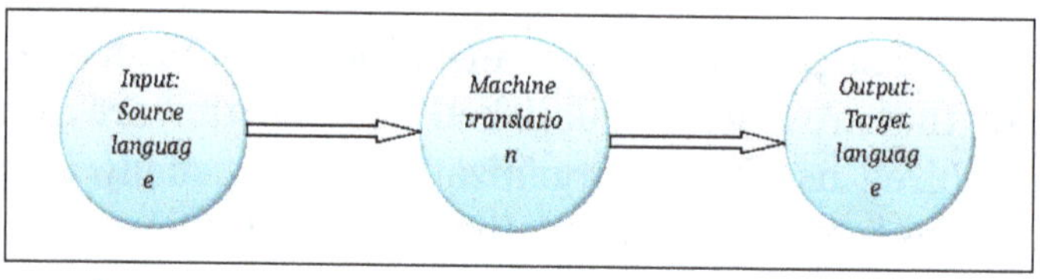

Architectures

The earliest historically is the "direct approach", adopted by most MT systems of what has come to be known as the first generation of MT systems. In response to the apparent failure of this direct architecture strategy, two types of "indirect architecture" were developed: the "transfer", and the use of an "interlingua" approaches. Systems of the latter architectures are sometimes referred to as second generation systems.

Direct Architectures

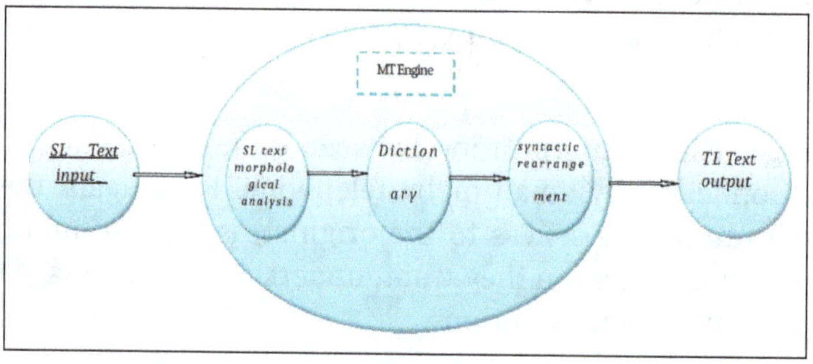

Direct MT is the one of the simplest machine translation architectures. In direct MT a direct word byword translation of the input source is carried out with the help of a bilingual dictionary and after which some syntactical rearrangement is made. The direct method lacks any kinds of intermediate stages in translation processes, where the processing of the SL input text leads "directly" to the desired TL output text. There is no analysis of syntactic structure or of semantic relationships. In other words, lexical identification depends on morphological analysis and leads directly to bilingual dictionary look-up providing TL word equivalences. Some local reordering rules follows to give more acceptable TL output, perhaps moving some adjectives verb particles, and then the TL text is produced. This approach is unidirectional and only takes one language pair into consideration at a time.

The severe limitations of this approach are obvious. It can be characterized as "word-for-word" translation with some local word-order adjustment. It gives the kind of translation quality that might be expected from someone with a very cheap bilingual dictionary and only the most basic knowledge of the grammar of the target language: frequent mistranslations at the lexical level and largely inappropriate syntax structures which mirrored too closely those of the SL. From a linguistic point of view what is missing is any analysis of the internal structure of the SL, particularly the grammatical relationships between the principal parts of the sentences. It continues to some extent in many unidirectional bilingual systems. In certain circumstances this approach is still valid today traces of the direct approach are found in systems such as Meteo-a successful MT system to translate weather forecasts.

Indirect Architectures

The failure of the first generation systems led to the development of more sophisticated linguistic models for translation. In particular, there was increasing support for the analysis of SL texts into some kind of intermediate representation a representation of its "meaning" in some respect which could form the basis of generation of the TL text. This is in essence the indirect method, which has two principal variants. The first is the interlingua approach also the first historically where the SL text is analyzed in a representation from which the TL text is directly generated. The interlingua architecture converts words into an intermediate language (IL), which is typically a universal language created for the system to use it as an intermediate for translation into more than one TL. It has an analyzer which produces the intermediate representation of the SL. The synthesizer takes over from the analyzer and produces TL sentences given by the analyzer.

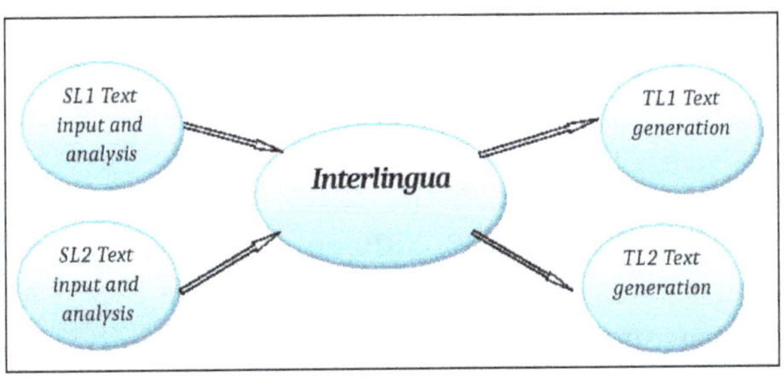

The intermediate representation includes all information necessary for the generation of the TL text without "looking back" to the original text. The representation is thus a projection from the SL text and at the same time acts as the basis for the generation of the TL text; it is an abstract representation of the TL text as well as a representation of the SL text. The method is interlingual in the sense that the representation is neutral between two or more languages. In the past, the intention or hope was to develop an interlingual representation which was truly "universal" and could thus be intermediary between any natural languages.

The advantage is that the addition of a new language to the system entails the creation of just two new modules: an analysis grammar and a generation grammar. By adding one analysts module, e.g. a German analysis grammar, the number of translation directions is increased from two (English to French, and French to English) to four (by the addition of German to French and German to English). The inclusion of another generation module, a German generation grammar, brings a further two pairs (English to German and French to German). The addition of two further modules for, say, Spanish, would increase the number of language pairs by another six (English, French and German into Spanish, and Spanish into English, French and German), and so on exponentially. While the addition of new languages may appear easy in an interlingual system, there are major disadvantages: the difficulties of defining an interlingua, even for closely related languages (e.g. the Romance languages: French. Italian, Spanish, Portuguese). A truly "universal" and language independent interlingua has defied (challenged) the best efforts of linguists and philosophers from the seventeenth century onwards. At present, interlingual systems are less ambitious.

The second variant of the indirect architectures is called the transfer method. In fact, all translation systems involve "transfer" of some kind, the conversion of SL text or representation into TL text or representation. Dictionary directly converts source into target whenever a sentence matches one of the transfer rules. SL dictionary, TL dictionary and a bilingual dictionary is used for this purpose. The translation mechanism is carried out in three phases. Firstly, the SL is converted into intermediate representation (Analysis) which is subsequently converted into TL representation in the second phase (Transfer). The third phase involves Generation of the final target language.

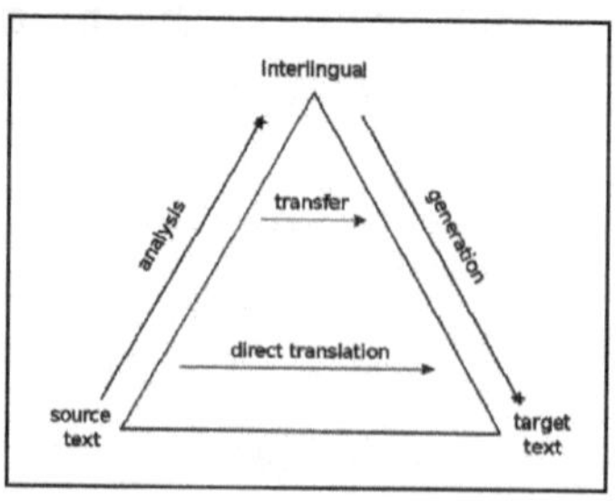

Unlike those in interlingual systems the transfer representations are language-dependent: the result of analysis is an abstract representation of the SL text, the input to generation is an abstract representation of the TL text. The function of the bilingual transfer modules is to convert SL (intermediate) representations into TL (intermediate) representations. Since these representations link separate modules (analysts, transfer, generation), they are also frequently referred to as interface representations. In comparison with the interlingua type of multilingual system there are clear disadvantages in the transfer approach. The addition of a new language involves not only the two modules for analysis and generation, but also the addition of new transfer modules, the number of which may vary according to the number of languages in the existing system: in the case of a two-language system, a third language would require four new transfer modules.

Paradigms

The architectural basis of the system is only one of many axes along which one might compare MT systems. Another important axis of comparison is that of research paradigm. It is important to understand the difference between the type of architecture and the type of paradigm: one does not presuppose the other. Architecture refers to the actual processing design (i.e., direct, transfer, and inetrlingua), whereas the paradigm refers to informational components that aid the processing design (knowledge-based, example-based, statistics-based, etc.) Research paradigms are classified into three categories:

- Those that propose to rely most heavily on linguistics techniques (linguistics paradigms).
- Those that do not use any linguistics techniques (non-linguistics).
- Those that use a combination of two (hybrid).

Linguistic Paradigms

Until recently, most MT researchers studied linguistic-based MT, i.e., translation on the basis of principles that are well-grounded in linguistic theory. Systems based on linguistic theory strive to use the rules of syntax, lexicon, and semantics to produce an appropriate TL realization of the SL sentence.

- Constraint-Based MT.
- Knowledge-Based MT.
- Lexical-Based MT.
- Rule-Based MT.
- Principle-Based MT.

Constraint-Based MT

CBMT techniques have shown up several different MT approaches. For ex., Shake-and-Bake approach demonstrates the full utility of constraint application. Initial approach in CBMT was using constraints on combination of lexical items, i.e., the Lexical Functional Grammar MT system. This system translates bidirectionally based on lexical functional grammar (LFG). In the LFG formalism, f-structure (functional structure) is a fundamental component of the translation. Because the LFG MT system is based on construction-specific representations, the mapping operations required in the transfer must be performed by transfer equations that relate source and target-language f-structures. The LFG MT framework makes an association between the syntactic structure and the f-structure using a set of mediating selectional constraints that are encoded as lexical entries.

The disadvantage of this approach is that the f-structure is tightly coupled with the syntactic structure of the language; thus if a particular concept can be syntactically expressed in more than one way, there will be more than one f-structure in this framework. A more refined version of this approach is currently used in the Verbmobil MT project.

Knowledge-Based MT

KBMT is a paradigm adopted by developers of numerous US systems including Pangloss at Carnegi Melon's Center for MT, ULTRA at New Mexico State's Computing Research Lab, Cyc-NL at CYCORP, Japangloss and GAZELLE (Univ of S. California), UNICON (Univ. of Pennsylvania), etc. KBMT paradigm is concentrated on the development of knowledge intensive morphological, syntactic and semantic information for lexicon. Tools have been developed for creating ontologies and have provided a framework for automatic lexical acquisition.

In general, the focus of research in KBMT has been on the development of underlying knowledge representation concepts. Little attention has been devoted to providing a systematic "linking" of these concepts to the syntax; thus, KBMT is complementary to the (less knowledge intensive). In its own, the KBMT provides higher-quality, fully-automated translations; however, the domains used for this approach are narrow and well-defined since the required amount of information would otherwise be large and cost-prohibitive with respect to indexing and searching. Disadvantage in this paradigm is that there no single systematic mapping between a concept and its surface realization.

Lexical-Based MT

LBMT overlaps heavily with several other approaches including RBMT, PBMT and SBMT. In general, a LBMT system refers to any system that supplies rules for relating the lexical entries of one language to the lexical entries of another language. Several researchers have adopted the lexical-based paradigm, but at different degrees of generality. One such system is LTAG (English-French and vice versa). System uses a transfer approach that uses synchronous tree-adjoining grammars to map shallow TAG derivations from one language into another.

The mapping is performed by means of a bilingual lexicon which directly associates source and target trees through links between lexical items and their arguments. Roughly each bilingual entry contains a mapping between a SL sentence and a TL sentence. One disadvantage of this approach is that it requires entire trees to be stored in the transfer dictionary for each source-to-target pair. This is significantly burdensome as the number of SL and TL begin to add up.

Rule-Based MT

The RBMT paradigm is associated with systems that rely on different linguistic levels of rules for translation between the SL and TL. The prototypical example of such a system is Roseta which divides translation rules into two categories:

- S-rules which are "non-meaningful rules" that map lexical items to syntactic trees.
- M-rules which are "meaning preserving rules" that map between syntactic trees to underlying meaning structures. In cases of syntactic mismatches between SL and TL representations, a "switch-rule" is invoked and normal processing is interrupted, control is then passed to a module that derives a new category that takes over the role of syntactic head.

One problem with this approach is that it leaves open the question of how grammar driven interrupts (that occur in case of mismatches) interact with idiosyncratic requirements of individual lexical items.

Principle-Based MT

PBMT paradigm has been developed by a number of researchers. PBMT is an alternative to RBMT in which rules are replaced by a small set of principles that cover morphological, grammatical, and lexical phenomena in a general fashion. An example of a PBMT paradigm is the PRINCITRAN MT system which is based on syntactic principles of Government-Binding Theory and lexical semantic principles of Lexical-Conceptual Structure. This system was originally designed for Korean-English MT, lexicons for Spanish and Arabic were subsequently developed for related NLP applications (ex., foreign language tutoring). In this system, structure building is deferred until underlying description satisfies a number of linguistic principles that are parametrized for ease of porting to new languages.

The processing mechanism is language independent and accommodates structurally different languages (ex., head-initial vs. head-final) with equally efficient run times. PBMT is considered to be a complementary to the KBMT and EBMT (example-based) paradigms in that it provides broad coverage of many different linguistic phenomena, but lacks deeper knowledge about the translation domain. There were efforts to combine the benefits of PBMT and KBMT techniques in a collaborative large-scale

Chinese-English MT effort between the University of Maryland and New Mexico State University.

Non-Linguistic Paradigms

Non-linguistic paradigms are those that are not based in linguistic theories or even linguistic properties of language. Such research paradigm has been made possible by the rapid advances in computational power and the availability of machine readable dictionaries and monolingual and bilingual corpora. The approaches all depend on existence of large text corpora which are used either for training data or databases of existing translations.

Corpus-based approaches to machine translation (statistical or example-based) tried, and partially succeeded to replace traditional rule-based approaches, beginning in the mid-1990s, following the developments in language technology. The main advantage of corpus-based machine translation systems is that they are self-customizing in the sense that they can learn the translations of terminology and even stylistic phrasing from previously translated materials. One of the many problems in the field of MT is that expressions (multi-word terms) convey ideas that transcend the meanings of the individual words in the expression. A sentence may have unambiguous meaning, but each word in the sentence can have many different meanings.

Autocoding (or automatic concept indexing) occurs when a software program extracts terms contained within text and maps them to a standard list of concepts contained in a nomenclature. The purpose of autocoding is to provide a way of organizing large documents by the concepts represented in the text. Autocoders transform text into an index of coded nomenclature terms (sometimes called a "concept index" or "concept signature").

Word sense disambiguation is a technique for assigning the most appropriate meaning to a polysemous word within a given context. Word sense disambiguation is considered essential for applications that use knowledge of word meanings in open text, such as machine translation, knowledge acquisition, information retrieval, and information extraction. Accordingly, word sense disambiguation may be used by many commercial applications, such as automatic machine translation intelligent information retrieval (helping the users of search engines find information that is more relevant to their search), text classification, and others.

By the turn of the century, this newer approach based on statistical models a word or phrase is translated to one of a number of possibilities based on the probability that it would occur in the current context has achieved marked success. The best examples substantially outperform rule-based systems. Statistics-based machine translation (SMT) also may prove easier and less expensive to expand, if the system can be taught new knowledge domains or languages by giving it large samples of existing human-translated texts. Despite some success, however, severe problems still exist: outputs are often ungrammatical and the quality and accuracy of translation falls well below that of a human linguist and well below demands of all but highly specialized commercial markets.

Statistics-Based MT

The production of translations based on statistical predictions techniques depends heavily on statistical analysis of bilingual parallel corpora. Earlier investigations on SBMT paradigm was held in late 1980s by IBM. In less than two decades, SBMT has come to dominate academic MT research, and has gained a share of the commercial MT market. Progress is rapid, and the state of the art is a moving target. SBMT treats translation as a machine learning problem. This means that we apply a learning algorithm to a large body of previously translated text, known variously as a parallel corpus, parallel text, bitext, or multitext. The learner is then able translate previously unseen sentences. With an SBMT toolkit and enough parallel text, we can build an MT system for a new language pair within a very short period of time perhaps as little as a day. For example, a Cebuano-to English SBMT system is reported to be have been built in a matter of weeks.

Workshops have shown that translation systems can be built for a wide variety of language pairs within similar time frames. The accuracy of these systems depends crucially on the quantity, quality, and domain of the data, but there are many tasks for which even poor translation is useful. A variant of Bayes' Rule is used to show that the probability that a string of words (T) is a translation of a given string of words (S) is proportional to the product of the probability that a string of words is a legal utterance in the TL and the probability that a string of words in the SL is a translation of the string of words in the TL.

$$P(T|S) \sim P(T)*P(S|T)$$

If the right hand probabilities are known, the translation is obtained by choosing T such that the left hand probability is maximized. Obviously, the probabilities for all strings in both languages cannot be known and consequently must be estimated for the approach to be tractable. The usual approach is to define approximate probabilistic models constructed from probabilities that can be directly estimated from existing data. This paradigm has been tested in the laboratory for French-English MT. The grand claim made for this approach that no lexicon or grammars are used, everything comes from statistical analysis of corpora, while this is strength of the approach, the weakness is that this corpora must exist. IBM later improved its systems by building hybrid systems adding morphological analysis, part-of-speech (POS) tagging, syntactic regularization, limited grammatical analysis and contextual marking.

Example-Based MT

The basic idea of EBMT assumes a database of parallel translations which is searched for the SL sentences and phrases closest matching a new SL sentence. The translation of the matched phrases are then modified and combined to form a transfer translation of the new sentences. A simple match would be an identical phrase except for a similar content word. The closeness of the match would be determined by the semantic "distance" between the two content words as measured by some metric based on a thesaurus or ontology. The translation would be the substitution of a translation of the different word in the translation of the best match.

The accuracy and quality of translation is heavily dependent on the size and coverage of the parallel database. Phrasal matching requires at least a rough syntactic analysis of the parallel translations as well as some semantic analysis to determine the closeness of the match. Sentence translation in EBMT requires that in addition to phrasal matching the syntactic structure of the SL sentence must be matched with sentences in the database. While full sentence matching has shown some success, most uses of EBMT are restricted to sub-problems such as function words, noun phrases, prepositional phrase attachment.

Hybrid MT Systems

However, many of non-linguistic-based paradigms had difficulty with some aspects of the MT process. For example, they cannot handle long range contextual dependencies or with complex sentences structures. It was quickly recognized that these non-linguistic-based paradigms could be combined with linguistic paradigms to exploit the strengths of each. The hybrid paradigm involves a mixing of MT paradigms (as well as mixing MT architectures). The usual approach is to use linguistic methods to obtain parses of the SL text and to use statistical or example techniques to resolve dependencies and phrasal translations, etc.

Hybrid methods are still fundamentally statistics-based, but incorporate higher level abstract syntax rules to arrive at the final translation. Such hybrids have been explored in the research community, but without any real success because it was difficult to merge the fundamentally different approaches. New algorithms exploit knowledge of how words, phrases and patterns should be translated; knowledge of how syntax-based and non-syntax based translation rules should be applied; and knowledge of how syntactically based target structures should be generated. Cross-lingual parsers of increasing complexity provide methods to choose different syntactic orderings in different situations.

Hybrid Machine Translation

Hybrid machine translation can be considered as the process, where several machine translation processes are being used inside one machine translation system to get a translation job done. It was proven that the single translation systems are not so effective. In fact, they were not in a position to provide the level of accuracy needed.

As a result, there emerged the need to come up with a new and accurate translation mechanism. That's where hybrid machine translations came into play. When multiple machine translation methods are used, there is a possibility to overcome the issues that are linked with single translation methods. As a result, the translators are capable of ending up with a highly accurate output. With that understanding in mind, let's deep dive and take a look at some of the most prominent hybrid translation methodologies that are being used as of now.

Multi-Engine Translation

The multi-engine translation approach to hybrid machine translation is associated with running multiple machine translation systems in parallel with each other. The final output is usually generated by the combined output of all the sub-systems involved in the process. Usually, the systems that use multi engine translation methods are rule based and statistical. However, the other combinations are explored as well. A group of researchers who come from the Carnegie Mellon University were able to end up with some success when they combined transfer based, example based, statistical and knowledge based translation sub-systems into one single machine translation system. This is one of the most widely used hybrid translation methodologies in today's world. Depending on the working mechanism, it can provide highly effective results to the translators with getting their translation work done. If you are a translator, you are encouraged to take a look at the very first thing, while you are deep diving into the hybrid translation methodologies.

Statistical Rule Generation

In this hybrid translation approach, statistical data is being used in order to generate syntactic and lexical rules. The input will then be processed along with the assistance of these rules. The functionality is pretty much similar to a rule based translator. This approach has the ability to avoid the time consuming and complex tasks of creating a set of fine-grained and comprehensive linguistic rules and extracting those rules via a training corpus. This approach still has many issues. If you are about to try it, you are encouraged to have a basic understanding of these issues as well.

In fact, most of the issues that the statistical rule generation hybrid translation method has been inherent from the basic principles that create it. For example, the accuracy of the translation heavily depends on the similarities that exist in between the text contained in the training corpus and the input text. Due to the same reason, the statistical rule generation hybrid translation method was able to achieve a high level of success in some of the domain-specific applications. On the other hand, it is not good in providing perfect results in a few other applications.

Multi-Pass

Multi pass can also be considered as a popular hybrid translation approach that you can find out there in the world. In this approach, the input is being processed serially for multiple times. Out of the techniques that are used in multi-pass translation, the most common technique is to pre-process the inputs along with the assistance of a rule based machine translation system. The output that comes from a rule based preprocessor is then being passed into the statistical machine translating system. This system is capable of providing a translator with the final translated output.

The multi pass translation technique is widely being used in order to limit the extent of information that a statistical system should consider. This will significantly reduce the processing power needed as well. On the other hand, it removes the need to have a rule based system in order to complete a translation for getting a document translated from one language to another. On the other hand, this translation approach is in a position to significantly reduce the human labor and effort that is needed to develop a system.

Dialogue Systems

A dialogue is considered as a two-way dynamic communication between speaker and hearer, where the roles of speaker and hearer keep interchanging. A dialogue is coherent when the participants share the textual, contextual and world knowledge. Studies have shown that conversations have a structure and the mechanism of turn taking is systematic. The simple 2-line dialogues given below give sufficient insight into issues related to pragmatics and discourse.

(i) A: Hi! How was your holiday?

B: With in-laws. What do you think it was like?

(ii) A: Hi! How was the movie?

B: It was good.

(iii) A: How come you are at home?

B: Today is Friday.

These dialogues show that knowing just the meaning of words or having knowledge of syntactic structures is not sufficient enough to understand each other. For instance, to understand B, A should know what it in (i) B and (ii) B refers to. In the same way, A should know the implication in (iii) B which is that schools/offices are closed on Fridays (in the Middle East) and so B is at home. Knowing the intention of the speaker and making correct inferences are very important as well, as seen in understanding the meaning of the phrase "It is cold" below.

(iv) A: It is cold.

B: Shall I turn off the air conditioner?

(v) A: It is cold.

B: Shall I heat it up in the microwave oven?

The phrase "It is cold" does not carry the same pragmatic force in (iv) and (v). The intention of speaker A was different in each context and B inferred the intention correctly. A difference also lies at the discourse level 'It' in (iv) is an empty pronoun, whereas 'It' in (v) refers to some exophoric noun phrase (that which is not mentioned in the text) a dish, perhaps. This difference is made out from B's response in each case. This level of language analysis is a challenge for machines.

Dialogue Systems is the most important application area of Computational Pragmatics which is a sub-field of Computational Linguistics. Computational Pragmatics draws on disciplines such as Pragmatics, Artificial Intelligence and Cognitive Science to study the research, implementation, and evaluation of dialogue systems or conversational agents. Studies in pragmatics related to speech-acts, indirect speech-acts, conversational implicatures etc. form the basis of Computational Pragmatics. Much progress has been made in the field of Dialogue Systems since Eliza, the first chatbot, was developed by Joseph Weizenbaum in the late 1960s. Eliza was based on Rogerian Psychotherapy and used pattern matching to carry on a limited form of conversation. It gave a feeling that it was 'human' as its answers showed its 'intelligence' in processing the input and generating suitable outputs. Today, there are much more sophisticated conversational agents available online serving a wide range of purposes. For example, many companies have chatbots serving as assistants and consultants in education, business, travel, hospitality, healthcare, and entertainment sectors. In recent times, one of the most successful applications of dialogue systems has been in car navigation. The machine helps the user not only by giving directions but also in making calls or choosing music. The following dialogue between User (U) and System (S) from CSLI Dialogue System for in-car devices gives a good idea of the extent of the usefulness of spoken dialogue systems.

1U: What music do you have?

2S: I have rock, soul ...

3U: What rock songs?

4S: Just a second: you have to turn left at the next intersection.

5U: OK.

6S: I have songs by U2, Cake, Green Day, Jet, ...

7U: Play something by them.

8S: OK. Playing xxx.

9U: Call John.

10S: Do you mean John Smith or John Barry?

11U: John Smith.

12S: Calling...

13U: I need somewhere for lunch.

14S: There is a highly rated vegetarian restaurant near here.

15U: What other cuisines?

16S: There are Italian, Japanese, Malaysian, Nepali, and Thai restaurants close by.

This particular spoken dialogue system has access to the car's internal databases such as the phone directory and the music playlist, and also has access to several web-based applications such as Google maps.

Types of Dialogue Systems

Research is continuing in several places across the world in building dialogue systems in different languages. Depending on the use and mode, the different systems available can be classified into the following types:

- Interactive Voice Systems (e.g., railway enquiry system asking the user to press certain numbers for accomplishing the task).
- Question-Answer Systems (e.g., START, a web-based question and answer system answering user's questions on movies, places, people etc).
- Natural Language Interfaces (e.g., tutoring systems and trip planning systems).
- Personal Assistants that understand user needs and tasks.
- Intelligent Tutoring that involves student engagement.
- Embodied Conversational Agents that engage via realistic and affective physical and facial gestures.
- Intelligent Systems for differing environments, such as the home or car that understands user situation and activity.

An alternative way of classifying dialogue systems is based on initiation techniques:

- Single initiative systems where the machine guides users through a series of scripted prompts as in telephone enquiry systems.

- Mixed initiative systems where both the users and machine can initiate the conversation in a cooperative and flexible way as in flight booking or car navigation.

A single initiative system limits the interaction, but the language processing is much better than in a mixed initiative system as the users' responses are predictable. However, researchers are more interested in developing mixed initiative systems as they are closer to the structure of human conversation. Conversation was more balanced in human-human situations in terms of the amount of speech, types of dialogue acts and with respect to initiative, while the system dominated in number of words and dialogue acts and in initiative in human-computer conversations.

Architecture of a Dialogue System

To understand dialogue systems better, I will draw on the architecture of a simple spoken dialogue system developed for the domain of railway reservations. The system has six modules, with the dialogue manager being the hub of the system. The dialogue manager plays an important role in interacting with the other modules. When the user utters a sentence, it is converted into text by the automated speech recognition (ASR) system. The text is given to the language understanding (LU) module where all the language specific tasks are completed.

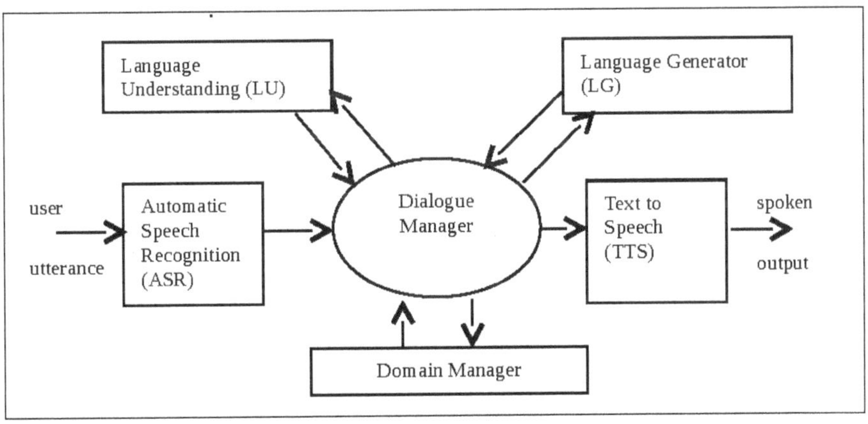

The output of this module is rich with linguistic information which helps the dialogue manager in proceeding to take the next step. For instance, it helps the dialogue manager to figure out the intention of the speaker and then draw appropriate inferences. Similarly, other tasks like ellipsis handling and anaphora resolution are dealt in this module. The domain manager gives the dialogue manager specific information based on the user's needs. Finally, the dialogue manager interacts with the language generator module to generate natural language sentences which the text to speech (TTS) module converts into spoken sentences.

Language Understanding Module

The task of the language understanding module is to process the output given by the ASR module. After the language processing is completed, the output representing the phonological, morphological, syntactic, semantic, pragmatic and discourse information is given to the dialogue manager for further operations. This module is the most challenging one as human language is complex and ambiguous. To understand language, different techniques, apart from linguistic knowledge and general knowledge, are needed. Examples like the following (taken from different sources including newspapers and everyday conversation) demonstrate the knowledge required by machines to process each one of these inputs when the context is missing.

- A nameless man/An aimless man (speech to text problem).
- She showed me the mouse. (Mouse = rodent or computer part).
- The leopard was spotted. (Spotted = adjective or verb).
- It is not my cup of tea. (Cup of tea = literal or figurative).
- If the boys don't like the new toys, throw them away. (Them refers to the boys or new toys).

The examples above reflect ambiguity at phonological, lexical, syntactic and discourse levels that can be resolved using contextual knowledge. The examples below have the context included to show that we process language easily only because we have internalised all the requisite knowledge.

- When shot at, the dove into the bushes. (Correct pronunciation of 'dove' according to the part of speech).
- Upon seeing the tear in the painting I shed a tear. (Correct pronunciation of 'tear' according to the meaning).

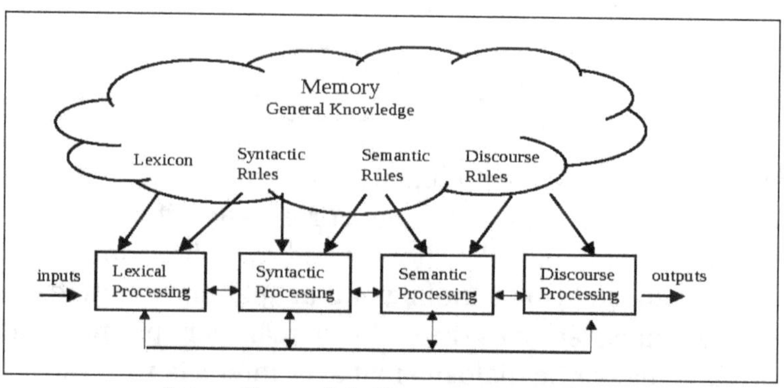

Interactive model of language processing.

It is interesting to see how humans process language so easily. Researchers have presents a cooperative model of language processing showing the interactions between the various types of knowledge. There is an interaction between two sources of knowledge: the input consisting of words and phrases and the information stored in one's memory. Then there are processes (lexical, syntactic, semantic and discourse) that interact with each other. The information is pooled from these different resources to generate an appropriate output.

We can understand the model if we take an example phrase, such as The Internet links. Depending on the words that follow, the meaning of the phrase changes as seen in The Internet links us to the world or The Internet links are given below. This shows that for language processing, interaction with all the available knowledge viz. lexical, syntactic, semantic and discourse is required simultaneously. This model is more cognitively efficient than a linear model which prefers language processing in a sequential manner first lexical, then syntactic and so on. For example, a linear model will analyse the first word The first, then The Internet and then The Internet links. If links is marked as a noun and the following word is us, then it is a wrong analysis. In the interactive model, there is no scope for such errors as it can look-ahead before analysing the current word. The interactive model is the most suitable one for the language understanding module in a dialogue system.

Issues Unresolved Computationally

Depending on the design requirements of the system, researchers have written new algorithms to solve differing linguistic issues or have adapted the algorithms written for specific applications. There are, however, some issues that remain unresolved, such as the techniques we use for sarcasm and humour in our conversation. There are also other issues related to kinesics and paralanguage which are important in communication, but are not handled computationally. For example, humans use many paralinguistic cues like hums, grunts, pauses, false starts, hedges, disfluencies, hesitations, temporal and prosodic features in their conversations. Some of these cues may have a linguistic meaning as well. A computational model for these features is still not available.

Dialogue Modeling Computationally

Currently, the available dialogue systems are for specific, limited domains. Building a general purpose dialogue system is far more challenging, as all the pragmatic and discourse issues, need to be solved. The following figure summarises some models that use different techniques such as finite state (where the structure is fixed and dialogue acts are represented as adjacency pairs, e.g., greeting-greeting, question-answer), frame-based (where the machine interacts in such a way that a template gets filled up) and plan-based techniques (where a plan may be decomposed into sequences of actions and sub-goals) to accomplish tasks such as booking tickets, enquiring about a product, designing house or helping in saving lives through the efficient use of information technology during a disaster. Figure also shows the range of systems currently available.

Technique Used	Example Task		Dialogue Phenomena Handled
Finite-state script	Long distance dialling	Least Complex	User answers questions.
Frame-based	Getting train timetable information		User asks questions, simple clarifications by system.
Set of contents	Travel booking agent		Shifts between predetermined topics.
Plan-based models	Kitchen design consultant		Dynamically generated topic structures, collaborative negotiation subdialogues.
Agent-based models	Disaster relief management	Most Complex	Different modalities (e.g. planned world and actual world).

All of the systems shown in figure can be classified as practical, goal-oriented dialogue systems with the structure of the dialogue being either task-oriented or information seeking. It is a fact that goal-oriented dialogue is simpler to implement than the general-purpose dialogue. The ultimate challenge is to devise a dialogue system that will not be limited by either domain or task. The dialogue systems built on the techniques mentioned above work well for limited domains such as travel, sports, tourism, health, etc. For any system to be judged intelligent, it should have the components. These are:

- Perception: The agent must be able to perceive the world around it.
- Beliefs: The agent must have a representation of the present state of the world.
- Desire/wants: The agent should have positive or negative responses to various states of the world, creating a way to compare the desirability of states.
- Planning/reasoning: The agent must be able to reason about ways to attain other states.
- Commitment: The agent must be able to decide to act to get to a different state.
- Intentions: The agent must be able to maintain the course of action decided on.
- Acting: The agent must be able to act and thus change its state.

Most of these features are seen in human conversation also. For successful conversation, even of a human-human type, recognizing the belief, desire and intention, all pertaining to the cognitive states, is important. A model along these lines is called the BDI (belief, desire and intention) model. It is an extremely powerful approach to dialogue act comprehension and speech act interpretation. It uses rich knowledge structures and powerful planning techniques. It addresses even subtle indirect uses of dialogue acts. It incorporates knowledge about the speaker's and hearer's intentions, actions, knowledge, and belief, that is essential for any complete model of dialogue. However, this model has its limitations. It requires that each utterance has a single literal meaning, which is considered by plan inference rules to produce a final non-literal interpretation.

An alternative model is cue based model. This model is based on the assumption that the listener uses different cues in the input to help decide how to build an interpretation. The surface input to the interpretive algorithm provides clues to structure-building, rather than providing a literal meaning which must be modified by purely inferential processes. The different sources of knowledge (cues) such as lexical, collocational, syntactic, prosodic, or conversational-structure cues are used in the cue-based model for detecting a speech act. Both these models generally use machine learning algorithms. For this purpose, a corpus of dialogues annotated with dialogue acts is required. Dialogue acts are speech acts marked with additional conversational functions and pragmatic force.

Representing Speech Acts as Dialogue Acts

An important resource to handle issues higher than the syntactic level is to have a corpus annotated for dialogue acts. Currently, much effort is going on in the annotation of corpora of dialogues. The machines are trained on the annotated corpora before they are developed into automated systems. A currently available tagging scheme is the DAMSL, Dialogue Act Markup in Several Layers, scheme. DAMSL is a dialogue act tagging scheme developed especially for task-oriented dialogue. By taking into account the content of the utterance and the intention of the speaker, the tags are classified into four main categories:

- Communicative Status: It records whether the utterance is intelligible and whether it was successfully completed.
- Information Level: A characterization of the semantic content of the utterance.
- The Forward Looking Function: How the current utterance constrains the future beliefs and actions of the participants, and affects the discourse.
- The Backward Looking Function: How the current utterance relates to the previous discourse.

The following conversation marked with the dialogue acts [in square brackets] is an example of an annotated dialogue.

A: I think we should meet soon. [Suggestion]

B: Yeah. [Agreement]

A: How about (pause) tomorrow? [Suggestion]

B: Hmm. Tomorrow I am busy. [Negation]

A: Whole day? [Negotiation begins]

B: Hmm. I have a class from 10 to 12 and then 2 to 4 a long meeting. [Elaboration]

A: How about at 12? [Insistence/Suggestion]

B: (Snigger) Lunchtime? [Dislike the option]

A: Yeah. (Smile) [Affirmation]

B: Okay then. [Agreement]

A: Don't worry. We will be back on time. I know this restaurant across the road. [Assurance/Suggestion]

B: Sounds good.

A machine trained on such annotated corpora should be able to conduct a successful conversation with humans. A computational linguist aims for the following type of conversation between a User (U) and a System (S). This conversation is based on a Wizard of Oz type of experiment for a prototypical flight reservation domain. The pragmatic and conversational techniques used are given in comments.

U1: Please book a ticket to London. //Violation of maxim of Quantity (less information is provided)//

S1: From Riyadh? //Information seeking//

U2: Yes. And one to Paris during Hajj vacation. //Ellipsis (one means one ticket)//

S2: You need to book one ticket to London and one ticket to Paris during Hajj vacation. //Seeking confirmation after ellipsis handling and context handling from previous turns//

U3: Yes. //Confirmation//

S3: When do you plan to travel? //Information seeking//

U4: Well, my first day of conference falls on 10 October. //Violation of maxim of clarity//

S4: Do you want to travel on 9 October? //Prediction//

U5: What is the flight's arrival time in London? //Query//

S5: On 9th October, British Airways has a flight reaching London at 5pm. Do you want me to check other airlines? //Options offered//

U6: No. This is perfect. //Confirmation//

S6: Okay. One ticket is booked on 9 October from Riyadh to London on British Airways. //Task completion//

U7: Good. //Confirmation//

S7: You want to make more bookings? //New task//

As can be seen, techniques related to conversation analysis (turn-taking, adjacency pairs), discourse analysis (ellipsis) and pragmatics (speech acts) as well as the integration of linguistic cues into computational models collaborate in making a successful dialogue.

References

- Introduction-to-Machine-Translation: inflibnet.ac.in, Retrieved 19, January 2020
- Hybrid-translation: agatotranslate.ae, Retrieved 15, March 2020

5

Speech Recognition and Processing

The methodologies and technologies which allow the recognition and translation of speech into text by computers are known as speech recognition. Most of the general-purpose speech recognition systems are developed through Hidden Markov Models. This chapter has been carefully written to provide an easy understanding of the varied facets of speech recognition and processing such as text to speech synthesis and Hidden Markov Model.

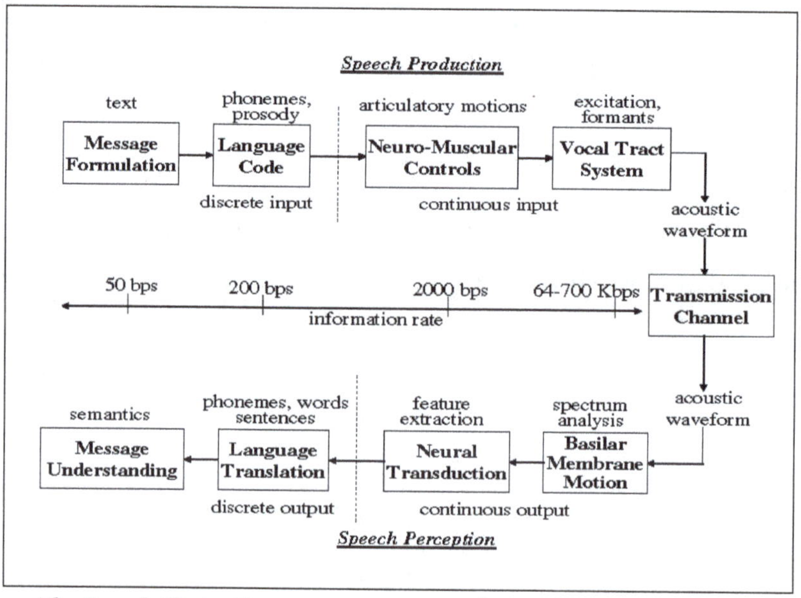

The Speech Chain: From message, to speech signal, to understanding.

Figure shows the complete process of producing and perceiving speech from the formulation of a message in the brain of a talker, to the creation of the speech signal, and finally to the understanding of the message by a listener. In their classic introduction to speech science, researchers have referred to this process as the "speech chain". The process starts in the upper left as a message represented somehow in the brain of the speaker. The message information can be thought of as having a number of different representations during the process of speech production.

For example the message could be represented initially as English text. In order to "speak" the message, the talker implicitly converts the text into a symbolic representation of the sequence of sounds corresponding to the spoken version of the text. This step, called the language code generator in figure, converts text symbols to phonetic symbols (along with stress and durational information) that describe the basic sounds of a spoken version of the message and the manner (i.e., the speed and emphasis) in which the sounds are intended to be produced. As an example, the segments of the waveform of figure are labeled with phonetic symbols using a computer-keyboard-friendly code called ARPAbet. Thus, the text "should we chase" is represented phonetically (in ARPAbet symbols) as [SH UH D – W IY – CH EY S].

The third step in the speech production process is the conversion to "neuro-muscular controls," i.e., the set of control signals that direct the neuro-muscular system to move the speech articulators, namely the tongue, lips, teeth, jaw and velum, in a manner that is consistent with the sounds of the desired spoken message and with the desired degree of emphasis. The end result of the neuro-muscular controls step is a set of articulatory motions (continuous control) that cause the vocal tract articulators to move in a prescribed manner in order to create the desired sounds. Finally the last step in the Speech Production process is the "vocal tract system" that physically creates the necessary sound sources and the appropriate vocal tract shapes over time so as to create an acoustic waveform, such as the one shown in figure that encodes the information in the desired message into the speech signal.

To determine the rate of information flow during speech production, assume that there are about 32 symbols (letters) in the language (in English there are 26 letters, but if we include simple punctuation we get a count closer to $32 = 2^5$ symbols). Furthermore, the rate of speaking for most people is about 10 symbols per second (somewhat on the high side, but still acceptable for a rough information rate estimate). Hence, assuming independent letters as a simple approximation, we estimate the base information rate of the text message as about 50 bps (5 bits per symbol times 10 symbols per second). At the second stage of the process, where the text representation is converted into phonemes and prosody (e.g., pitch and stress) markers, the information rate is estimated to increase by a factor of 4 to about 200 bps. For example, the ARBAbet phonetic symbol set used to label the speech sounds in figure contains approximately $64 = 2^6$ symbols, or about 6 bits/phoneme (again a rough approximation assuming independence of phonemes). In figure, there are 8 phonemes in approximately 600 ms. This leads to an estimate of $8 \times 6/0.6 = 80$ bps. Additional information required to describe prosodic features of the signal (e.g., duration, pitch, loudness) could easily add 100 bps to the total information rate for a message encoded as a speech signal.

The information representations for the first two stages in the speech chain are discrete so we can readily estimate the rate of information flow with some simple assumptions. For the next stage in the speech production part of the speech chain, the representation becomes continuous (in the form of control signals for articulatory motion). If they could be measured, we could estimate the spectral bandwidth of these control signals and appropriately sample and quantize these signals to obtain equivalent digital signals for which the data rate could be estimated. The articulators move relatively slowly compared to the time variation of the resulting acoustic waveform. Estimates of bandwidth and required accuracy suggest that the total data rate of the sampled articulatory control signals is about 2000 bps. Thus, the original text message is represented by a set of continuously varying signals whose digital representation requires a much higher data rate than the information rate that we estimated for transmission of the message as a speech signal. Finally, the data rate of the digitized speech waveform at the end of the speech production part of the speech chain can be anywhere from 64,000 to more than 700,000 bps.

We arrive at such numbers by examining the sampling rate and quantization required to represent the speech signal with a desired perceptual fidelity. For example, "telephone quality" requires that a bandwidth of 0–4 kHz be preserved, implying a sampling rate of 8000 samples/s. Each sample can be quantized with 8 bits on a log scale, resulting in a bit rate of 64,000 bps. This representation is highly intelligible (i.e., humans can readily extract the message from it) but to most listeners, it will sound different from the original speech signal uttered by the talker. On the other hand, the speech waveform can be represented with "CD quality" using a sampling rate of 44,100 samples/s with 16 bit samples, or a data rate of 705,600 bps. In this case, the reproduced acoustic signal will be virtually indistinguishable from the original speech signal.

As we move from text to speech waveform through the speech chain, the result is an encoding of the message that can be effectively transmitted by acoustic wave propagation and robustly decoded by the hearing mechanism of a listener. As we move from text to sampled speech waveform, the data rate can increase by a factor of 10,000. Part of this extra information represents characteristics of the talker such as emotional state, speech mannerisms, accent, etc., but much of it is due to the inefficiency of simply sampling and finely quantizing analog signals. Thus, motivated by an awareness of the low intrinsic information rate of speech, a central theme of much of digital speech processing is to obtain a digital representation with lower data rate than that of the sampled waveform.

The complete speech chain consists of a speech production/generation model, as well as a speech perception/recognition model. The speech perception model shows the series of steps from capturing speech at the ear to understanding the message encoded in the speech signal. The first step is the effective conversion of the acoustic waveform to a spectral representation. This is done within the inner ear by the basilar membrane, which acts as a non-uniform spectrum analyzer by spatially separating the spectral components of the incoming speech signal and thereby analyzing them by what amounts to a non-uniform filter bank. The next step in the speech perception process is a neural transduction of the spectral features into a set of sound features (or distinctive features as they are referred to in the area of linguistics) that can be decoded and processed by the brain.

The next step in the process is a conversion of the sound features into the set of phonemes, words, and sentences associated with the in-coming message by a language translation process in the human brain. Finally, the last step in the speech perception model is the conversion of the phonemes, words and sentences of the message into an understanding of the meaning of the basic message in order to be able to respond to or take some appropriate action. Our fundamental understanding of the processes in most of the speech perception modules in figure is rudimentary at best, but it is generally agreed that some physical correlate of each of the steps in the speech perception model occur within the human brain, and thus the entire model is useful for thinking about the processes that occur.

There is one additional process shown in the diagram of the complete speech chain in figure that we have not discussed namely the transmission channel between the speech generation and speech perception parts of the model. In its simplest embodiment, this transmission channel consists of just the acoustic wave connection between a speaker and a listener who are in a common space. It is essential to include this transmission channel in our model for the speech chain since it includes real world noise and channel distortions that make speech and message understanding more difficult in real communication environments. More interestingly for our purpose here it is in this domain that we find the applications of digital speech processing.

Applications of Digital Speech Processing

The first step in most applications of digital speech processing is to convert the acoustic waveform to a sequence of numbers. Most modern A-to-D converters operate by sampling at a very high rate, applying a digital lowpass filter with cutoff set to preserve a prescribed bandwidth, and then reducing the sampling rate to the desired sampling rate, which can be as low as twice the cutoff frequency of the sharp-cutoff digital filter. This discrete-time representation is the starting point for most applications. From this point, other representations are obtained by digital processing. For the most part, these alternative representations are based on incorporating knowledge about the workings of the speech chain as depicted in figure. It is possible to incorporate aspects of both the speech production and speech perception process into the digital representation and processing. It is not an oversimplification to assert that digital speech processing is grounded in a set of techniques that have the goal of pushing the data rate of the speech representation to the left along either the upper or lower path in figure.

Speech Coding

Perhaps the most widespread applications of digital speech processing technology occur in the areas of digital transmission and storage of speech signals. In these areas the centrality of the digital representation is obvious, since the goal is to compress the digital waveform representation of speech into a lower bit-rate representation. It is common to refer to this activity as "speech coding" or "speech compression".

Figure shows a block diagram of a generic speech encoding/decoding (or compression) system. In the upper part of the figure, the A-to-D converter converts the analog speech signal $x_c(t)$ to a sampled waveform representation $x[n]$. The digital signal $x[n]$ is analyzed and coded by digital computation algorithms to produce a new digital signal y[n] that can be transmitted over a digital communication channel or stored in a digital storage medium as $\hat{y}$ [n]. As we will see, there are a myriad of ways to do the encoding so as to reduce the data rate over that of the sampled and quantized speech waveform x[n]. Because the digital representation at this point is often not directly related to the sampled speech waveform, y[n] and $\hat{y}$ [n] are appropriately referred to as data signals that represent the speech signal. The lower path in figure shows the decoder associated with the speech coder. The received data signal $\hat{y}$ [n] is decoded using the inverse of the analysis processing, giving the sequence of samples $\hat{x}$ [n] which is then converted (using a D-to-A Converter) back to an analog signal $\hat{x}_c$ (t) for human listening. The decoder is often called a synthesizer because it must reconstitute the speech waveform from data that may bear no direct relationship to the waveform.

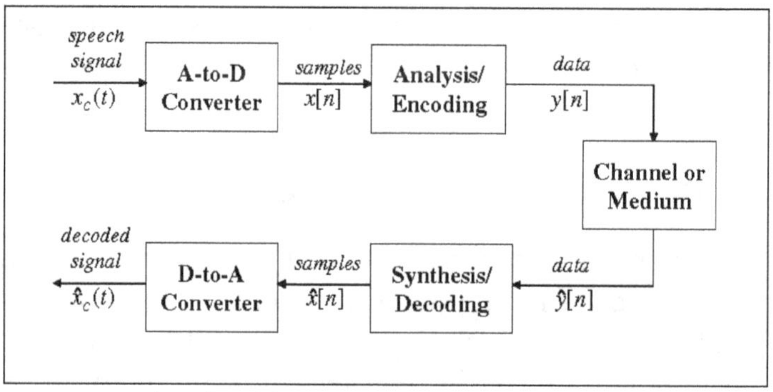

Speech coding block diagram: Encoder and decoder.

With carefully designed error protection coding of the digital representation, the transmitted (y[n]) and received ($\hat{y}$ [n]) data can be essentially identical. This is the quintessential feature of digital coding. In theory, perfect transmission of the coded digital representation is possible even under very noisy channel conditions, and in the case of digital storage, it is possible to store a perfect copy of the digital representation in perpetuity if sufficient care is taken to update the storage medium as storage technology advances. This means that the speech signal can be reconstructed to within the accuracy of the original coding for as long as the digital representation is retained. In either case, the goal of the speech coder is to start with samples of the speech signal and reduce (compress) the data rate required to represent the speech signal while maintaining a desired perceptual fidelity. The compressed representation can be more efficiently transmitted or stored, or the bits saved can be devoted to error protection.

Speech coders enable a broad range of applications including narrowband and broadband wired telephony, cellular communications, voice over internet protocol (VoIP) (which utilizes the internet as a real-time communications medium), secure voice for privacy and encryption (for national security applications), extremely narrowband communications channels (such as battlefield applications using high frequency (HF) radio), and for storage of speech for telephone answering machines, interactive voice response (IVR) systems, and prerecorded messages. Speech coders often utilize many aspects of both the speech production and speech perception processes, and hence may not be useful for more general audio signals such as music. Coders that are based on incorporating only aspects of sound perception generally do not achieve as much compression as those based on speech production, but they are more general and can be used for all typcs of audio signals. These coders are widely deployed in MP3 and AAC players and for audio in digital television systems.

Hidden Markov Model

The HMM is based on augmenting the Markov chain. A Markov chain is a model that tells us something about the probabilities of sequences of random variables, states, each of which can take on values from some set. These sets can be words, or tags, or symbols representing anything, like the weather. A Markov chain makes a very strong assumption that if we want to predict the future in the sequence all that matters is the current state. The states before the current state have no impact on the future except via the current state. It's as if to predict tomorrow's weather you could examine today's weather but you weren't allowed to look at yesterday's weather.

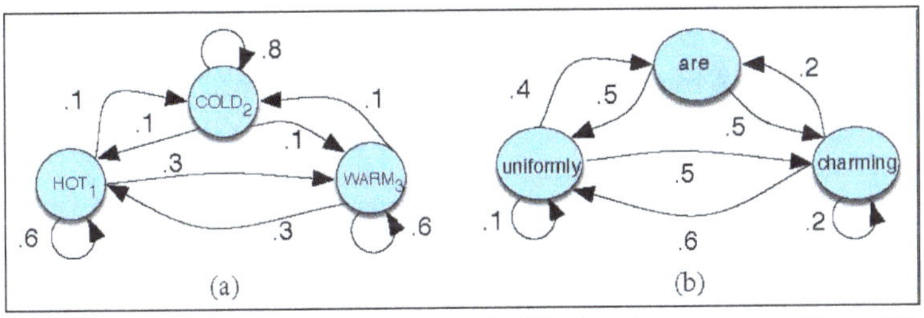

A Markov chain for weather (a) and one for words (b), showing states and transitions. A start distribution π is required; setting π = [0.1, 0.7, 0.2] for (a) would mean a probability 0.7 of starting in state 2 (cold), probability 0.1 of starting in state 1 (hot), etc.

More formally, consider a sequence of state variables $q_1,q_2,\ldots,q_i$. A Markov model embodies the Markov assumption on the probabilities of this sequence: that Markov assumption when predicting the future, the past doesn't matter, only the present.

$$\text{Markov Assumption}: P(q_i = a \mid q_1 \ldots q_{i-1}) = P(q_i = a \mid q_{i-1})$$

Figure shows a Markov chain for assigning a probability to a sequence of weather events, for which the vocabulary consists of HOT, COLD, and WARM. The states are represented as nodes in the graph, and the transitions, with their probabilities, as edges. The transitions are probabilities: the values of arcs leaving a given state must sum to 1. Figure shows a Markov chain for assigning a probability to a sequence of words $w_1 \ldots w_n$. This Markov chain should be familiar; in fact, it represents a bigram language model, with each edge expressing the probability $p(w_i \mid w_j)$. Given the two models in figure, we can assign a probability to any sequence from our vocabulary. Formally, a Markov chain is specified by the following components:

$Q = q_1 q_2 \ldots q_N$	A set of N states
$A = a_{11} a_{12} \ldots a_{n1} \ldots a_{nn}$	A transition probability matrix A, each a_{ij} representing the probability of moving from state i to state j, s.t $\Sigma_{j=1}^{n} a_{ij} = 1 \ \forall i$
$ð = ð_1, ð_2, \ldots, ð_N$	An initial probability distribution over states. π_i is the probability that the Markov chain will start in state i. Some states j may have π_i=0, meaning that they cannot be initial states. Also, $\Sigma_{i=1}^{n} ð_i = 1$

A Markov chain is useful when we need to compute a probability for a sequence of observable events. In many cases, however, the events we are interested in are hidden: we don't observe them directly. For example we don't normally observe part-of-speech tags in a text. Rather, we see words, and must infer the tags from the word sequence. We call the tags hidden because they are not observed. A hidden Markov model (HMM) allows us to talk about both observed events and hidden events (like part-of-speech tags) that we think of as causal factors in our probabilistic model. An HMM is specified by the following components:

$Q = q_1 q_2 \ldots q_N$	A set of N states
$A = a_{11} a_{12} \ldots a_{n1} \ldots a_{nn}$	A transition probability matrix A, each a_{ij} representing the probability of moving from state i to state j, s.t $\Sigma_{j=1}^{n} a_{ij} = 1 \ \forall i$
$O = o_1 o_2 \ldots o_T$	A sequence of T observations, each one drawn from a vocabulary $V = v_1, v_2, \ldots, v_V$
$B = b_i(o_t)$	A sequence of observation likelihoods, also called emission probabilities, each expressing the probability of an observation o_t being generated from a state i
$ð = ð_1, ð_2, \ldots, ð_N$	An initial probability distribution over states. π_i is the probability that the Markov chain will start in state i. Some states j may have π_i=0, meaning that they cannot be initial states. Also, $\Sigma_{i=1}^{n} ð_i = 1$

A first-order hidden Markov model instantiates two simplifying assumptions. First, as with a first-order Markov chain, the probability of a particular state depends only on the previous state:

$$\text{Markov Assumption}: P(q_i \mid q_1 \ldots q_{i-1}) = P(q_i \mid q_{i-1})$$

Second, the probability of an output observation o_i depends only on the state that produced the observation qi and not on any other states or any other observations:

$$\text{Output Independence}: P(o_i \mid q_1 \ldots q_i, \ldots, q_T, o_1, \ldots, o_i, \ldots, o_T) = P(o_i \mid q_i)$$

Imagine that you are a climatologist in the year 2799 studying the history of global warming. You cannot find any records of the weather in Baltimore, Maryland, for the summer of 2020, but you do find Jason Eisner's diary, which lists how many ice creams Jason ate every day that summer. Our goal is to use these observations to estimate the temperature every day. We'll simplify this weather task by assuming there are only two kinds of days: cold (C) and hot (H). Given a sequence of observations O (each an integer representing the number of ice creams eaten on a given day) find the 'hidden' sequence Q of weather states (H or C) which caused Jason to eat the ice cream. Figure shows a sample HMM for the ice cream task. The two hidden states (H and C) correspond to hot and cold weather, and the observations (drawn from the alphabet O = {1,2,3}) correspond to the number of ice creams eaten by Jason on a given day.

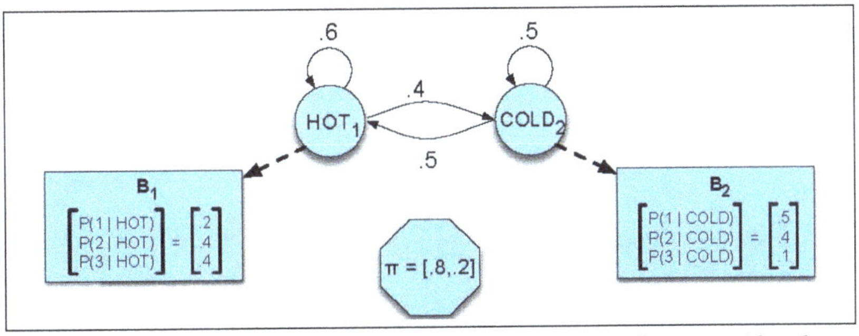

A hidden Markov model for relating numbers of ice creams eaten by Jason (the observations) to the weather (H or C, the hidden variables).

Hidden Markov models should be characterized by three fundamental problems:

Problem 1 (Likelihood):	Given an HMM λ = (A,B) and an observation sequence O, determine the likelihood P(O|λ).
Problem 2 (Decoding):	Given an observation sequence O and an HMM λ = (A,B), discover the best hidden state sequence Q.
Problem 3 (Learning):	Given an observation sequence O and the set of states in the HMM, learn the HMM parameters A and B.

Our first problem is to compute the likelihood of a particular observation sequence. For example, given the ice-cream eating HMM in figure, what is the probability of the sequence 3 1 3? More formally Computing Likelihood:

> Given an HMM λ = (A,B) and an observation sequence O, determine the likelihood P(O|λ).

For a Markov chain, where the surface observations are the same as the hidden events, we could compute the probability of 3 1 3 just by following the states labeled 3 1 3 and multiplying the probabilities along the arcs. For a hidden Markov model, things are not so simple. We want to determine the probability of an ice-cream observation sequence like 3 1 3, but we don't know what the hidden state sequence is. Let's start with a slightly simpler situation. Suppose we already knew the weather and wanted to predict how much ice cream Jason would eat. This is a useful part of many HMM tasks. For a given hidden state sequence (e.g., hot hot cold), we can easily compute the output likelihood of 3 1 3. Let's see how. First, recall that for hidden Markov models, each hidden state produces only a single observation. Thus, the sequence of hidden states and the sequence of observations have the same length.

Given this one-to-one mapping and the Markov assumptions expressed in Markov Assumption : $P(q_i \mid q_1 \ldots q_{i-1}) = P(q_i \mid q_{i-1})$, for a particular hidden state sequence $Q = q_0, q_1, q_2, \ldots, q_T$ and an observation sequence $O = o_1, o_2, \ldots, o_T$, the likelihood of the observation sequence is $P(O \mid Q) = \prod_{i=1}^{T} P(o_i \mid q_i)$.

The computation of the forward probability for our ice-cream observation 3 1 3 from one possible hidden state sequence hot hot cold is shown in Equation below. Figure below shows a graphic representation of this computation.

$$P(3\,1\,3 \mid \text{hot hot cold}) = P(3 \mid \text{hot}) \times P(1 \mid \text{hot}) \times P(3 \mid \text{cold})$$

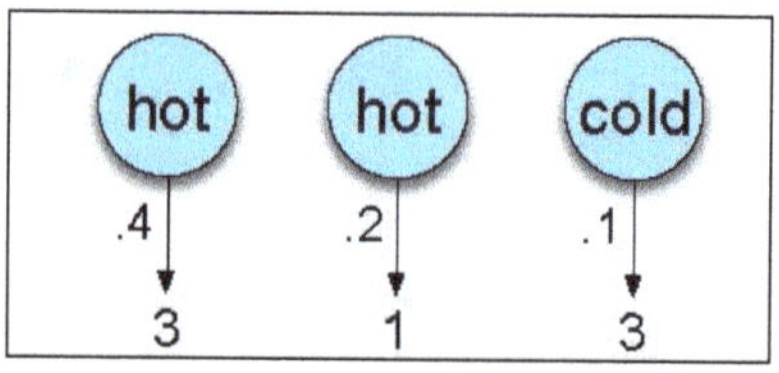

The computation of the observation likelihood for the ice-cream events 3 1 3 given the hidden state sequence hot hot cold.

But of course, we don't actually know what the hidden state (weather) sequence was. We'll need to compute the probability of ice-cream events 3 1 3 instead by summing over all possible weather sequences, weighted by their probability. First, let's compute the joint probability of being in a particular weather sequence Q and generating a particular sequence O of ice-cream events. In general, this is:

$$P(O,Q) = P(O \mid Q) \times P(Q) = \prod_{i=1}^{T} P(o_i \mid q_i) \times \prod_{i=1}^{T} P(q_i \mid q_{i-1})$$

The computation of the joint probability of our ice-cream observation 3 1 3 and one possible hidden state sequence hot hot cold is shown in Equation below. Figure below shows a graphic representation of this computation.

$$P(3\,1\,3, \text{hot hot cold}) = P(\text{hot} \mid \text{start}) \times P(\text{hot} \mid \text{hot}) \times P(\text{cold} \mid \text{hot})$$
$$\times P(3 \mid \text{hot}) \times P(1 \mid \text{hot}) \times P(3 \mid \text{cold})$$

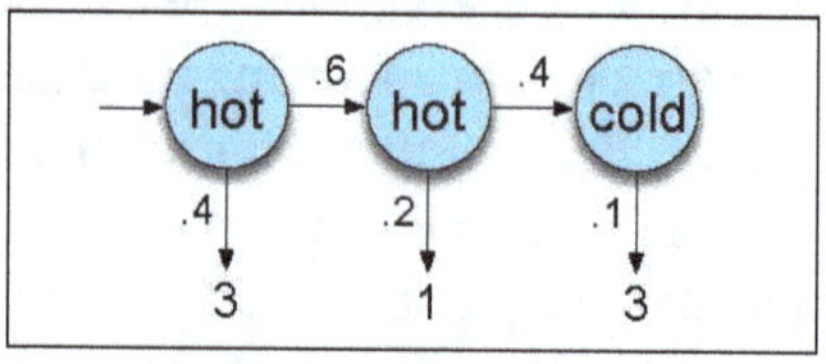

The computation of the joint probability of the ice-cream events 3 1 3 and the hidden state sequence hot hot cold.

Now that we know how to compute the joint probability of the observations with a particular hidden state sequence, we can compute the total probability of the observations just by summing over all possible hidden state sequences:

$$P(O)=\sum_{Q}P(O,Q)=\sum_{Q}P(O|Q)P(Q)$$

For our particular case, we would sum over the eight 3-event sequences cold cold cold, cold cold hot, that is:

$$P(3\,1\,3)=P(3\,1\,3,\text{cold cold cold})+P(3\,1\,3,\text{cold cold hot})+P(3\,1\,3,\text{hot hot cold})+...$$

For an HMM with N hidden states and an observation sequence of T observations, there are N^T possible hidden sequences. For real tasks, where N and T are both large, N^T is a very large number, so we cannot compute the total observation likelihood by computing a separate observation likelihood for each hidden state sequence and then summing them. Instead of using such an extremely exponential algorithm, we use an efficient $O(N^2T)$ algorithm called the forward algorithm. The forward algorithm is a kind forward algorithm of dynamic programming algorithm, that is, an algorithm that uses a table to store intermediate values as it builds up the probability of the observation sequence. The forward algorithm computes the observation probability by summing over the probabilities of all possible hidden state paths that could generate the observation sequence, but it does so efficiently by implicitly folding each of these paths into a single forward trellis. Figure shows an example of the forward trellis for computing the likelihood of 3 1 3 given the hidden state sequence hot hot cold.

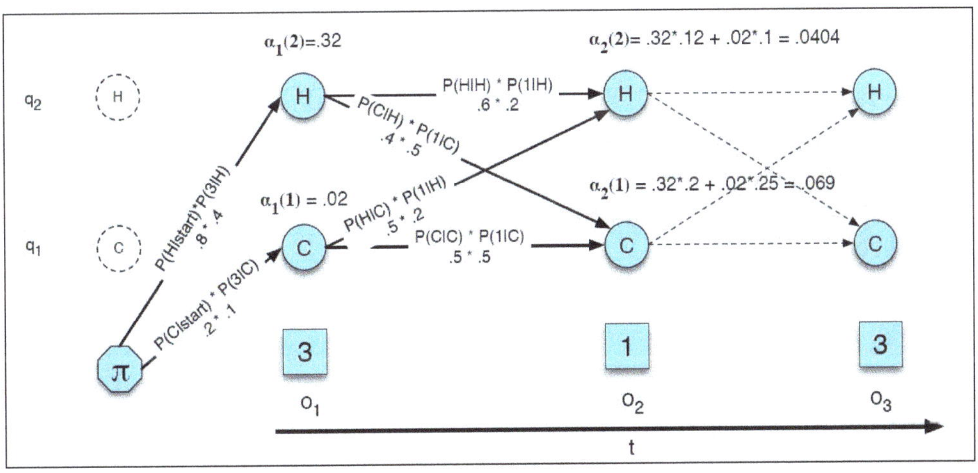

The forward trellis for computing the total observation likelihood for the ice-cream events 3 1 3. Hidden states are in circles, observations in squares. The figure shows the computation of αt(j) for two states at two time steps. The computation in each cell follows Equation: $\alpha_t(j)=\sum_{i=1}^{N}\alpha_{t-1}(i)a_{ij}b_j(o_t)$. The resulting probability expressed in each cell is Equation: $\alpha_t(j)=P(o_1,o_2...o_t,q_t=j|\lambda)$.

Each cell of the forward algorithm trellis $\acute{a}_t(j)$ represents the probability of being in state j after seeing the first t observations, given the automaton λ. The value of each cell $\acute{a}_t(j)$ is computed by summing over the probabilities of every path that could lead us to this cell. Formally, each cell expresses the following probability:

$$\acute{a}_t(j) = P(o_1, o_2 \ldots o_t, q_t = j \mid \lambda).$$

Here, $q_t = j$ means "the tth state in the sequence of states is state j". We compute this probability $\acute{a}_t(j)$ by summing over the extensions of all the paths that lead to the current cell. For a given state q_j at time t, the value $\acute{a}_t(j)$ is computed as, $\acute{a}_t(j) = \sum_{i=1}^{N} \acute{a}_{t-1}(i) a_{ij} b_j(o_t)$. The three factors that are multiplied $\acute{a}_t(j) = \sum_{i=1}^{N} \acute{a}_{t-1}(i) a_{ij} b_j(o_t)$ in in extending the previous paths to compute the forward probability at time t are:

$\acute{a}_{t-1}(i)$	The previous forward path probability from the previous time step.
a_{ij}	The transition probability from previous state q_i to current state q_j.
$b_j(o_t)$	The state observation likelihood of the observation symbol o_t given the current state j.

Consider the computation in figure above of $\alpha_2(2)$, the forward probability of being at time step 2 in state 2 having generated the partial observation. We compute by extending the α probabilities from time step 1, via two paths, each extension consisting of the three factors above: $\alpha_1(1)'P(H|C)'P(1|H)$ and $\alpha_1(2)'P(H|H)'P(1|H)$. Figure below shows another visualization of this induction step for computing the value in one new cell of the trellis. We give two formal definitions of the forward algorithm: The pseudocode in given below where forward[s,t] represents $\alpha_t(s)$ and a statement of the definitional recursion here.

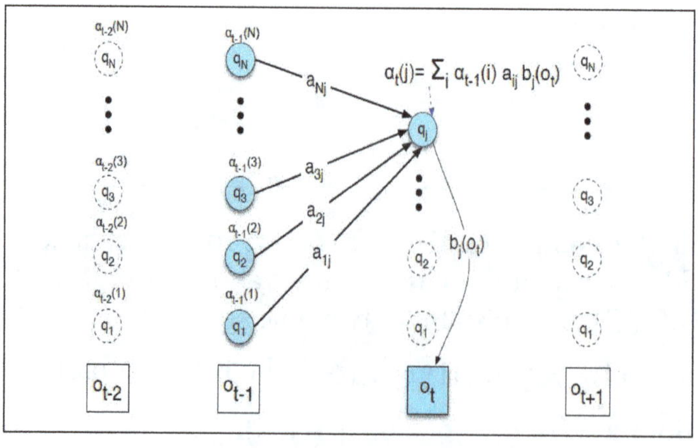

Visualizing the computation of a single element $\alpha_t(i)$ in the trellis by summing all the previous values α_{t-1}, weighted by their transition probabilities a, and multiplying by the observation probability $b_i(o_t)$. For many applications of HMMs, many of the transition probabilities are 0, so not all previous states will contribute to the forward probability of the current state. Hidden states are in circles, observations in squares. Shaded nodes are included in the probability computation for $\alpha_t(i)$.

```
function FORWARD(observations of len T, state-graph of len N) returns forward-prob
  create a probability matrix forward[N,T]
  for each state s from 1 to N do                                  ;initialization step
        forward[s,1] ← π_s * b_s(o_1)
  for each time step t from 2 to T do                              ;recursion step
        for each state s from 1 to N do
              forward[s,t] ← Σ_{s'=1}^{N} forward[s',t-1] * a_{s',s} * b_s(o_t)
  forwardprob ← Σ_{s=1}^{N} forward[s,T]                           ;termination step
  return forwardprob
```

- Initialization: $\acute{a}(_1)j = \pi_j b_j(o_1) \quad 1 \le j \le N.$
- Recursion: $\acute{a}(_t)j = \sum_{i=1}^{N} \acute{a}_{t-1}(i)\, a_{ij}\, b_j(o_t); \quad 1 \le j \le N, 1 \le t \le T.$
- Termination: $(P\ O|)\lambda = \sum_{i=1}^{N} \alpha_T(i).$

Text to Speech Synthesis

Speech is the most basic form of communication between human beings. Every human being cannot read and write, however, can communicate using speech. Probably, because of its high influence on the day-to-day life of human being, speech processing has been a subject of research from the decades. Speech synthesis in general means synthetic production of speech with the help of machines. This synthesis can be by a decoder based on the parameters it has received on transmission line. Such examples include speech synthesis by linear prediction (LP) analysis, more specially the use of codecs. Apart from this approach, speech synthesis may refer to synthesis carried by a computer to estimate some kind of a presentation of the speech signal given a text input. The latter part is known as the text-to-speech (TTS) synthesis. More often TTS is referred to as speech synthesis.

A text-to-speech (TTS) synthesis system is a system to which a text is provided and in response to the text, a speech sound is produced by the computer. A TTS synthesis system must be able to read any given text, it must be intelligible and must be natural sounding. The goal of TTS is the automatic conversion of written text into corresponding speech signal. A TTS system takes as input a sequence of words and converts them to speech. A text-to-speech synthesizer is a computer-based system that should be able to read any text whether it was directly introduced into the computer or through character recognition system (OCR). The speech synthesis field has witnessed much advancement in the past few decades. Due to the increasing applications of TTS, research activity in this area is also increasing. TTS system is widely useful for the people with disabilities. TTS systems find its applications in screen readers to be useful for usage of computer system by visually challenged person. Apart from this, recently, new and emerging applications of TTS are developing such as voice cloning, voice reconstruction for people with vocal disability, aid people with speech impairment personalized speech-to-speech translation, environment adaptive speech synthesis systems, intelligent communicative robots and personal assistant. It is also used for public announcement at railway stations; in retrieving information over telephone services such as banking services, in-car navigation, in call centers, etc.

In a very broad classification, the TTS technology can be divided into two broad categories, i.e., model-based (which models the speech production mechanism, i.e., articulatory or model-based that models the transfer function of vocal tract based on source-filter-model, i.e., formant synthesis), concatenative speech synthesis (that uses prerecorded samples derived from natural speech) and statistical parametric speech (SPS) synthesis.

Overview of Text-to-Speech (TTS) System

The goal of TTS is the automatic conversion of written text into corresponding speech. The speech synthesis field has witnessed much advancement in the past few decades. A general TTS synthesizer comprises of a text analysis module and digital signal processing (DSP) module. Figure shows the functional diagram of a very general TTS synthesizer. The text analysis module produces a phonetic transcription of the text read, together with the desired intonation and rhythm (i.e., prosody). The DSP module produces the synthetic speech corresponding to the transcription produced by text analysis module.

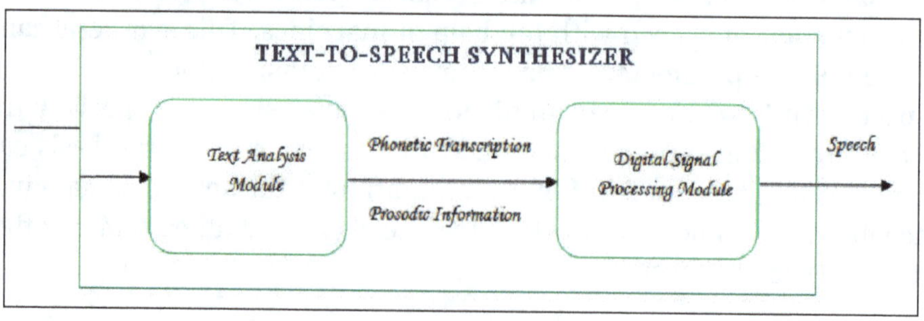

General TTS system.

Text Analysis Module

Figure shows the skeleton of a general text analysis module. The text analysis stage is extremely difficult, as this stage needs to produce all the information required by DSP module (for producing speech) from merely text only. However, a mere text does not contain all of the information needed to produce speech. The first block of the text analysis module is Text-to-Phonetics (T2P) block which converts the input text-to-phonetic transcription and the second block is Text-to-Prosody which produces prosodic information.

- Text-to-Phonetics: The Text-to-Phonetics block can be further broken down into text normalization module and a word pronunciation module.
    - Text Normalization: A text normalization module organizes the input text into manageable lists of words. It identifies numbers, abbreviations, acronyms and idiomatic and expands them into full text. This is commonly done by using regular grammars.
    - Word Pronunciation: Once the sequence of words has been generated using text normalization module, their pronunciation can be determined. A simple Letter-to-Sound (LTS) rule may be applied where words are pronounced as they are written. Where this is not the case, a morpho-syntactic analyzer may be used. A morpho-syntactic analyzer tags the speech with various identities, such as prefixes, roots and suffixes, and organizes the sentences into syntactically related groups of words, such as nouns, verbs, and adjectives. The pronunciation of these can then be determined using a lexicon.

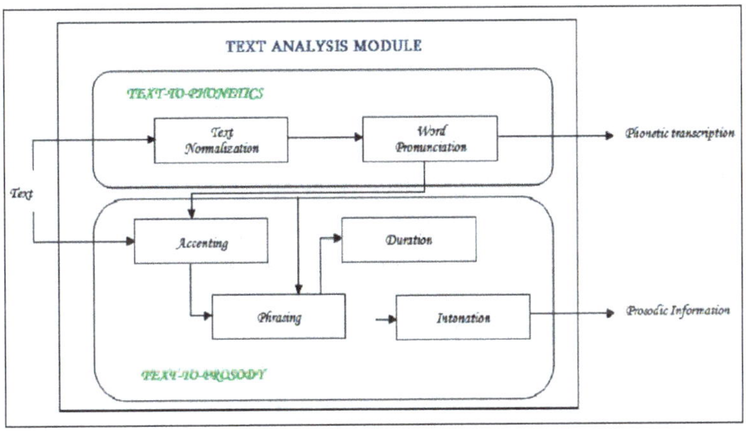

Text analysis module of a general Text-to-Speech (TTS) system.

- Text-to-Prosody: The term prosody refers to certain properties of the speech signal such as audible changes in the pitch (i.e., intonation), loudness, tempo, duration, stress and rhythm. The naturalness of speech can be described mainly in terms of prosody. Prosodic events are also referred to as suprasegmental phenomena as these events appear to be time-aligned with syllables or group of syllables, rather than with segments (sounds, phonemes). The pattern of prosody is used to communicate the meaning of sentences. The Text-to-Prosody block produces prosody information using the text and output of the word pronunciation module. This block can be further broken down into smaller processes that determine accenting, phrasing, duration, and intonation for each sentence. Following is the brief description of these four processes:

- Accenting: Accent or stress assignment is based on the category of the word. For example, content words (such as nouns, adjectives and verbs) tend to be accented and function words (such as prepositions and auxiliary verbs) are usually not accented. This information is used for predicting the intonation and duration.

- Phrasing: Sentences are broken down into phrasal units and phrase boundaries are assigned to the text. These boundaries indicate pauses and the resetting of intonation contours.

- Intonation: Intonation clarifies type and meaning of the sentence (neutral, imperative or question). In addition, intonation also conveys information about the speaker characteristics (such as gender and age) and emotions. The intonation module generates a pitch contour for the sentences. For example, the sentences "Open the door" and "Open the door?" have very different prosody. In terms of intonation contour (defined as rise and fall of the pitch throughout the utterance), the first sentence is declarative and has a relatively flat pitch contour, whereas the second is questioning and exhibits a rise in pitch at the end of the phrase.

- Duration: Segmental duration is an essential aspect of prosody. It affects the overall rhythm of the speech, stress and emphasis, the syntactic structure of the sentence, and the speaking rate. There are many factors which contribute to the duration of a speech segment. Some of them are the identity of the phone itself, the identity and characteristics of neighboring phones, the accent status of the syllable containing the phone, its phrase position and the speaking rate and dialect of the speaker.

Digital Signal Processing (DSP) Module

The DSP module uses the phonetic transcription and prosodic information produced by text analysis module to produce speech. This can be done in two ways:

- By using the series of rules which formally describes the influence of one phoneme on the other (i.e., the coarticulation effect).

- By storing numerous instances of each speech sound unit and using them as they are, as ultimate acoustic units.

Two main classes of TTS systems have emerged, namely, synthesis-by-rule and synthesis-by-concatenation. Figure shows a general DSP module.

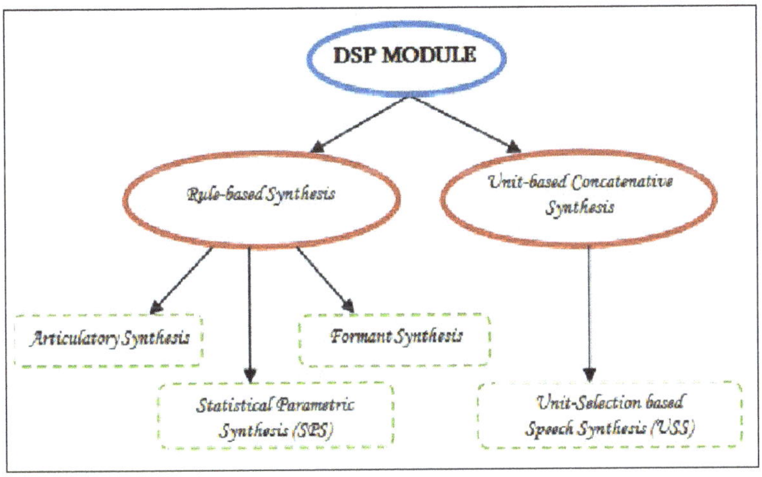

Types of Synthesis Techniques

Previously speech synthesis techniques were classified into articulatory, formant and concatenative speech synthesis. The concatenative speech synthesis method was the most popular method. With the advancement of statistical modeling of the speech production mechanism, the statistical approach of using hidden Markov model (HMM) based and further using deep neural network (DNN) in speech synthesis.

Articulatory Synthesis

The articulatory synthesis attempts to ideally model the complete human vocal organs (i.e., the human articulators and vocal folds) that produce speech as perfectly as possible. The articulatory control parameters include lip aperture, lip protrusion, tongue tip position, tongue tip height, tongue position and tongue height. It has the advantage of accurate modeling of transients due to abrupt area changes due to continuous vocal tract movement. Therefore, ideally it should be the most adequate method to produce high-quality synthetic speech. On the other hand, it is also one of the most difficult methods to implement. The first articulatory model was based on a table of vocal tract area functions from larynx to lips for each phonetic segment. The articulators are usually modeled with a set of area functions between glottis and mouth. For rule-based synthesis the articulatory control parameters may be for example lip aperture, lip protrusion, tongue tip height, tongue tip position, tongue height, tongue position and velic aperture. Phonatory or excitation parameters may be glottal aperture, vocal fold tension, and lung pressure.

During the process of speech generation, the vocal tract muscles cause the articulators to move and hence, the shape of the vocal tract changes, which results in production of different sounds. During speaking, the moment of the vocal tract is obtained from the data for articulatory model is generally derived from X-ray analysis of natural speech. However, this data is usually only 2D when the real vocal tract is naturally 3-D, so the rule-based articulatory synthesis is very difficult to optimize due to the unavailability of sufficient data of the motions of the articulators during the production of speech. In addition, another disadvantage with articulatory synthesis is that Xray data do not describe information about the masses or degrees of freedom of the articulators. In addition, the movements of tongue are so complicated that it is almost impossible to model them precisely. The articulatory synthesis is quite rarely used in present systems; however, since the analysis methods are developing fast and the computational resources are increasing rapidly, it might be a potential synthesis method in the future.

Sinewave Synthesis

Sinewave synthesis is a method for synthesizing speech by replacing the formants (the resonances in the vocal tract model) with pure tone whistles. It is based on the assumption that the speech signal can be represented in terms of sine waves having varying frequencies and also varying amplitudes. Therefore, a speech signal s(n) can be modeled as the sum of N no. of sinusoids,

$$s(n) = \sum_{i=1}^{N} A_i \cos(\omega_i n + \phi_i)$$

Where A_i, ω_i and φ_i represents the amplitude, frequency and phase of the sinusoid component. These parameters are estimated from the discrete Fourier transform (DFT) of windowed signal frames. The peaks of the spectral magnitude are selected from each frame. The basic model is also known as the McAulay/Quatieri sinusoidal model. The basic model has also some modifications such as ABS/OLA (Analysis by Synthesis/Overlap Add) and Hybrid/Sinusoidal Noise models. However, such a model works well with representing periodic signals, such as vowels and voiced consonants only and it will not work with the representation of unvoiced speech.

Formant Synthesis

Formant synthesis is based on the source-filter model of speech. It is based on the model that the human vocal tract system has several resonances and these resonances in the system results in various characteristics of speech sounds. The vocal tract can be assumed to be a cascade of several resonators in case of speech production of various periodic sounds. However, for nasalized sounds, the nasal cavity comes into picture and the tract can be modeled as a parallel resonant structure. Therefore, there are two basic structures in general, parallel and cascade, but for better performance some kind of combination of these is usually used. Formant synthesis also provides infinite number of sounds which makes it more flexible than (for example, concatenation methods).

The lower formants are known to carry the information of the sound and the higher formants carry speaker information. At least three formants are generally required to produce intelligible speech and up to five formants to produce high quality speech. Each formant is usually modeled by a 2nd order digital band-pass resonator, where a complex conjugate pole-pair corresponds to a formant frequency. The pole angle corresponds to the angular frequency and the distance of the pole from the unit circle (in z plane) corresponds to the -3 dB bandwidth specified. From the two basic structures of a cascade and parallel architecture, there has been no conclusion as to which of these two structures should be used for speech synthesis. It is easy to see that good results with only one basic method is difficult to achieve so some efforts have been made to improve and combine these basic models. In 1980 Dennis Klatt proposed a more complex formant synthesizer which combined both the cascade and parallel synthesizers with additional resonances and anti-resonances for nasalized sounds, sixth formant for high frequency noise, a by-pass path to give a flat transfer function, and a radiation characteristics. The system used quite complex excitation model which was controlled by 39 parameters updated every 5 ms. The quality of Klatt Formant Synthesizer was very promising and the model has been incorporated into several present TTS systems, such as MITalk, DECtalk, Prose-2000, and Klattalk. Parallel and cascade structures can also be combined by several other ways. One solution is to use so called PARCAS (Parallel-Cascade) model introduced and patented by Laine for SYNTE3 speech synthesizer for Finnish.

Concatenation Synthesis

Concatenative speech synthesis is one of the currently used systems. It is based on concatenating pre-recorded speech to produce the desired utterances. In concatenative speech synthesis approach, there is no need to determine speech production rules. Hence, concatenative synthesis is simpler than rule-based synthesis. Concatenative synthesis generates speech by connecting natural, prerecorded speech sound units. These sound units can be words, syllables, half syllables, phonemes, half-phone, diphones or triphones. The joining of natural speech utterances helps to achieve very high natural sounding speech. However, the joints of speech sound units need to be smooth to avoid abrupt changes or glitches in the synthetic speech signal. The main challenges in this approach are the prosodic modification to speech units and resolving discontinuities at unit boundaries or joints. Prosodic modification results in artifacts in the speech which in turn make the speech sound unnatural. Unit selection-based speech synthesis technique, which is a kind of concatenative synthesis, solves this problem by storing numerous instances of each unit with varying prosodies. The unit that best matches the target prosody is selected and concatenated. Depending on the unit selected, large speech corpus is required to be labeled, which is very tedious and time-consuming. These types of TTS systems are more natural sounding. However, the memory requirement of such synthesis techniques is very large and hence, may find difficulty in being portable to hand-held devices.

HMM-Based Speech Synthesis System

Instead of storing whole speech database in this method, statistically meaningful model parameters are stored and used to synthesize speech waveforms. To build unit-selection system on one speaker data requires about 8-10 hours of speech database. In addition, syllable or phoneme coverage in database is very uneven. Apart from it, in concatenative approach, system will recreate units from what we have recorded. Furthermore, in this approach, we are effectively memorizing the speech data whereas in statistical approach, we are attempting to learn general properties of the speech data. Hidden Markov Model (HMM) -based speech synthesis system (HTS) comes under the category of statistical parametric speech synthesis (SPS) methods. Basic idea is to generate average of some similar sounding speech segments.

Spectrum and excitation parameters are first extracted from speech database. Mel frequency cepstral coefficients (MFCC) and their dynamic features are generally taken as spectrum (i.e., vocal tract system) parameters and log(F_0) and it's dynamic features are taken as excitation (i.e., speech source) parameters. Then, these features are modeled by context-dependent HMMs. Here, spectrum, excitation and duration are going to be modeled in a unified framework. After the training at the time of synthesis, first given sentence, which has to be synthesized, its corresponding utterance is converted to context-dependent phoneme sequence. Then, according to the phoneme sequence, utterance HMM is constructed by concatenating context-dependent HMMs. Then state duration of HMMs is determined. Then using speech parameter generation algorithm, spectrum and excitation parameters are generated. Finally, using Mel log spectrum approximation (MLSA) filter speech waveform is generated.

Evaluation of TTS

TTS systems need to be properly evaluated so that the gap of natural speech and synthetic speech can be identified and should be taken care by developing proper methods in each modeling block of TTS systems. TTS systems evaluation includes finding effectiveness of individual building blocks of TTS as well as final outcome the synthetic speech. Evaluation of TTS blocks includes text normalization, pitch and duration modeling, waveform generation through vocoder, speech parameter generation algorithm, and many other blocks of system. Quality of synthesized speech has been evaluated primarily using subjective listening tests (for example, Mean Opinion Score (MOS)). Objective tests are also conducted to give further support to subjective tests and may give other attributes of speech quality which may not be captured by the human listeners.

Speaker Recognition

Speech recognition is the process of deciphering the linguistic message carried by an acoustic signal generated by human speech production apparatus. A schematic of speech recognition is shown in figure. The speech signal can be viewed as a sequence of acoustic patterns that are arranged according to linguistic rules such as grammar. The word "recognition" indicates the recapitulation of known sound patterns based on cognitive models of these sounds. Thus, speech recognition involves forming and using models of speech sounds and their sequences. The decoding of the linguistic information from the speech signal by machine is called Automatic Speech Recognition (ASR).

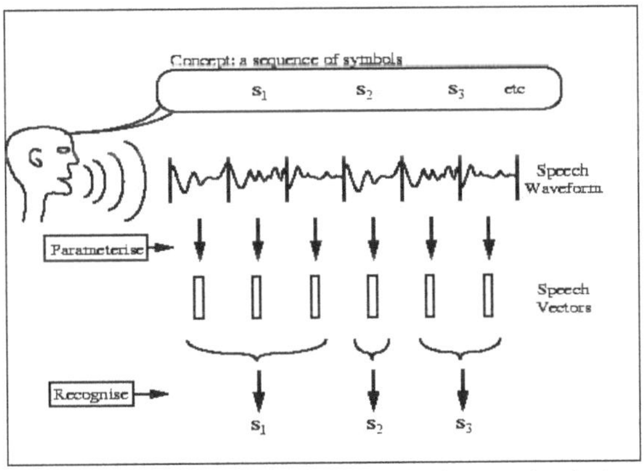

Computer decoding of linguistic message encoded by human brain in speech waveform.

Automatic speech recognition is a special case of pattern recognition. There are two phases in the life-cycle of a supervised pattern recognition system: training and testing. Training phase involves building (or training) mathematical models of different pattern classes using known examples of patterns belonging to each class. During the testing (or recognition) phase, a test pattern is compared with trained models of all classes. The test pattern is declared to belong to the class to which it matches best. The accuracy of the classification will be good if the comparison is made in the space of features that are useful for discrimination between classes. Hence a pattern or a signal is, in general, processed to extract useful features. As shown in figure, a supervised pattern recognition system consists of 3 processing blocks:

- Signal processing (feature extraction).
- Training of class models.
- Matching features of a test pattern with trained models.

In this processing block, features are computed from short segments of speech. Most popular feature set comprises 13 Mel Frequency Cepstral Coefficients (MFCC) as well as the slopes and curvatures of their temporal trajectories. The sequence of such 39-dimensional feature vectors are computed at the rate of 100 times per second.

Recognition of Static Patterns

A spoken word is represented by a temporal sequence of feature vectors. Such sequential patterns are called dynamic patterns. On the other hand, feature vector of a single segment of a speech sound is called a static pattern. Here, we will consider recognition of static patterns such as vowels. Let us start with recognition of one vowel spoken in isolation (i.e., no other sound is uttered). In the previous module, we learnt that formant frequencies characterise vowels well. They can be used as signatures of vowels to recognise the class label of an unknown spoken vowel. Figure shows the time waveform and spectrogram of a spoken word "aayiye". The first 2 formant frequencies of the 3 vowels are also listed. The pairs of formant frequency values for different vowels are fairly distinct. Since each vowel is characterised by two features, every utterance of a vowel can be represented as a point in 2-dimensional plane.

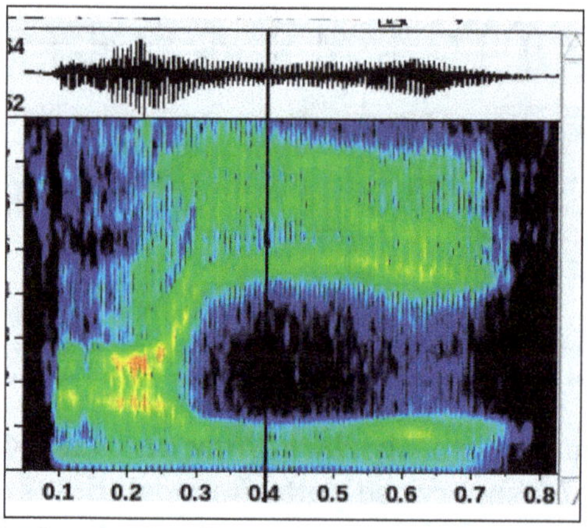

Values of first 2 formant frequencies of the 3 vowels of the word "aayiye".

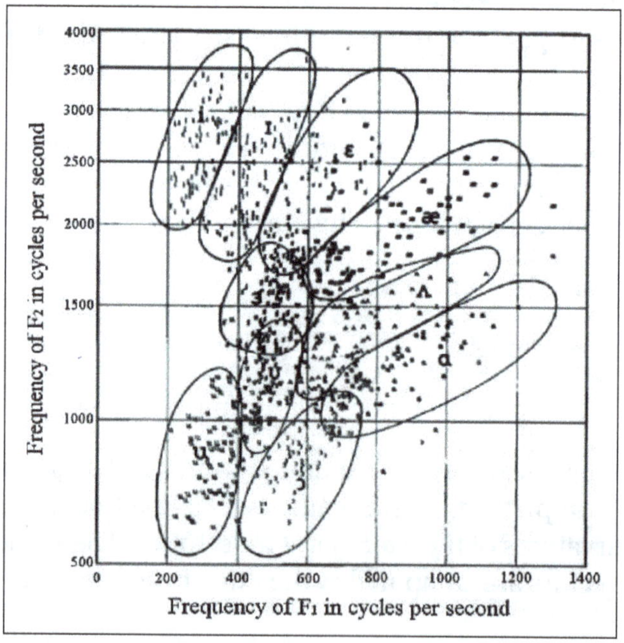

The frequencies of first two formants (F1 and F2) of American vowels, each spoken by 100 speakers. The points belonging to a vowel form group or cluster in this 2-dimensional feature vector space.

Figure shows the first (F1) and second formant frequencies (F2) of American English vowels; each vowel was spoken by 100 speakers: men, women and children. Thus, for every vowel, there are 100 points in this figure. The formant frequencies of a given vowel can vary due to differences in physiology (e.g., length of vocal tract) of speakers.

Yet, points belonging to a given vowel are generally closer than the points belonging to another vowel. Thus, vowels form clusters in the F1-F2 plane as can be seen from the figure. For each of the vowel, one can locate the centre of the respective cluster, and store the F1 and F2 values of the cluster centre. The cluster centres can be used as representatives of representative vowels; these are also called reference patterns. This completes the model generation step; now, the system is ready to recognise a spoken vowel whose class label is unknown.

When the waveform of a segment of spoken vowel is given to the system, the values of F1 and F2 of this new (also called test) vowel is computed. These two values represent a test point in the F1-F2 plane. Let dk denote the distance of the test point from the centre of kth vowel cluster. The system computes such distances corresponding to each and every vowel. The system recognises the test vowel as belonging to m^{th} vowel class if the test point is closest to the centre of the mth vowel class. This recognition decision criterion can be written mathematically as follows: Assign test point to m^{th} vowel class if $d_m < d_k$ for all values of $k \neq m$.

Statistical Model

In figure, points belonging to vowel "uu" exhibit more variation along the vertical axis than the horizontal axis. In contrast, the variation is more along the horizontal axis in case of vowel "ae". In other words, the variations of features (values of F1 or F2) are vowel dependent. The vowel sounds are likely be modelled better if we consider the variation of data points (second order statistics). Visually, the clusters do not have a circular shape; quite a few have elliptical shapes of differing orientations. The vowel recognition accuracy increases when the vowel classification criterion takes such unequal and vowel class dependent variation of features into account. This can be accomplished by dividing the distance by the variance along the axis. Mahalanobis distance is one such distance measure, and is defined as follows:

$$d(\vec{x}, \vec{y}) = \sqrt{\sum_{i=1}^{N} \frac{(x_i - y_i)^2}{s_i^2}}$$

Here, x_i and y_i are ith co-ordinates of test point and centre of a cluster (pattern class) respectively, and s_i^2 is the variance of the class along ith axis. This formula applies to N-dimensional feature space. A point in N-dimensional space can also be considered as a N-dimensional vector starting at the origin and ending at the point. Then, the above distance measure can be viewed as a measure of dissimilarity in N-dimensional vector space.

Probabilistic Model

Inspection of figure shows that the clusters of neighbouring vowels are not separated, but they do overlap. This leads to errors in vowel recognition. In such cases, if a test data falls in the overlap region, we cannot determine the class label of the test data with certainty. On the other hand, we can compute the conditional probability (called likelihood) of the test data belonging to any class, provided we train probabilistic models for each class. The most popular probability distribution is Normal distribution (also known as Gaussian distribution) which is defined as follows:

$$f(x \mid \mu, \sigma) = \frac{1}{\sigma\sqrt{2\pi}} e^{-\frac{(x-\mu)^2}{2\sigma^2}}$$

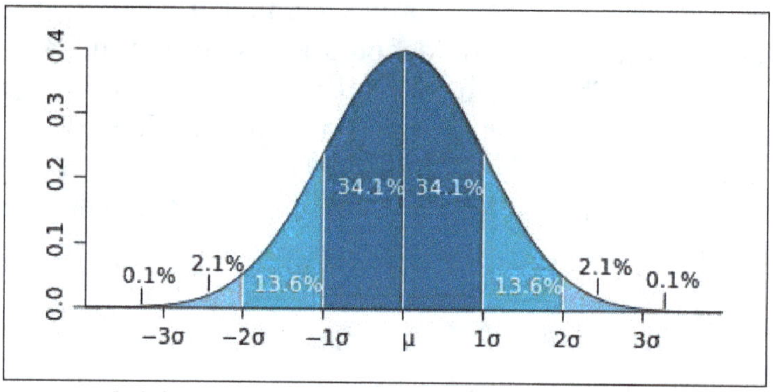

Probability density function of standard normal variate.

Here x and μ denote the co-ordinates of the test point and the mean (centre) of the class respectively, and σ^2 denotes the variance of the class. If we compute mean and variance of feature vectors derived from several utterances of a vowel, we have trained a Gaussian model for that vowel. Similarly, Gaussian models can be for each of the vowel class using training data. When a waveform of a test speech (i.e., the class label is not known) is given, we compute the test feature vector x. We can compute the likelihood of x belonging k^{th} vowel class; let us denote this likelihood by $L(x, C_k)$. Then, we assign the test data to that class whose likelihood of generating x is the highest. This classification criterion is known as Maximum Likelihood criterion and is mathematically written as follows: Assign test data x to m^{th} vowel class if $L(x, C_m) > L(x, C_k)$ for all values of $k \neq m$. The maximum likelihood criterion can be applied to multi-dimensional feature vectors by employing multivariate normal distribution.

Gaussian Mixture Model

A multivariate normal distribution is a good probabilistic model provided the distribution of data points is in the form of a regular ellipse. If we inspect the shape of the cluster of vowel "a" in figure, it is not even elliptical in shape. It is more like the shape of a bean. In such situations, a normal distribution is a poor model of the class. However, the bean shaped cluster can be represented as a sum of two overlapping ellipses. Following this analogy, an irregular shaped distribution of data points can be modelled by a collection (or a mixture) of possibly overlapping Gaussian distributions. Such a model is known as Gaussian Mixture Model (GMM).

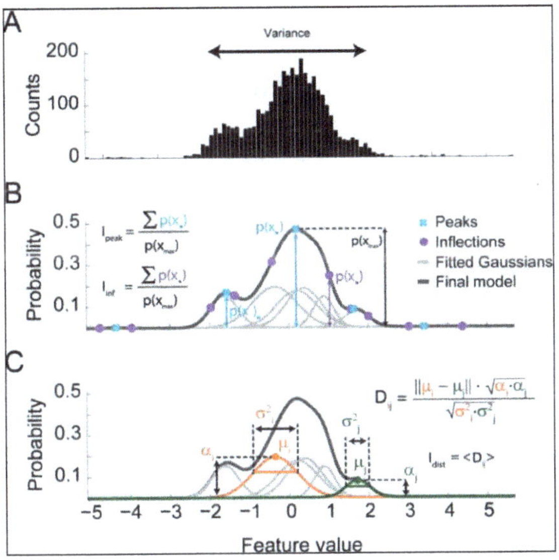

When the shape of distribution does not match the bell shape of normal distribution, a mixture of Gaussians model the data better. The top pane shows the histogram of a cepstral coefficient. A mixture of 10 Gaussians (bottom pane) represents the data better.

Figure illustrates the need for employing GMMs for modelling speech sounds. The top pane of Figure shows the histogram of a cepstral coefficient. The histogram has multiple peaks; the histogram is not symmetric. Consequently, a single normal distribution (middle pane) models the data poorly than a mixture of 10 Gaussians (bottom pane). GMMs are used extensively in ASR. Figure below is another illustration of utility of GMMs for modelling data clusters whose shape does not follow normal distribution. The data can be better modelled as a mixture of 4 normal distributions (represented graphically as 4 ellipses of different location, size and orientations) as shown in the lower pane of figure.

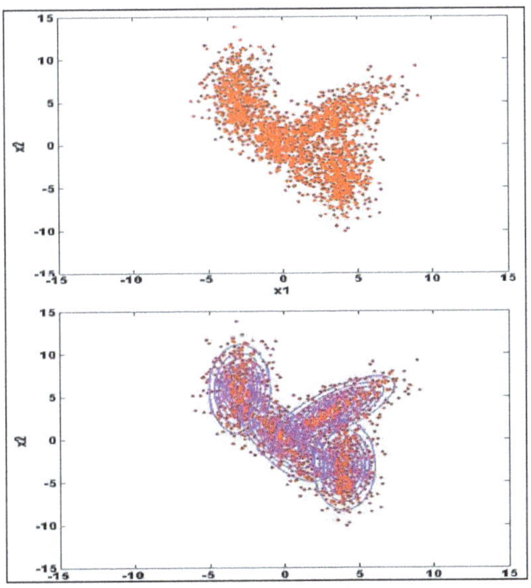

The shape of the cluster of data is not elliptical; so, a single Gaussian distribution does not model data well. A set of 4 Gaussians model the data well as shown in the lower pane.

Artificial Neural Network

Human brain, a mass of highly interconnected network of neural tissues, has evolved over time to acquire the capability to recognize patterns, static or time varying. Artificial Neural Network (ANN) is a simple mathematical model that simulates known properties of neural cells in human brain. Similar to brain, ANNs consist of a massively parallel system with large number of interconnected processing units. The processing units are arranged in layers. Fig. 8 shows a neural network with 3 layers. A unit in a layer receives input from all units in the preceding layer and computes weighted sum of these inputs. This weighted sum is passed through a non-linear function; if the output of the non-linear function is greater than a threshold, it sends a signal to the units in the next layer. Initially, the weights between interconnections are set to small random values. The neural net is fed with training data (the inputs); the output of the single node in the final layer is compared with the known desired/correct value of the input data. The difference is called the error; this error is used to update the weights using a procedure known as 'error back propagation' algorithm.

Neural networks have been used for various problem solving tasks. In particular, it has been successfully used for several pattern recognition tasks such as recognition of handwritten characters, speech sounds, detecting abnormality of human heart etc. Neural networks having more than 2 layers can even draw non-linear boundaries (in feature space) between classes as shown in figure.

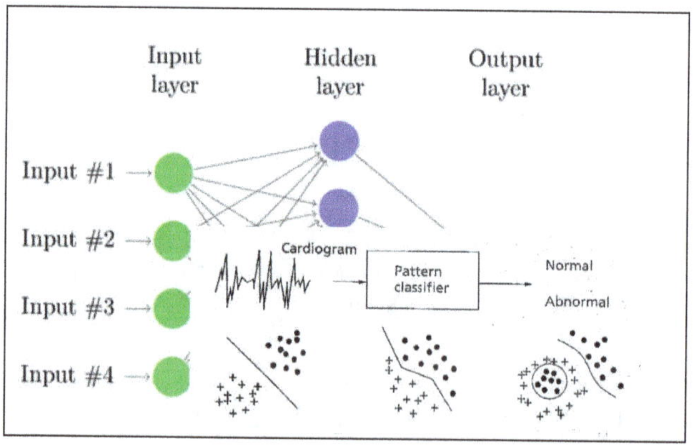

Trained Neural networks can classify data into various categories by drawing boundaries between the classes in the feature space. When the number of layers is 3 or more it can separate arbitrarily shaped convex regions.

In the recent past, a method of effective training artificial neural networks having a large number (as high as 20) of neuron layers has been proposed. These are called Deep Neural Networks (DNN). The word deep refers to the depth (number of layers) of neural network. DNNs together with hidden Markov models have increased the accuracy recognising speech sounds, which in turn has led to increased speech recognition accuracy.

Support Vector Machine

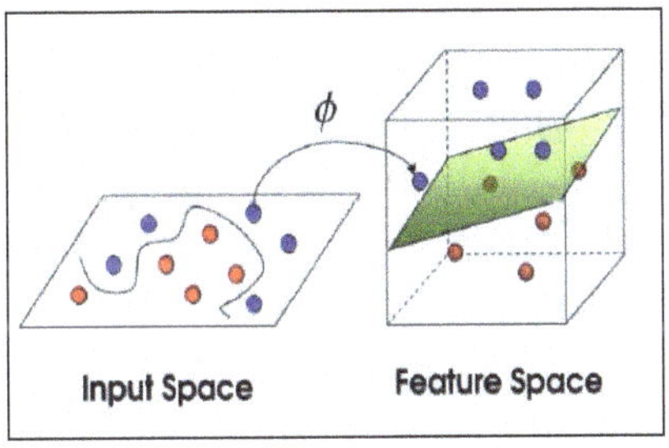

SVM linearly separates data after a non-linear transformation.

Support vector machine (SVM) is a binary classifier based on kernel functions. Even if the boundary between data of two classes is highly irregular, transformation of input data vector to a much larger dimensional space using an appropriate non-linear kernel function enables SVM to draw a linear boundary between the classes in the 'feature space'. This is illustrated in figure.

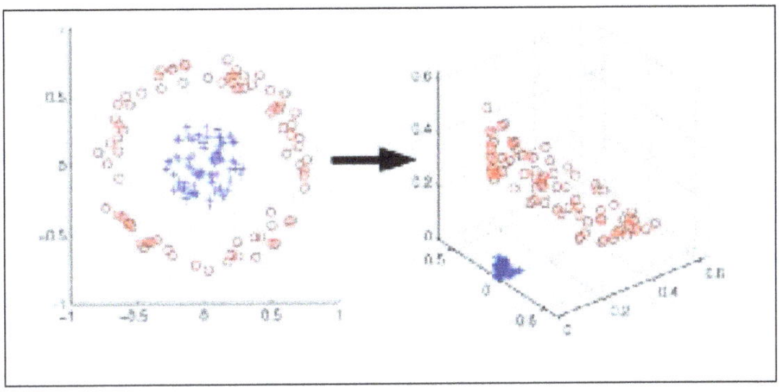

A circular boundary in the input space becomes linear boundary in higher dimensional space after quadratic transformation.

Figure demonstrates the power of SVM. Theoretically, one needs infinite number of linear lines to approximate a circular boundary between two classes when data of one class is surrounded by that of the other as shown on the left of figure. A quadratic transformation converts input data (in 2- dimensional space) to feature in 3-dimensional space where the two classes are linearly separable (both x_2 and y_2 are small for blue data). SVMs have been more successful than multi-layer perceptron type neural networks; they have been used in applications such as automatic speaker verification.

Challenges in Matching of Sequential Patterns

Here, we select the problem of recognising a spoken word for illustrating the challenges in the task of recognising sequential patterns. An example is the case of name dialling, where you can speak the name of a friend to call/dial that friend. When you speak the name of a friend near the mobile phone, the input speech data is processed to compute a sequence of MFCC-like feature vectors. Let us denote this sequence by x_1, x_2, ..., x_N,

Where x_i is the feature vector, computed from ith short segment of input speech. Here, N is the length of the sequence, and depends on the duration of the utterance. The process of recognition proceeds as follows: The feature vector sequence computed just now (called the test sequence) is compared with the reference feature sequences of all the words known to the ASR system. In the name dialling example, these reference feature sequences were computed, in advance, from spoken names of your friends: one reference sequence for each friend. The phone calls that friend whose reference sequence is closest (i.e., matches best) to the test sequence. Such a procedure of finding the reference sequence (also called reference template) that matches best with the test sequence is called Template Matching.

$$d = |x-y| = \sqrt{\sum_{i=1}^{n} |xi-yi|^2}$$

In template matching, the core task is to compute the similarity between a reference sequence (y_1, y_2, ..., y_M of length M) and the test sequence (x_1, x_2, ..., x_N of length N). If the lengths of the two sequences are equal (i.e., M=N), one can compute the distance between the sequences by summing the distance between pairs of feature vectors, and computing the square root. However, in many cases, a difficulty arises when the length of test sequence is not equal to that of the reference sequence. This happens while comparing a short spoken word with a long spoken word. Then, it is not clear which pair of feature vectors have to be considered for pairwise distance computation.

Another situation of unequal lengths of reference and test sequences is when a given word, spoken slowly (for example, by an elder person), is to be compared with the same word spoken rapidly. In other words, speaking rates can cause unequal lengths when the same word is spoken by different persons. One simple solution to this problem, is to normalise the length of reference sequence with that of the test sequence. If the length of the reference sequence is 150 (feature vectors) and the length of the test sequence is 100, one can drop every 3rd feature vector of the reference sequence. Then, the length of the reference sequence also becomes 100, and the distance between the two sequences can be computed using the procedure outlined in the previous para. On the other hand, if the reference sequence is shorter than the tests sequence, a few frames of the reference sequence can be repeated. Such proportional 'warping' of reference sequence so that its length becomes equal to that of the test sequence is called linear warping.

This figure illustrates the need for non-linear warping of time. The top graph shows the waveform when the initial part of the word ("ahmed") was spoken slower than the later part of the word "ahmedabad". The bottom graph shows the waveform of the same word spoken rapidly initially and slowly later. In both the waveforms, the locations of the individual sounds are shown. Correct matching of the two time waveforms demands aligning the initial 0.55 seconds of the upper waveform with the initial 0.30 seconds of the lower waveform: a clear illustration of the need for non-linear warping in speech recognition. The linear warping method fails in many cases due to varying speaking rate within a word. For example, a speaker might have stressed a syllable resulting in relatively longer duration of that syllable. Figure illustrates the need for non-linear warping of reference sequences in ASR. The word "ahmedabad" was spoken twice by the same speaker. The first time, the person spoke the first two syllables slowly, and the later syllables rapidly (upper waveform). The second time, the person spoke the first two syllables rapidly, and the later syllables slowly (lower waveform). The duration of both the utterances was about 1 second. Yet, a visual inspection of the two waveforms as well as the time-aligned transcriptions clearly show the need for aligning the initial 0.55 seconds of the upper waveform with the initial 0.30 seconds of the lower waveform in order to correctly align the two time waveforms.

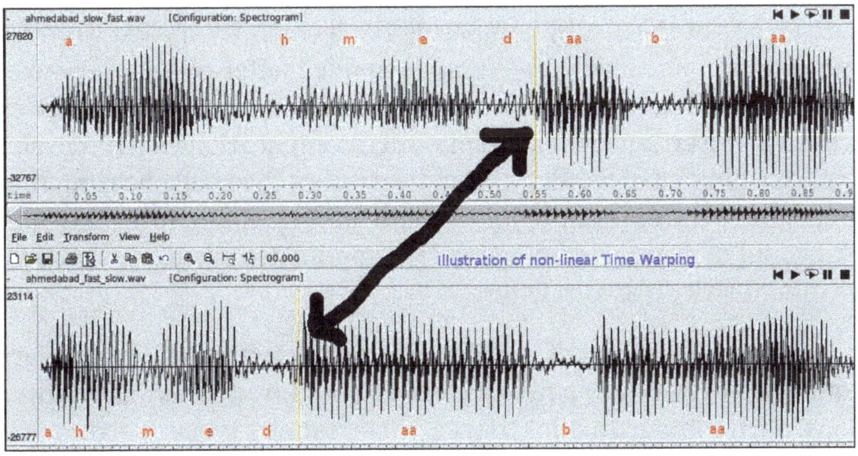

Figure illustrates the need for non-linear warping even in case of two utterance of a single word. Here, a human can visually align the two sequences. However, the alignment process becomes uncertain while aligning/matching time waveforms of two different words. Since computers solve problems following a step-by-step procedure, we need a principled approach for solving the challenge of matching two sequences of possibly unequal length or/and content (sound sequence in case of ASR). A naive approach is to allow arbitrary time warping. Then we have to compute the distance of a test feature vector with every reference vector, resulting in huge computational load. A principle, called dynamic programming, avoids repetitive calculations in such a naïve approach, and reduces the amount of computations (linear in the length of sequences). Such a computationally efficient procedure as applied to time warping of sequences is called Dynamic Time Warping.

Dynamic Time Warping

Speech recognition following the template matching approach involves comparing the feature vector sequence of a test utterance (whose content/transcription is unknown) with reference feature sequences of each and every word in the vocabulary of the ASR system. Since speaking rates vary among speakers, a nonlinear warping (expansion or contraction) of reference sequence is needed for its correct alignment and matching with the test sequence. A computationally efficient procedure for executing this task of aligning non-linearly warped temporal sequences (speech feature vector sequences) is called Dynamic Time Warping (DTW). Understanding the application of DTW for ASR involves a couple of equations. For the sake of simplicity, let us appreciate the principle of dynamic programming through an illustration of its application to the task of spell checking.

We use word processors for typing and formatting textual data. If we make a spelling mistake, the software places a red wavy line below the erroneous word. If we right click on that word, a pop up window shows a sorted list of candidate correct words. The word at the top of the list is the most probable correct word as determined by the software. The software arrives at this list by comparing the incorrectly spelled word with (effectively all the) words in its dictionary. A simple minded letter-by-letter comparison may not be apt since letters may be missed (called a deletion error) or extra letters may be inserted (called an insertion error). Despite such complications and large size of modern dictionaries (millions of words), the software does the spell checking rapidly. This is possible thanks to the application of dynamic programming principle to the task of spell checking and offering a list of correction candidates sorted according to certain criterion of dissimilarity between letters.

A word is a sequence of letters of the alphabet. So, determining the similarity of two words is equivalent to comparing two sequences, possibly of different lengths and letter compositions. Such comparison has to take into account 3 types of errors:

- Deletion error (a letter has not been typed).
- Insertion error (an extra letter has been typed).
- Substitution error (an incorrect letter has been typed).

Each error results in decrease in similarity between the pair of words being compared. Equivalently, every error increases the dissimilarity between the words. The cost of an error can be set according to the severity of the type of the error. The sum of costs of all errors in the optimal alignment of two words can be considered as the distance (a measure of dissimilarity) between the two words. For a word containing a spelling error in the document, the words in the dictionary can be arranged according to decreasing distances. A few candidate words, sorted according to decreasing distance, can be listed in the pop-up window. It is best to understand this procedure by considering an illustrative example as shown in figure. While typing the word "pattern", student has made all 3 types of spelling errors:

- Insertion error: typed extra "p" and "r".
- Deletion error: forgot to type the second "t".
- Substitution error: type "a" instead of "e" after "t".

In order to compute the total (also called "global") distance between two sequences, one has to add the "local" distances (i.e., costs of errors, if any) of all the points along the optimal alignment path. The local distance between a (pink) letter in reference word and a (blue) letter in the test word is the cost of mismatch between the two letters. Such local distances (denoted by symbol d) set in this example are listed in Table. As expected, serious error are assigned higher cost.

Table: Local distance (d) or cost of a spelling error is listed for different types of errors. Cost is zero when there is no error. Cost is higher when a vowel is substituted by a consonant.

First letter	Second letter	distance
a letter	same letter	0
a vowel	different vowel	1
a consonant	different consonant	1
a consonant	a vowel	2

First, let us compute the local costs between every pair of letters, one (pink coloured) letter from the reference sequence along the vertical axis and another (blue coloured) letter from the test sequence along the horizontal axis. For example, if we consider the first letters in both words, they ("p") are same; the cost is zero according to 1st row table of. This value is written in the (lower left) cell in green colour. This value, 0, is the distance between the letter in the row (1st row from bottom) and column (1st column from left) of the cell. Let us move along the 1st column upwards. Let us compute such local distance for the cell in the 2nd row and 1st column. The letter in the 1st column is "p" and letter in the 2nd row is "a". Since "p" is a consonant and "a" is a vowel, the distance is 2. This computation procedure continues; local distance in a cell of xth row and y^{th} column is the distance between the of xth letter of the reference word and y^{th} letter of the test word. Figure shows "local distance" values of many cells. In reality, not all values need to be computed resulting in reduction of computation.

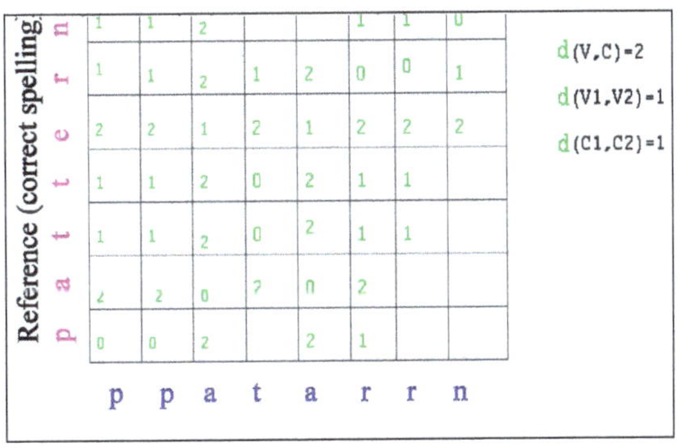

A table/grid showing the "local" distance between a (pink) letter in the correct (reference) word and a (blue) letter in the incorrect (test) word.

The distance between two sequences of letters is defined as the sum of the local distances in the cells along the optimal path. The matching path starts from the lower left cell and ends at the upper right cell. The matching path cannot turn left or down because time cannot flow backwards. The matching path that has the lowest total or ("global") distance is the optimal path. Dynamic programming computes the total (also called "cumulative") distance of the optimal path recursively by computing the cumulative distance of best paths ending at every cell in the grid. Let D(x, y) denote the cumulative distance of the optimal path starting at lowermost left cell (1,1) and ending at the cell (x, y). This quantity, D(x, y), can be computed from similar quantity of the cells to its left and below, using the recursive equation.

$$D(x,y)=d(x,y)+\text{minimum}\{D(x-1,y),D(x-1,y-1),D(x,y-1)\}$$

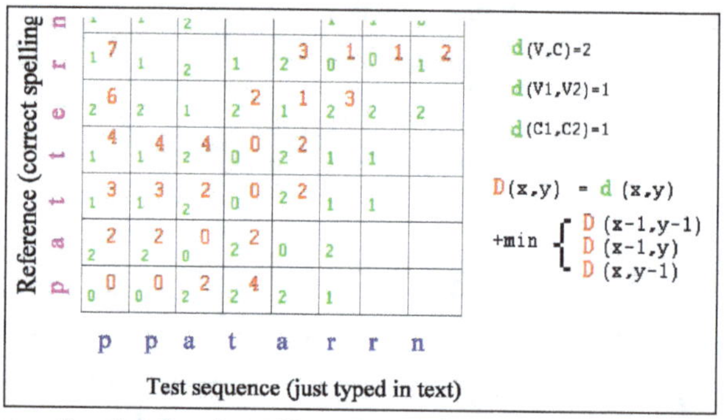

The cumulative distance of optimal path ending at every cell are written in red colour inside the cell. On the lower right of the image is the recursive equation of calculating the value in a cell [D(x,y)] using the corresponding values in the cells below or left or diagonally below.

The D(x, y) values are computed column-wise starting from the leftmost column. D(1, 1) is simply d(1,1) since the path starts here. A valid path from cell (1,1) to cell (2,1) [i.e., 2nd row and 1st column] is a vertical path from (1,1) to (1,2). So,

D(2,1) = d(2,1) + D(1,1)

= 2 + 0

= 2

This value of D(2,1) is written red colour inside the cell (2,1). Similarly, D(3,1) = d(3,1)+D(2,1) = 1+2 = 3. Continuing in this manner, D values can be computed for all cells in the 1st column. Then, we calculate D values for the cells in the 2nd column. There is only one valid path starting from (1,1) to (1,2); this path is the horizontal path from (1,1) to (1,2). So, D(1,2) = d(1,2) + D(1,1) = 0+0 = 0. This value is written in red colour in the cell (1,2).

Table: The 3 rows show the steps in computation of cumulative costs of 3 valid paths ending in cell (2,2). The D(2,2) is the minimum of the 3 values in the last column.

Path to (2,2)	Cost calculation	Cumulative cost
Diagonal from (1,1)	d(2,2) + D(1,1)	2 + 0 = 2
Horizontal from (2,1)	d(2,2) + D(2,1)	2 + 2 = 4
Vertical from (1,2)	d(2,2) + D(1,2)	2 + 0 = 2

There are 3 valid paths starting from (1,1) and ending at cell (2,2). These paths and the corresponding cumulative costs are shown in Table. We need to choose that path which gives the least cumulative cost. In this particular case, there are two paths with the minimum cost (2). In such cases, the diagonal path coming directly from (1, 1) is preferred. This minimum value of cumulative distance of partial optimal path starting from (1, 1) and ending in cell (2, 2) is written in red colour inside the cell. Sometimes, the fact that the optimal path to (2, 2) came from (1, 1) is also stored as a 'back pointer'. This helps in determining the boundary between sounds in continuous speech.

This recursive process of computing cumulative distance of partial optimal path to a cell is repeated to compute such distances (written in red colour) for all cells. Such value (in red colour) on the top right cell is the distance between two sequences of letters. In particular, 1 is the distance (a measure of dissimilarity) between the correct spelling of the word "pattern" and the incorrect spelling "ppatarrn". Similar idea applies in case of speech recognition. A reference sequence of a word is the sequence of MFCC based cepstral vectors of that word spoken during training phase. The local distance, d(x,y) is the (weighted) Eucledian distance between x^{th} reference vector and the yth test vector computed from the test speech. The 'red' value is the distance between the test word and this reference word. Such distances are calculated for each reference word in the vocabulary of the system. The reference word that has the smallest distance to the test word is declared as the word spoken by the speaker.

DTW for Connected Word Recognition

The DTW technique can be extended to recognize connected words such as a spoken number a sequence of digits. However, the extension of DTW to continuous speech encounters a serious hurdle. A reference template has to be constructed for each word of the language. Moreover, the template of a word would not capture variations that are inherent in natural speech. The problem is partially solved either by storing multiple reference templates for a word or by generating a representative template. Yet, these would be static templates that capture some variations in the pronunciation of the word. On the other hand, sophisticated statistical models can capture these variations more efficiently.

References

- Digital-speech-processing-course, Rabiner: ece.ucsb.edu, Retrieved 19, July 2020
- Hidden-Markov-Models: stanford.edu, Retrieved 26, March 2020

6

Diverse Aspects of Computational Linguistics

Some of the prominent aspects of computational linguistics are chunking and shallow parsing, syntactic parsing, word sense disambiguation, etymological annotation, extratextual annotation and computational lexicology. The chapter closely examines these aspects of computational linguistics to provide an extensive understanding of the subject.

Chunking and Shallow Parsing

A chunk is a single word or group words conveying a single meaning. A chunk consists of a single content word surrounded by a constellation of function words. Chunks are normally taken to be a 'correlated group of words'. But identification of chunk boundaries can prove challenging. These different definitions give rise to question like which word to include in a chunk, which to exclude or when to begin a new chunk. According to Paninian Grammar, a chunk can be defined as a minimal (non-recursive) phrase (partial structure) consisting of correlated, inseparable words/entities, such that word-relations inside a chunk are not distorted. Chunking gives a sense about the compositionality of a sentence. The parse tree of a sentence can be represented with chunks as its nodes and interaction between them.

Chunking

Text chunking subsumes a range of tasks. The simplest way of finding 'noun groups' or 'base NP's is to identify non-recursive noun phrases up to the head (for English). Some systems can consist of additional chunk types, such as verb groups, adjective or preposition groups or may split the sentence into chunks of different types:

[NP He] [VP reckons] [NP the current account deficit] [VP will narrow] [PP to] [NP only $1.8billion] [PP in] [NP September].

In any case, chunks are non-recursive structures which can easily be handled by finite-state methods. Quite high performance on automatic NP chunking can be obtained with a small number of regular expressions. With a larger rules of Constraint Grammar, Voutilainen obtained a recall score of 98% and precison score 95-98% for noun chunks.

Need for Chunking

Full parsing requires more computational power to represent the syntactic and semantic meaning for a sentence. This process can be expensive with less robustness. The parse trees generated by a parser can lack semantic coherence. Partial parsing can be achieved with less computation, is more robust, and is sufficient for many applications (Information Retrieval, Information Extraction, Named Entity Recognition, Question Answering). It can also act as the first step in case of full parsing. Chunks containing proper nouns, date/time expressions have very different syntax or structure as compared to normal noun chunks with one nominal expression. Chunk lengths can also vary across languages. Agglutinative languages have less number of words per chunk, while synthetic languages tend to have more function words. NP chunkers can be modified and can use different techniques to help identify these special NPs where tedious, clumsy regular expressions are not sufficient for the identification task. As English is a fixed word order language, chunks can be identified by creating a specialized grammar to identify different combination of categories that are present in a chunk. One of the many possible ways of doing this is by creating a context-free grammar and a finite state automata that parses that grammar.

Learning Methods for Chunking

A simple context-free grammar is adequate to describe the structure of the chunks. In his paper on POS tagging, Church describes a method for finding base noun phrases. For each pair of parts of speech, we determine the probability that there is an open bracket (the start of a base NP) between the two words, and the probability that there is a close bracket (end of a base NP) between the two words. Church conducted an informal test (243 NPs) and reported very good results (238 correct). However, his notion of chunks is more restrictive than what is desired for doing further more complicated analyses, so the results don't represent the applicability of this technique. The identification of chunks is assisted by the use of part-of-speech (POS) tagging of individual words. As an example, consider the following rewrite rules for English. These are sufficient to capture most of the NP chunks.

$$NP \rightarrow DT\ NN$$

$$NP \rightarrow NN \mid NNP$$

$$NP \rightarrow DT\ JJ\ NN$$

1. Chunking for English: Chunking refers to the process of identifying constituents in a sentence. Chunks roughly correspond to prosodic phrases. Pauses most likely fall between chunks. The famous example that Abney gave for chunks is as follows: [I begin] [with an intuition]: [when I read] [a sentence], [I read it] [a chunk] [at a time]. Chunk Parsing becomes difficult for long sentences where there are attachment ambiguities. English can posit a lot of prepositional phrases in a sentence. Then the ambiguity lies in the decision of whether to attach the PP to a preceding verb phrase or a noun phrase.

These selections can sometimes be tricky and automatic chunk identification is prone to failure if the context is not taken into consideration. Looking at nearby words (context) is important in identifying chunk boundaries, so that the correct semantic meaning of the sentence is maintained.

The co-occurrence of chunks is not just determined by the syntactic categories, they are also sensitive to the precise words that head them. You would see in later sections that different grammar formalisms may choose different words as "heads" to roughly comparable noun phrases in two languages. Moreover, The order of chunks is much more flexible than the order of the words within the chunks. There is psychological evidence for the existence of chunks. Gee and Grosjean in 1983 introduced the term performance structures consisting of word clusters collected from various experimental data like pause in reading, naive sentence diagramming. They break the input string after each syntactic head which was a content word.

2. Chunking for Free word order languages: For free word order languages like many Indian Languages, creating a grammar can be time consuming as different categories occur at different positions in the sentence. This usually results in a very large set of rewrite rules. We will end up including rules for different positions in a sentence in the grammar which will make it difficult for generalization. The most common and frequent chunks are verb and noun chunks. In Indo-Aryan Languages, a verb chunk includes a main verb followed by auxiliary verbs. Similarly the noun chunk contains a noun followed by post positions. A noun chunk can also contain other modifiers like adjectives, particles, conjunctions. Dravidian Languages are morphologically richer than the Indo-Aryan Languages. The auxiliary verbs are not present as separate tokens, they are attached to the main form as TAM(tense-aspect-modality) markers or suffixes. The same is also applicable for noun chunks. The post positions are actually vibhakti or case markers. These post positions are attached to the head noun as suffixes.

Chunks are local word groups which can be formed using surface information of the words present in the sentence, the chunk notion provides sufficient information so that they can be computationally useful for Paninian Karaka Theory. Chunks do not provide finer shades of semantics information, they are useful syntactic constructs. The task of a Chunker is to group words occuring in a sequence into a cohesive unit, but it is not a replacement for a morph analyzer. A morph analyzer analyzes each token, lemmatizes them, provide GNP (Gender-Number-Person), TAM information depending on the category of the word.

Chunking depends on the POS Tags of the words to mark the chunk boundaries. Chunking is the subsequent step to POS Tagging in case of shallow parsing. Rule-based chunking involves Linguists or Language experts creating an exhaustive grammar with a long list of hand-written rules for identification of chunks. But with evolution of statistics, probabilistic models are able to find the underlying structure of the sentence, therefore identify the chunk and chunk boundaries. Chunking can be posed as a supervised classification task where a large labeled corpus with annotated chunk boundaries is provided to the classifier. POS Tag of the individual words act as a distinguishing feature for chunking.

The motive behind chunking lies in capturing regularity of the chunks over different sentences so that a grammar explaining this structure is learnt. This is called grammar induction. The representation of a chunk containing a single head word finds its use in Paninian Karaka Theory. The chunks have syntactic as well as semantic information encoded within them. This in turn facilitates in treebank creation where interchunk dependencies (relations between different chunks) are annotated. After Noam Chomsky's generative grammar gained traction in the late 1950's, sets of rules in the grammar were used to identify the structure of sentences. Each sentence was represented as a derivation tree with each node pointing to a syntactic category.

The syntactic category can either be a lexical category (POS Tag) or phrasal category. The lexical words are the leaves of the syntactic tree and represent the terminals. The lexical categories and phrasal categories are at higher levels and represent the non-terminals. But the phrases were recursive in nature which led to its computational limitations. The one-to-many relation of the rewrite rules made the constituent identification much more difficult.

Constituents

Constituency is a very integral notion of syntax. A constituent may consist of one or more words acting as a single unit or phrase. The constituent as a whole can move around in a sentence without affecting the meaning of the sentence. But individual words in a constituent cannot exist as stand-alone entities and impact the grammaticality of the sentence. On sunday morning, a big rally was held in the stadium. A big rally was held in the stadium on sunday morning. A big rally was held on sunday morning in the stadium. "On sunday morning" acts as a constituent, it can be placed at the beginning or at the end or in the middle of the sentence without affecting the meaning. *On sunday, a big rally was held in the stadium morning. Individual words cannot be split from the constituent and placed anywhere in the sentence. The above sentence is ungrammatical.

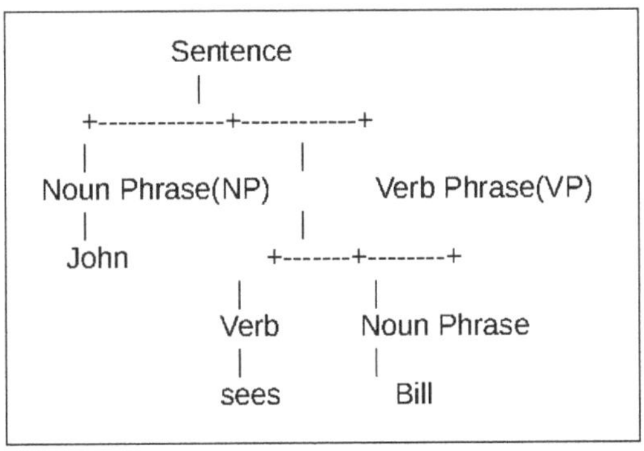

The constituents in the above parse tree are shown below:

NP $\rightarrow$ John

VP $\rightarrow$ Verb NP $\rightarrow$ sees Bill

NP $\rightarrow$ Bill

The constituents are formed following a simple phrase structure grammar.

1. Identification of Constituents: The main evidence for constituents is that they appear in similar kind of syntactic environments. The ordering of words inside a constituent is crucial, changing the order may render it ungrammatical. There are some standard constituency tests like topicalization, clefting, pro-form substitution, passivization, answer ellipsis to identify constituents in a sentence.

2. Why do constituents matter: Constituents are usually word groups in a sequence. As they act as a unit, they have a role in determining the syntax and semantics of a sentence. In Machine Translation systems, 2 kinds of models are predominantly used - word-based and phrase-based models. Word-based models take care of individual translations of word pairs between a source and a target language. The translation of words in a sentence can be combined to have a translation of sequence of words (there is no grammatical constraint for phrases in phrase-based models) for corresponding word sequence in the aligned sentence.

The most used constituent modeling in English is CFG or context-free grammar. Most rules are of the form A $\rightarrow$ b where A is a non-terminal and b being a string of terminals and non-terminals In case of natural languages, the non-terminals refer to the phrases or syntactic categories and terminals refer to the actual tokens or words present in a sentence. Let us consider the sentence John went to the market. An example of CFG for parsing the above sentence is:

S $\rightarrow$ NP VP

NP $\rightarrow$ DT NN | NNP

VP $\rightarrow$ V PP

PP $\rightarrow$ P NP

DT $\rightarrow$ the

NN $\rightarrow$ market

NNP $\rightarrow$ John

V $\rightarrow$ went

P $\rightarrow$ to

Shallow Parsing

Shallow parsing of a sentence involves tokenization, Part Of Speech (POS) tagging and chunking (constituent identification). Tokenization can be done by employing regular expressions and a set of language specific rules. The most widely used machine learning techniques for POS Tagging and chunking are Conditional Random Fields (CRF), Maximum Entropy models, Hidden Markov Models etc. For each of these methods, the words and their features are presented as samples. The features of a word that help identify its POS or chunk tags include suffixes, prefixes, lemma, root form and character length of a word. The POS tag of a word is influenced by its neighboring words. These neighboring words can also be presented as features of a word. In case of chunking, the word itself and its tag are the most important and are presented as sample. The tags used for chunking are one of B(Beginning), I(Inside) or O(Outside) of any chunk (NP, VP, PP etc.). All the models used for POS Tagging and Chunking consider them as a sequence labelling task. A sequence labeling task is a prediction task of a sequence of tags given a sequence of words. These methods use a large corpus of words for training the models. These trained models can then be used for shallow parsing new sentences. The following figure shows a common shallow parsing pipeline.

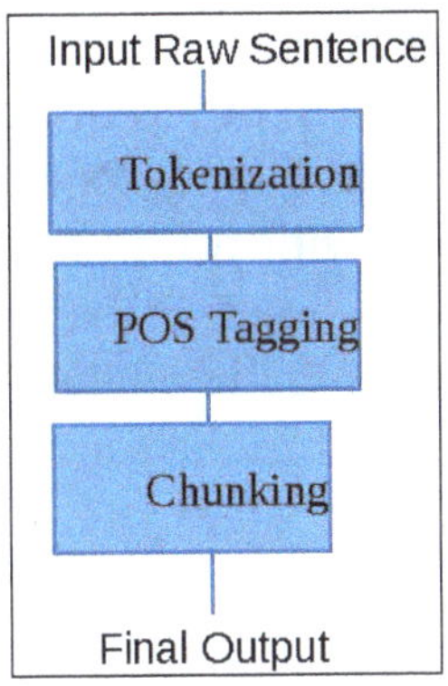

Issues in Shallow Parsing

As shallow parsing follows a pipeline structure, errors in one stage affect the outcomes of the next stage. This is called "Error Propagation". The best performing POS Tagging and Chunking techniques use statistical methods for pre-dicting labels and there remain chances of error if words present inside a sentence are less frequent. These errors can arise due to various reasons. One of the reasons is inconsistent annotation in the training corpus. A manually annotated corpus is passed through several passes of human validation to remove such errors. The POS Tagging and Chunking models can also incorporate salient properties of a language. A model created for English may perform badly for prediction tasks in Hindi as Hindi is mor-phologically richer than English and suffix features would provide much more infor-mation for Hindi than they would for English. The morphological features for a word act as discriminating features while predicting the label of the word. While creating an efficient shallow parser, one needs to care for many factors. Language structure, sub-word features, morphological affixes and contextual ambiguity resolution are a few among those.

Syntactic Parsing

Syntactic parsing is the most common form of text annotation of a written corpus after part-of-speech (POS) tagging of words. It does some kind of syntactic analysis of sentences in texts according to the grammar of a given language and tries to identify the phrases and clauses that are used as building blocks to construct sentences in a language. The motivation of syntactic parsing is to understand and explicate how the constituents are arranged in particular syntactic orders to form sentences and what kinds of relational interface and dependency role these constituents play in final realisation of sentences. Syntactic analysis of sentences can be done either manually with data and information collected from traditional grammars or automatically by a computer with a set of grammatical rules formulated with information obtained from traditional or modern grammar formalisms.

Whether the analysis of sentences is done manually, automatically, or by combining both the techniques, the ultimate result is a parsed version of the original text in which individual words are parsed with information to exhibit both their syntactic properties and functions in the language. The main difference between a tagged text with that of a parsed text is the scope or significance of analysis of the respective texts. In case of a tagged text, the tag list is meant to provide information about the individual words and their parts-of-speech in the text, while in case of a parsed text, parsing provides information to identify the structural or syntactic relationships of the groups of words (e.g., phrases, clauses, etc.) that are used within the sentences.

Ambiguity of the Term

The term 'parsing' is ambiguous in nature as it refers to three significantly different concepts in traditional grammar, natural language processing and cognitive linguistics. In traditional grammar it refers to the act of identifying subject(s) and predicates, phrases and clauses, main clause and subordinate clauses and how these are interlinked to frame a sentence. It also involves the act of understanding the exact meaning of a sentence or several meanings embedded within single surface construction (e.g., Time flies like and arrow). In the area of computational linguistics and natural language processing, it refers to the scheme of formal analysis of sentences by computer based on a set of predefined syntactic rules. The rules are modeled in the form of an algorithm that is capable of interpreting syntactic structures and recognizing constituents like phrases and clauses as well as their nature of syntactic dependencies in construction of the sentences. This results in a parsed tree showing their syntactic relation to each other in a hierarchical order containing both syntactic and semantic information.

In the area of cognitive linguistics (psycholinguistics as well) it refers to the act of language comprehension in all its syntactic-semantic nuances. Here it tries to explore how people analyze sentences or phrases in terms of grammatical constituents. This helps to identify the parts-of-speech of words as well as the syntactic relations of larger constituents like phrases and clauses through the event of which comprehension of meaning becomes possible. All the three different senses of the term however indicates one single thing - the formation of sentences in a natural language is actually a highly complex process with involvement of several constituents and their interlinear relations acting as a thread for binding them. The parser, as a strategy or tool, tries to understand how these relations are evolved and maintained in the whole act of meaningful sentence formation and comprehension.

Transition of the Concept

In traditional grammatical enterprise the term 'parsing' referred to the concept of breaking down a sentence into possible minimum elements in the form of words and identification of part-of-speech of the words with proper reference to their form, function, and syntactic relationship with each other in formation of sentence and expressing its meaning. Based on this assumption, for centuries, parsing has been treated as a part of traditional grammar education where a learner is taught to take a word of a sentence, analyze its lexico-grammatical identity, assign it to a particular part-of-speech, specify its grammatical category, and list its grammatical relations with other words. It also involved the act of identifying subject and various types of object for a verb as well as specifying the words which concord with others in unique grammatical relations. A crucial part of teaching of parsing was to identify the major components of a sentence, namely, subject, predicate, main clause, subordinate clause, etc., that are arranged in specific syntactic order in sentence with single/several meanings. For instance, let us refer to the following sets of data to understand how learners are taught to parse a sentence in traditional grammar teaching method.

Table: Parsing a sentence in traditional grammar teaching method.

Sentence	: The man killed a snake that entered the room
Subject	: The man
Object	: snake
Predicate	: killed a snake that entered the room
Main clause	: The man killed a snake
Subordinate clause	: that entered the room
Main verb	: killed
Lexical Verbs	: killed, entered

In modern linguistics parsing usually refers to the computer-aided syntactic analysis of language. In this scheme parsing is defined as the decomposition of complex structures of sentences into their constituent parts where "the complex structures under consideration are natural language sentences and constituent parts are the building blocks in a syntactic analysis, from clauses and phrases down to words and morphemes". In most cases, the algorithm for parsing is designed based on a formal structural model known as Context Free Phrase Structure Grammar with the following rudimentary rules that work as pillars for symbolic representation of a natural sentence.

Table: Rudimentary rules of Context Free Phrase Structure Grammar.

(1)	S → NP + VP
(2)	NP → (Det) + (Adj) + N
(3)	VP → (Aux) + V + (NP) + (PP) + (NP)
(4)	PP → Prep NP
(5)	Det → a, an, the, that, some ....
(6)	Adj → big, small, tall, high, good ....
(7)	N → man, student, cow, time .....
(8)	Aux → will, can, may, shall ....
(9)	Verb → eat, run, fall, call, give .....
(10)	Prep → in, at, by, for, with ....

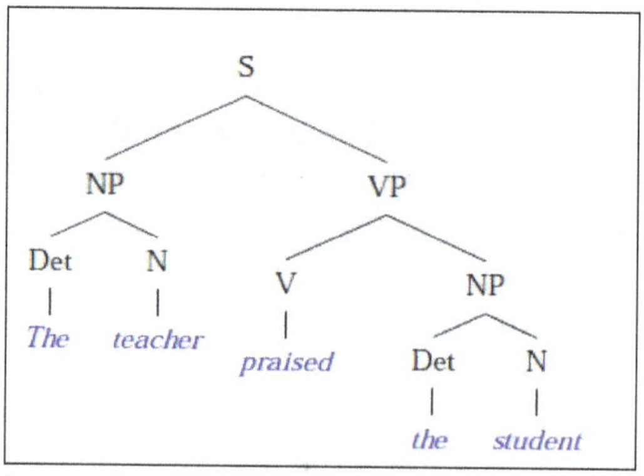

A simple parsed tree diagram of a simple declarative sentence.

For advanced parsers, context-free grammars are not much useful as these grammars cannot express all of the requirements of a language. Moreover, context-free grammars usually fail to remember the presence of a construct over an arbitrarily long input. For instance, it is quite common in a natural language that a named entity is often declared before it is referenced in subsequent part of a text. In such a situation a context-free grammar may not be able to refer to the named entity quite accurately as it is mentioned long ago at the earlier part of a sentence. On the other hand, the more powerful grammar formalisms that can handle this constraint quite elegantly, may not parse efficiently as more powerful grammar formalisms are more complex in nature as they usually put up many context-based constraints that require additional contextual information for accurate parsing outputs. To avoid such complexities it is always better to adopt a simple and common strategy to create skeleton parse with a context-free grammar, as it accepts a superset of desired language constructs along with some invalid constructs. At later stage, unwanted constructs may be filtered out from the output database through contextualized semantic analysis of the parsed strings.

Goals of Parsing

Technically, parsing refers to the practice of assigning syntactic structure to texts, performed after identification of basic morphosyntactic categories in sentence. It involves automatic context-bound as well as context-free syntactic analysis by using information acquired from word-level processing. Based on different models of grammar analysis a parsing scheme tries to bring in morphosyntactic categories into a higher level of syntactic relationship with each other. Whatever be the parsing model, the approach, technique, and methodology of a parser, in essence, are the followings:

- Identification of words used in a sentence.
- Assignment of appropriate syntactic descriptions to words.
- Grouping of multiword units (i.e., collocation, phrase and clause).
- Identification of word-group boundaries (e.g., phrase, clause, etc.).
- Allocation of groups to clause components.
- Identification of main syntactic constituents.
- Naming of the constituents accordingly.

Most of the parsing systems developed so far aims to use some existing linguistic formalism (e.g., principles of Government and Binding theory, rules of context-free phrase structure grammar, etc.) to express the inherent syntactic relations underlying the constituents used in a sentence. This has been the normal practice, since it is believed that implementation of parsers based on certain grammar formalism will be more convenient and useful for encoding the syntactic relations as well as for achieving higher level of success. However, application of grammatical formalism does not produce commendable degree of success, which eventually leads linguists to design methods based on exclusively human-created rule sets. A large part of sets, however, are man-made that seek to encode human knowledge to construct a creditable parser.

Parser

Developed with a set of machine readable syntactic rules of a natural language a parser is a software which takes natural texts as input data and generates structure of sentences in the form of parse trees, abstract syntax trees, or other hierarchical structures to give structural representation of the input sentences with special attention on correct syntactic representation of the constituents. Since it is a long and hierarchical process carried out by an algorithm, a computer system may depend on some preceding or following operations (lexical analysis, POS tagging, collocation, tokenization, chunking, etc.) that may be directly linked with a parser for better understanding of sentence structures by a machine. All these steps may be carried out in sequential order or may be combined into a single operational interface with several small steps operating in a parallel synchronized fashion.

Parsers are normally programmed to work automatically or semi-automatically controlled by a 'parser generator' both in supervised and non-supervised manners. The input to a parser is often provided in the form of a text that is rendered into computer language as a computer can hardly comprehend a natural language text produced in existing scripts. In advanced schemes, texts may be supplied in a natural language more in the form of a less structured textual data the result of which will be the extraction of a part of the text or the components form it rather than formation of parsed trees of the input sentences. Parsers can work in different manners and sequences. Given below is the list of works normally a parser carries out once a natural language text is given to the system as an input:

- Detecting the end of sentences: Once a paragraph of a text is inserted in the form of a string variable input, the parser tries, in a simple and limited way, to divide the paragraph into sentences with the use of an algorithm based on the information of sentence splitter like : '.', '!', '?', etc. In most cases, more or less correctly, it identifies the end of a sentence, unless specified otherwise. While there is a good number of punctuations that can end sentences, this technique may not be able to recognize that these can also appear in the middle of sentences too.

- Tokenizing sentences: Having isolated a sentence, the parser will apply some NLP techniques on the text to split sentences into 'tokens' that is, words, word groups and punctuations. Again, since this split method alone is not adequate to achieve high rate of accuracy, it takes help from tokenization and collocation methods to carry out the task. This task also may involve activities relating to POS tagging of words so that words in sentences are properly marked out and put to tokenization.

- Part-of-speech tagging: Part-of-speech tagging is the act of assigning a part-of-speech to each word used in a sentence of a text. Having obtained an array of tokens from the tokenization process, the parser can feed that array to the part-of-speech tagger, which tags the words based on the actual syntactic-semantic functions of the words in the sentence. The POS tags are returned in an array of the same length as the tokens array, where the tag at each index of the array matches the token found at the same index in the tokens array. The POS tags consist of coded abbreviations conforming to a particular tagging scheme designed elaborately taking languages into consideration.

The parser labels the words with their actual part-of-speech tags, such as, /N/ (noun), /FV/ (verb), /ADJ/ (adjective), and /ADV/ (adverb), /PP/ (preposition), etc. At this stage it also takes into account those words that exhibit several different syntactic categories, such as, back (N and FV), right (N and ADJ), still (ADJ and ADV), bank (N and FV) and labels them accordingly. At this stage, moreover, a parser can either guess the categories of unknown words (/N/, /FV/, /Adj/, etc.) or simply leave them unmarked due to lack of adequate information for identification of their lexico-syntactic function.

- Chunking larger units: The parser may take support of a chunking tool to group the tokens of a sentence into larger chunks, each chunk corresponding to a syntactic unit, such as, a noun phrase (NP), a verb phrase (VP), or a prepositional phrase (PP), etc. after POS tagging. This is the next step on the way to full parsing, but it can also be useful in itself when we look for units of meaning in a sentence larger than the individual words. To perform the chunking task, a parser may require a POS tagged set of tokens.

- Finding out verbs in sentences: The next step a parser does in a sentence is to find out the finite verbs (FVs). This is useful for a number of reasons. First, the verb is the key to the whole clause so it makes sense to get it sorted out first. Also, sentences containing multiple clauses can most easily be identified by locating all the verbs. In identifying the verbs the parser may need to learn that a single clause can contain up to three auxiliary verbs in addition to the lexical verb (i.e., the main verb). At this stage it is the lexical verb that is the main concern of a parser. The strategic way to find lexical verbs in a sentence like the following is to notice where the lexical verbs, tagged with inflectional suffixes (-s, -ed, -ing, -en) appear in the sentence.

  She is planning to leave early from work as she has to go to hospital to see her mother.

  But it has some limitations as stated below:

  - Some verbs do not require suffixes (e.g., leave, go and see in the example above).

  - All of these suffixes also appear on nouns for various reasons.

  It is also useful for the parser to consider auxiliary verbs (e.g., be, am, is, are, was, were, have, etc.) and modal verbs (e.g., can, may, might, will, should, aught, etc.) as these are often used as main verbs in a sentence when lexical verbs are absent.

- Identifying non-finite clauses: The parser has to identify all non-finite clauses because non-finite clauses are always subordinate in a sentence. Finding subordinate clauses makes it much easier for a parser to sort out how different elements within a sentence are related to each other and how these are organized in construction of a grammatically valid sentence. The non-finite clauses generally contain non-finite verbs. These verbs are usually in their infinitive, present participle or past participle form that are not supported by any auxiliary verb. However, there are also examples of subordinate clauses containing finite verbs. So this procedure alone will not help a parser to identify all subordinate clauses used in sentence. The parser may require additional lexica-grammatical information to mark out subordinate clauses.

- Finding basic constituents: The next step a parser does is to identify the basic constituents and establish their transitivity type. Since transitivity varies based on the nature of a verb (i.e., intransitive, transitive, ditransitive, etc.), a parser has to know the transitivity of the main verb so that it is able to identify the number of arguments the main verb is able to carry in the sentence. This is handy at the time of identifying the main clause as well as the subordinate clauses used in a sentence. The final output of a parser is the combination of results of several text processing operations eventually leading to decomposing a sentence into clauses, clauses into phrases, phrases into smaller building blocks (multiword units) all marked with specific symbols used for syntactic parsing.

Types of Parsing

Since the majority of parsing schemes are based on a form of context-free phrase-structure grammar, they normally have the same goal and motivation for identification of constructs as well as marking them. All the parsing systems are, however, not identical in form, methodology, and representation. The main differences lie in:

- The number of constituent types, which a system employs.
- The ways in which constituent types are allowed to combine with each other.

Within the broad framework of context-free phrase structure grammar, an important distinction is made between full parsing and skeleton parsing. The full parsing scheme aims at providing as detailed as possible an analysis of the sentence structure.

Table: Full parsing of a sentence.

SAMPLE TEXT	Another new style feature is the wine-glass or flared heal, which was shown teamed up with pointed, squared, and chisel toes.
FULL PARSING	[S[Ncs another_DT new_JJ style_NN feature_NN Ncs] [Vzb is_BEZ Vzb] [Ns the_AT1 [NN/JJ& wine-glass_NN [JJ+ or_CC flared_JJ JJ+]NN/JJ&] heal_NN ,_, [Fr [Nq which_WDT Nq] [Vzp was_BEDZ shown_VBN Vzp] [Tn [Vn teamed_VBN Vn] [R up_R] [P with_INN [NP [JJ/JJ/NN& pointed_JJ ,_, [JJ- squared_JJ JJ-] ,_, [NN+ and_CC chisel_NN NN+] JJ/JJ/NN&] toes_NNS Np]P]Tn]Fr]Ns] ._. S]

The skeleton parsing, on the other hand, tends to use a less finely distinguished set of syntactic constituent types and ignores the internal structure of the certain constituent types used in the sentences.

Table: Skeleton parsing of an English sentence.

SAMPLE TEXT	Nemo, the killer whale, who'd grown too big for his pool on Clacton Pier, has arrived safely at his new home in Windsor safari park.
SKELETON PARSING	[S[N Nemo_NP1 ,_, [N the_AT killer_NN1 whale_NN1 N] ,_, [Fr[N who_PNQS N][V 'd_VHD grown_VVN [J too_RG big_IJ [P for_IF [N his_APP$ pool_NN1 [P on_Il [N Clacton_NP1 Pier_NNL1 N]P]N] P]J]V]Fr]N] ,_, [V has_VHZ arrived_VVN safely_RP[P at_Il [N his_ APP$ new_lJ home_NN1 [P in_Il [N Windsor_NP1 [N safari_NN1 park_NNLl]N]P]N]P]V] ._.S]

The parsing outputs are most often post-edited by human analysts because automatic parsing has a lower success rate than POS tagging. The disadvantage of full parsing lies in irregularity on behalf of the system engaged in parsing or processing texts. Although more detailed guidelines are provided to overcome limitations, ambiguities are bound to occur when multiple interpretations are possible for a single phrase or a clause. Implementation of parsing systems for corpora of Indian languages is still a far-sighted dream although some efforts are made in this direction in the form of the ILMT (Indian Languages Machine Translation) project, where sentences in Indian languages have been parsed following the dependency grammar formalism. We have to do more intensive research into the area before we can think of developing good parsers for Indian languages.

Treebank

A comprehensive parsing scheme usually assigns phrase marker or labelled bracket to each sentence of a text in the manner of a phrase structure. The resulting 'parsed corpus' is generally known as a Treebank, because both syntactic and semantic structures are represented compositionally as a tree structure, and it projects a lay out similar to tree diagrams used in Phrase Structure Grammar.

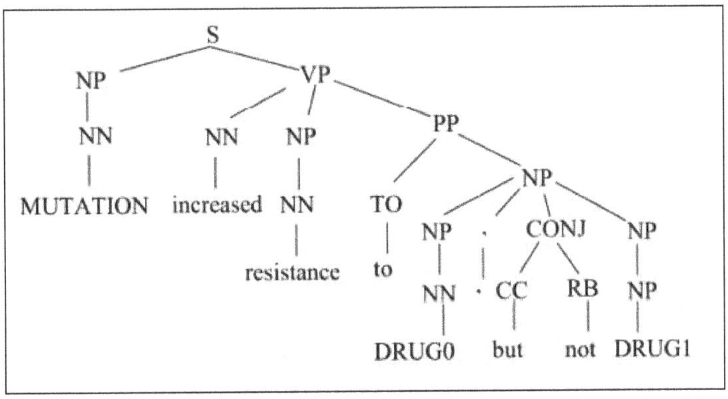

Penn Treebank output of the Stanford parser (Sample Treebank).

Since visual representation of a tree structure is rarely found in text annotation and sentence parsing, the identical information is represented using sets of labelled brackets. Thus, the sentence Pearl sat on a chair will appear in a treebank in the following way. Here morphosyntactic information is attached to the words by underscore characters

While the constituents are indicated by opening and closing square brackets annotated at the beginning and at the end with the phrase type e.g. [S ... S].

```
Input Sentence         : Pearl sat on a chair
Bracketing format: [S[NP Pearl_NP1 NP][VP sat_VVD [PP on_II [NP a_AT1 chair_NN1
NP]PP] VP]S]

[S
        [NP Pearl_NP1 NP]
                [VP sat_VVD
                        [PP on_II
                                [NP a_AT1 chair_NN1 NP]
                        PP]
                VP]
S]
```

Treebank with labelled brackets.

Treebanks are useful resources that can provide annotations of natural languages at various levels of structure: word level, phrase level, sentence level, and sometimes at the level of function-argument structure. Due to these advantages, treebanks have become crucially important for the development of data-driven approaches to natural language processing, human language technologies, grammar extraction, and linguistic research in general. There are a several on-going projects on compilation of representative treebanks for the languages like Spanish, Bulgarian, Portuguese, Dutch, and others that still lack them. Also a number of projects are going on for compilation of treebanks for specific purposes for those languages that have already have them (e.g., English, German, French, Russian, etc.), the most famous one is the Penn Treebank Project at the University of Pennsylvania, USA followed by other treebank projects at Lancaster University, UK, Lund University, Sweden, Tokyo University, Japan, Hong Kong university, Hong Kong etc.

The Tuebingen Treebank of Written German is a manually annotated German newspaper corpus based on data taken from daily issues of the 'die tageszeitung'. The annotation scheme has distinguished the four major levels of syntactic constituency: lexical, phrasal, topological, and clausal. In addition to the constituent structures, annotated trees contain edge labels between node labels, which encode grammatical functions. The treebank currently comprises approximately 95,595 sentences. On the other hand, the Tuebingen Partially Parsed Corpus of Written German is a collection of articles from newspapers, which is annotated with clause structure, topological fields, and chunks, in addition to more low-level annotation including the parts-of-speech as well as the morphological ambiguity classes. All the texts are processed automatically, starting from paragraph, sentence and token segmentation. The tokens have included information about some regular types of named entities, including dates, telephone numbers, and number/unit combinations.

Treebank for Indian languages are yet to come up. However, the ILMT project, in a consortium mode, has produced some parsed trees for various Indian languages at different nodal centres located at IIT-Bombay, IIIT-Hyderabad, IIT-Kharagpur, IIIMT-Trivandum, and others. It is expected that this project may result in formation of a useful treebank for Indian languages in near future. The regular practice of building syntactically parsed corpora has proved that aiming at more detailed description of data becomes more and more theory-dependent (e.g., Prague Dependency Treebank, Italian Treebank, Turkish Treebank, Polish Treebank, Bulgarian Treebank, etc.). Therefore the development of treebanks and formal linguistic theories need to be more tightly connected in order to ensure the necessary information flow between them.

Utility of Parsing

Recent advancement in the area of natural language processing and computational linguistics has given birth many application areas of a parser in understanding the text as well as in applying information extracted from text through parsing. Given below are some of the immediate areas where parser has a pertinent role to play:

- Information and document retrieval: Here the recognition and parsing of noun phrases is of special relevance for documents identification and retrieval of information from them.
- Question answering: Here the system relies on deep parsing and semantic interpretation of texts for formulation of answers with information retrieved from texts. Statistics-based systems use web to find answers to queries by means of partial parsing and matching.
- Terminology extraction: Either shallow or full parser is used for cross-lingual information retrieval and scientific and technical terms extraction.
- Lexicon induction: Here lexical information such as collocation, lexical association, multiword units as well as the argument structure of predicates are acquired from corpora through parsing.
- Text summarization: Here parsing is applied at the sentence and discourse level to produce shorter grammatical versions of sentences as well as to compress several sentences into one.
- Knowledge extraction: It often uses shallow parsing for the analysis of NPs and verbal groups (VPs) but sometimes uses full parsing scheme coupled with semantic analysis of texts.
- Optical Character Recognition: Here morphological processing and syntactic parsing are used to correct recognition problems of characters and character combinations.
- Speech recognition: Natural language syntactic structures are analysed for developing powerful language models for recognising the word strings used in spoken texts.

- Speech understanding: Parser is used for interactive speech-based systems that require speech processing, robustness and the ability to deal with speech disfluencies.
- Bilingual text alignment: Parser supports a wide range of multilingual applications such as cross-lingual information retrieval, bilingual lexicography, bilingual (translated) text alignment at phrase level, translation verification, etc.
- Machine translation: The interlingua, transfer-based, example based, and statistical machine translation systems depend heavily on deep parsing applied on input sentences from the source language to generate equivalent outputs in target language.
- Speech translation: Parser here helps to combine approaches of speech recognition and machine translation into one frame to translate source speech into target speech.

Word Sense Disambiguation

In natural language processing, word sense disambiguation (WSD) is the problem of determining which "sense" (meaning) of a word is activated by the use of the word in a particular context, a process which appears to be largely unconscious in people. WSD is a natural classification problem: Given a word and its possible senses, as defined by a dictionary, classify an occurrence of the word in context into one or more of its sense classes. The features of the context (such as neighboring words) provide the evidence for classification. A famous example is to determine the sense of pen in the following passage:

Little John was looking for his toy box. Finally he found it. The box was in the pen. John was very happy.

WordNet lists five senses for the word pen:

- Pen: A writing implement with a point from which ink flows.
- Pen: An enclosure for confining livestock.
- Playpen, pen: A portable enclosure in which babies may be left to play.
- Penitentiary, pen: A correctional institution for those convicted of major crimes.
- Pen: Female swan.

Research has progressed steadily to the point where WSD systems achieve consistent levels of accuracy on a variety of word types and ambiguities. A rich variety of techniques have been researched, from dictionary-based methods that use the knowledge encoded in lexical resources, to supervised machine learning methods in which a classifier is trained for each distinct word on a corpus of manually sense-annotated examples, to completely unsupervised methods that cluster occurrences of words, thereby inducing word senses. Among these, supervised learning approaches have been the most successful algorithms to date. Current accuracy is difficult to state without a host of caveats. On English, accuracy at the coarse-grained (homograph) level is routinely above 90%, with some methods on particular homographs achieving over 96%. On finer-grained sense distinctions, top accuracies from 59.1% to 69.0% have been reported in recent evaluation exercises (SemEval-2007, Senseval-2), where the baseline accuracy of the simplest possible algorithm of always choosing the most frequent sense was 51.4% and 57%, respectively.

Applications

Machine translation is the original and most obvious application for WSD but WSD has actually been considered in almost every application of language technology, including information retrieval, lexicography, knowledge mining/acquisition and semantic interpretation, and is becoming increasingly important in new research areas such as bioinformatics and the Semantic Web.

- The utility of WSD: There is no doubt that the above applications require and use word sense disambiguation in one form or another. However, WSD as a separate module has not yet been shown to make a decisive difference in any application. There are a few recent results that show small positive effects in, for example, machine translation, but WSD has also been shown to hurt performance, as is the case in well-known experiments in information retrieval. There are several possible reasons for this. First, the domain of an application often constrains the number of senses a word can have (e.g., one would not expect to see the 'river side' sense of bank in a financial application), and so lexicons can and have been constructed accordingly. Second, WSD might not be accurate enough yet to show an effect and moreover the sense inventory used is unlikely to match the specific sense distinctions required by the application. Third, treating WSD as a separate component or module may be misguided, as it might have to be more tightly integrated as an implicit process (i.e., as mutual disambiguation, below).

- Machine translation: WSD is required for lexical choice in MT for words that have different translations for different senses. For example, in an English-French financial news translator, the English noun change could translate to either changement ('transformation') or monnaie ('pocket money'). However, most translation systems do not use a separate WSD module. The lexicon is often pre-disambiguated for a given domain, or hand-crafted rules are devised, or WSD is folded into a statistical translation model, where words are translated within phrases which thereby provide context.

- Information retrieval: Ambiguity has to be resolved in some queries. For instance, given the query "depression" should the system return documents about illness, weather systems, or economics? Current IR systems (such as Web search engines), like MT, do not use a WSD module; they rely on the user typing enough context in the query to only retrieve documents relevant to the intended sense (e.g., "tropical depression"). In a process called mutual disambiguation, reminiscent of the Lesk method, all the ambiguous words are disambiguated by virtue of the intended senses co-occurring in the same document.
- Information extraction and knowledge acquisition: In information extraction and text mining, WSD is required for the accurate analysis of text in many applications. For instance, an intelligence gathering system might need to flag up references to, say, illegal drugs, rather than medical drugs. Bioinformatics research requires the relationships between genes and gene products to be catalogued from the vast scientific literature; however, genes and their proteins often have the same name. More generally, the Semantic Web requires automatic annotation of documents according to a reference ontology. WSD is only beginning to be applied in these areas.

Methods

There are four conventional approaches to WSD:

- Dictionary: and knowledge-based methods: These rely primarily on dictionaries, thesauri, and lexical knowledge bases, without using any corpus evidence.
- Supervised methods: These make use of sense-annotated corpora to train from.
- Semi-supervised or minimally-supervised methods: These make use of a secondary source of knowledge such as a small annotated corpus as seed data in a bootstrapping process, or a word-aligned bilingual corpus.
- Unsupervised methods: These eschew (almost) completely external information and work directly from raw unannotated corpora. These methods are also known under the name of word sense discrimination.

Dictionary- and Knowledge-Based Methods

The Lesk method is the seminal dictionary-based method. It is based on the hypothesis that words used together in text are related to each other and that the relation can be observed in the definitions of the words and their senses. Two (or more) words are disambiguated by finding the pair of dictionary senses with the greatest word overlap in their dictionary definitions. For example, when disambiguating the words in pine cone, the definitions of the appropriate senses both include the words evergreen and tree (at least in one dictionary).

An alternative to the use of the definitions is to consider general word-sense relatedness and to compute the semantic similarity of each pair of word senses based on a given lexical knowledge-base such as WordNet. Graph-based methods reminiscent of spreading-activation research of the early days of AI research have been applied with some success. The use of selectional preferences (or selectional restrictions) are also useful. For example, knowing that one typically cooks food, one can disambiguate the word bass in I am cooking bass (i.e., it's not a musical instrument).

Supervised Methods

Supervised methods are based on the assumption that the context can provide enough evidence on its own to disambiguate words (hence, world knowledge and reasoning are deemed unnecessary). Probably every machine learning algorithm going has been applied to WSD, including associated techniques such as feature selection, parameter optimization, and ensemble learning. Support vector machines and memory-based learning have been shown to be the most successful approaches, to date, probably because they can cope with the high-dimensionality of the feature space. However, these supervised methods are subject to a new knowledge acquisition bottleneck since they rely on substantial amounts of manually sense-tagged corpora for training, which are laborious and expensive to create.

Semi-Supervised Methods

The bootstrapping approach starts from a small amount of seed data for each word: either manually-tagged training examples or a small number of surefire decision rules (e.g., play in the context of bass almost always indicates the musical instrument). The seeds are used to train an initial classifier, using any supervised method. This classifier is then used on the untagged portion of the corpus to extract a larger training set, in which only the most confident classifications are included. The process repeats, each new classifier being trained on a successively larger training corpus, until the whole corpus is consumed, or until a given maximum number of iterations is reached. Other semi-supervised techniques use large quantities of untagged corpora to provide co-occurrence information that supplements the tagged corpora. These techniques have the potential to help in the adaptation of supervised models to different domains. Also, an ambiguous word in one language is often translated into different words in a second language depending on the sense of the word. Word-aligned bilingual corpora have been used to infer cross-lingual sense distinctions, a kind of semi-supervised system.

Unsupervised Methods

Unsupervised learning is the greatest challenge for WSD researchers. The underlying assumption is that similar senses occur in similar contexts, and thus senses can be induced from text by clustering word occurrences using some measure of similarity of context. Then, new occurrences of the word can be classified into the closest induced clusters/senses. Performance has been lower than other methods, above, but comparisons are difficult since senses induced must be mapped to a known dictionary of word senses. Alternatively, if a mapping to a set of dictionary senses is not desired, cluster-based evaluations (including measures of entropy and purity) can be performed. It is hoped that unsupervised learning will overcome the knowledge acquisition bottleneck because they are not dependent on manual effort.

Evaluation

The evaluation of WSD systems requires a test corpus hand-annotated with the target or correct senses, and assumes that such a corpus can be constructed. Two main performance measures are used:

- Precision: the fraction of system assignments made that are correct.
- Recall: the fraction of total word instances correctly assigned by a system.

If a system makes an assignment for every word, then precision and recall are the same, and can be called accuracy. This model has been extended to take into account systems that return a set of senses with weights for each occurrence. There are two kinds of test corpora:

- Lexical sample: the occurrences of a small sample of target words need to be disambiguated.
- All-words: all the words in a piece of running text need to be disambiguated.

The latter is deemed a more realistic form of evaluation, but the corpus is more expensive to produce because human annotators have to read the definitions for each word in the sequence every time they need to make a tagging judgement, rather than once for a block of instances for the same target word. In order to define common evaluation datasets and procedures, public evaluation campaigns have been organized. Senseval has been run three times: Senseval-1, Senseval-2, Senseval-3, and its successor, SemEval, once.

Why is WSD Hard?

Words are typically assumed to have a finite and discrete set of senses, a gross simplification of the complexity of word meaning, as studied in lexical semantics. While this characterization has been fruitful for research into WSD per se, it is somewhat at odds with what seems to be needed in real applications. WSD is hard for many reasons, three of which are discussed here:

- A sense inventory cannot be task-independent: A task-independent sense inventory is not a coherent concept: each task requires its own division of word meaning into senses relevant to the task. For example, the ambiguity of mouse (animal or device) is not relevant in English-French machine translation, but is relevant in information retrieval. The opposite is true of river, which requires a choice in French (fleuve 'flows into the sea', or rivière 'flows into a river').

- Different algorithms for different applications: Completely different algorithms might be required by different applications. In machine translation, the problem takes the form of target word selection. Here the "senses" are words in the target language, which often correspond to significant meaning distinctions in the source language (bank could translate to French banque 'financial bank' or rive 'edge of river'). In information retrieval, a sense inventory is not necessarily required, because it is enough to know that a word is used in the same sense in the query and a retrieved document; what sense that is, is unimportant.
- Word meaning does not divide up into discrete senses: Finally, the very notion of "word sense" is slippery and controversial. Most people can agree in distinctions at the coarse-grained homograph level (e.g., pen as writing instrument or enclosure), but go down one level to fine-grained polysemy, and disagreements arise. For example, in Senseval-2, which used fine-grained sense distinctions, human annotators agreed in only 85% of word occurrences. Word meaning is in principle infinitely variable and context sensitive. It does not divide up easily into distinct or discrete sub-meanings. Lexicographers frequently discover in corpora loose and overlapping word meanings, and standard or conventional meanings extended, modulated, and exploited in a bewildering variety of ways. The art of lexicography is to generalize from the corpus to definitions that evoke and explain the full range of meaning of a word, making it seem like words are well-behaved semantically. However, it is not at all clear if these same meaning distinctions are applicable in computational applications, as the decisions of lexicographers are usually driven by other considerations.

Etymological Annotation

A simple look at the vocabulary of any natural language will invariably show that a large part of its vocabulary is actually obtained from foreign languages, besides having its own lexical stock inherited from native ancestral languages. Also analysis of the lexical stock will show that most of the words are naturalized to such an extent that it is almost difficult to trace their source of origin. This leads us to the concept of Etymological annotation where the basic task is to tag etymological information to words and terms used within corpora with regard to their source of origin (or antiquity) for future reference and application.

Etymological annotation on corpora is necessary for each natural language because the event of lexical borrowing is an inevitable linguistic phenomenon through which each natural language passes for its continuous growth and survival. In fact, many advanced languages like English, German, Spanish, French, Italian, Japanese, Chinese, Portuguese, Hindi, Bangla, Marathi, Tamil, Telugu, etc. which are proud of having large pool of vocabulary, gladly admit the truth that much of their vocabulary are obtained from other languages both native and foreign. For instance, Hindi language has a large stock of words in its vocabulary and a major part of it is obtained from Sanskrit, English, Arabic, Persian, Spanish, German, Urdu, Punjabi, Gujarati, Kashmiri, Bangla, etc. Since there is hardly any well-documented record (for most of the languages) to show which lexical items are inherited or borrowed from which languages into the vocabulary of a language, it is difficult for investigators to find how the vocabulary of a language has evolved across space and time on different diachronic scales.

Here arises the functional relevance of etymological annotation on language corpora. A carefully constructed annotation scheme helps solving the problem of etymological indeterminacy with proper documentation of etymological information for each word used in a piece of text, as each word in the corpora is annotated with a specific tag of its source language. The process may be initially carried out manually for developing a trial database for machine learning as well as for tagging automation in subsequent stages. The ultimate goal is to develop a system for automatic etymological annotation of corpora of a language utilizing information and knowledge found from a supervised machine learning system.

We would work here an etymological annotation scheme in which we would try to annotate the source of words used in a text to identify as well as record the 'mother language' from where these words are obtained and used. This annotation is necessary because a large quantity of vocabulary of a language is actually obtained from various other languages. Moreover, the actual source of origin of words used in a language needs to be properly annotated for future linguistic works. In next two sections, we would focus on vocabulary classification of lexical stock of a language with reference to etymology, and design a tagset for etymological annotation.

Vocabulary Classification

Vocabulary classification is one of the most important processes of language analysis in the area of descriptive and historical linguistics. In language technology and computational linguistics also, it has turned up as an important strategy for language-specific lexical information retrieval and knowledge representation. In our present scheme of work, vocabulary classification is simply indispensable because the subsequent stages of tagset development and etymological annotation are invariably dependent on proper classification of vocabulary of a language. In the act of vocabulary classification, we first identify the source of origin of a word and then annotate it accordingly.

For instance, within a modern Hindi text we can annotate the word 'skul'/ENG/ "school" as an English word, because although the word is a part of the present Hindi vocabulary to naturalization, the mother source of the word is English. Therefore, it is annotated as an English word, and not as a Hindi word. If we try to use hierarchical tagging, then it should carry tags of both the languages. Through this process, we can learn words of which ancestry are used in the language and what kind of morphophonemic changes these words have undergone in the process of naturalization.

The primary goal of vocabulary classification is to capture the information of the source language of a particular word that has come to be used in another language. For instance, in a language like Bangla, a large part of its present vocabulary is actually derived from various other languages, such as, Sanskrit, Arabic, Persian, English, Hindi, Portuguese, Dutch, etc. besides having words inherited from its native sources. A simple analysis of modern Bangla text can show that most of the words are actually used in naturalized form due to which it is tough to trace their actual origin or etymological ancestry. This is a crucial challenge that motivates us to introduce the concept of etymological annotation where, at the time of corpus annotation, we assign etymological information to words with regard to their antiquity for future reference and application.

Etymological information of words can be properly tagged in a piece of text in accordance with origin of words, which may, at subsequent stages, help the language investigators know from which source languages these words have come into a language. For example, based on traditional scheme of vocabulary classification, we can classify the lexical stock of the Indian languages into three broad types. Given below is an etymology-based classified list of words obtained from a Bangla text corpus to show how the vocabulary of modern Bangla is made up with words of different languages (one/two words are given from each language for reference only):

1. Native stock: This includes words inherited from 'mother language' as well as from local dialects and others. For instance, in Bangla, words obtained from Sanskrit, Tatsama, Tadbhaba, Deshi, and regional dialects are put into this category. Examples:

Bangla	: rāstā "road", ghar "house".
Tatsama	: akṣi "eye", agni "fire".
Tadbhaba	: āj "today", āṭ "eight".
Indigenous	: ḍiṅgi "canoe", jhol "broth".

2. National stock: It includes words and terms obtained from other regional and national languages. For instance, in Hindi, it covers words taken from Urdu, Hindi, Bangla. Punjabi, Marathi, Tamil, Telugu, Malayalam, Odia, etc. Examples:

Hindi	: kāmāi "absence", lāgātār "continuous".
Tamil	: curuṭ "cigar", khokā "boy".
Santhali	: kurāṭ "axe", biṛā "bundle'.

3. Foreign stock: It includes words borrowed from foreign languages. For instance, in

Bangla, words borrowed from Arabic, Persian, English, French, Chinese, etc. are put in this category. Examples:

English	: āpil "appeal", āpel "apple".
Arabic	: ārji "request", kisyā "story".
Persian	: kharid "buy", cāmac "spoon".
Portuguese	: ālmāri "almirah", cābi "key".
German	: jār "Tsar", nātsi "Nazi".
French	: ā̃tel "intellectual', byāle "ballet".
Dutch	: hartan "harten", ruitan "ruhiten".
Spanish	: kamreḍ "comrade", ārmā āḍ "armada".
Italian	: kompāni "company", gejeṭ "gazette".
Russian	: spuṭnik "sputnik", glāsnast "glasnost".
Australian	: kyāṅgāru "Kangaroo".
Japanese	: hārākiri "suicide", hāiku "haiku".
Chinese	: cā "tea", cini "sugar".
Burmese	: ghughni "curry", luṅgi "lungi".
Tibetan	: iyāk "yak", lāmā "Llama".
Peruvian	: kuināin, "quinine".
African	: jebrā "Zebra", bhubhujelā "vuvuzela".
Hybrid	: slibhhīn "sleeveless", oṣṭhogrāphy, "art of kissing".
Unknown	: harpoon "harpoon".

For a language or other this scheme of classification may be modified based on the name of the source languages from where words are inherited and borrowed. For instance, while English will include many Scandinavian, Greek, Latin, French, German, Spanish, Italian and other languages into its list of source languages, a South Asian language like Malayalam will include many Dravidian languages, Sanskrit, English, and other Indian languages.

Defining Etymological Annotation Tagset

Since most of the living languages have directly or indirectly obtained words from other languages besides using their own stock, it is expected that at the time of etymological annotation, information about the source of words should be accurately tagged in the text corpus. Therefore, we need to have a well-defined tagset that can be uniformly applied to annotate words found in the corpus. For Indic languages we can think of using the following tagset for words coming from various languages across the world.

Table: Language-based tagset for etymological annotation.

No.	Language	Tag	No	Language	Tag
1.	African	/AFR/	16	Japanese	/JPN/
2.	Arabic	/ARB/	17	Native	/NTV/

3.	Assamese	/ASM/	18	Odia	/ODI/
4.	Australian	/AUS/	19	Persian	/PRS/
5.	Bengali	/BNG/	20	Peruvian	/PRV/
6.	Burmese	/BRM/	21	Portuguese	/PRG/
7.	Chinese	/CHN/	22	Russian	/RSN/
8.	Dialectal	/DLT/	23	Santhali	/SNT/
9.	Dutch	/DTH/	24	Spanish	/SPN/
10.	English	/ENG/	25	Tadbhaba	/TDV/
11.	French	/FRN/	1	Tamil	/TAM/
12.	German	/GMC/	27	Tatsama	/TSM/
13.	Hindi	/HND/	28	Telugu	/TLG/
14.	Hybrid	/HRB/	29	Tibetan	/TBT/
15.	Italian	/ITL/	30	Unknown	/UNN/

If such tags are attached with words in the corpus it will be easier to know the actual etymological source of the words used in a language. However, it should be kept in mind that annotating such information automatically or manually with the words is not a trivial task, as it asks for sound knowledge of etymological information of words on the part of the text annotators. Therefore, only those people who are well versed with the history of origin of words may be asked to do the said task. Also, supporting information may be retrieved from etymological dictionaries available in a language to verify as well as to authenticate the information about the origin of words before these are annotated in the corpus.

Although the tagset proposed in the table above is primarily meant to tag single-level information to the words coming from different languages, one can also extend the scheme for encoding subsequent layers of etymological information of words. In fact, the language tags that are proposed here can roughly indicate the source language from where a particular word is borrowed. This, however, asks for a second layer of annotation (in a hierarchical order) to capture the information of origin of a word as well as the process of derivation, alternation, and euphonic changes it might have undergone in the borrower's language with a possibility for semantic change. For instance, consider the borrowed Bangla word māine "monthly salary" as described below. Etymologically the word is derived from the Persian word māhiyānā "month". In this case at least the word has undergone both phonological and semantic change after it is borrowed into Bangla. This information may be tagged with the word in a manner like the following:

- māine/PRS_BNG/

  This indicates etymological hierarchy of the word. This kind of hierarchical annotation may be useful in case of those portmanteau words where the lexical items of two different languages are combined to together to form a compound word, as the following examples show:

  - sinemākhor/ENG_BNG/ "cinema addict"

- klāśghar/ENG_BNG/ "class room",
- no bai/ENG_BNG/ "notebook"
- bho dātā/ENG_BNG/ "voter", etc.

Now we will briefly discuss the actual process of assigning etymological tag to words in a sample Bangla text corpus; lexical level data and information obtained from this sample tagged corpus; and the application benefits of etymologically annotated corpora.

Process of Etymological Annotation

Annotation can be done either manually or automatically. It is, however, better to annotate a text in a supervised or semi-supervised manner for the first time so that the reliability of an annotated text is beyond question. Then the tagged text is authentically used as a trial database for development of an automatic annotation system or tool.

At the time of automatic annotation, on the other hand, a system has to be designed, which will annotate single word units as well as multiword units in the corpus with appropriate etymological information. For this, the system needs to be supported with a Machine Readable Etymological Dictionary (MRED) where each word is tagged with its relevant etymological information. Moreover, the system has to be trained in such a way that it is able to retrieve relevant etymological information from the MRED and use it to annotate the words in corpora. The process of automatic annotation may be carried out following the following algorithm made with eight steps:

- Step 1: Preparation of a MRED with etymological information of each word of a language.
- Step 2: Integration of the MRED with an Etymological Annotation system.
- Step 3: Run the Etymological Annotation system on a normalized corpus.
- Step 4: The system encounters a word in the corpus.
- Step 5: Matches the word with the lexical stock in the MRED.
- Step 6: Extracts etymological information from the MRED.
- Step 7: Annotates the word in the corpus with relevant etymological information.
- Step 8: Generates the annotated output.

The process, however, may be monitored by experts when the system runs on a corpus. When the process runs, it encounters words of different forms and structures in corpora, such as, inflected words, non-inflected words, naturalized words, frozen words, abbreviated words, compounded words, reduplicated words, multiword strings, and hybrid words, etc. At the initial stage, with reference to the MRED, the system will annotate all single words as well as compound words (both inflected and non-inflected) used in corpora to record their sources of origin. In case of ambiguity, the system will directly refer to the etymological dictionaries to dissolve confusion in proper identification of the source language of a word. If a word is left untouched in the corpora, it will be verified, validated and augmented (if needed) in the MRED. Gradually, through continuous process of modification and up-gradation the system will succeed in annotating all the words in the corpora vis-à-vis in the language.

At the initial stage, we have to take only the surface level information of etymology which may appear inadequate in subsequent stages of text annotation. To overcome this, the decision to mark words as having specific origin may be supported with the information obtained from some authoritative etymological dictionaries available in a language by which any doubt regarding the origin of those words that travel back and forth in the course of its use in a language will be dissolved. The annotated text corpora thus developed will offer important information to enrich both man and machine. In case of man, the corpora will provide a clear picture about the ratio of load of words of different origins in the language. On the other hand, it will make a machine robust to identify the major patterns of distribution of words of different etymology in the corpora. Based on this information, a system developer will build up useful prediction strategies on the overall patterns of occurrence of words of different origin in a language.

Some Findings from the Tagged Corpus

For our initial study we tagged words at the etymological level in a modern Bangla newspaper text corpus made with 1,00,000 (one lakh) words. The results obtained from this tagged corpus shows that the percentage of used words belonging to different etymological antiquities are quite useful to shed some new lights on the present status of the language as well as on the patterns of lexical stock being used in formation of text in the language.

Table: Percentage of words of different etymology in a Bangla newspaper text corpus.

Words of different Etymology	Total Words	%-age
Sanskrit (Tatsama) words	10,000	10%
Bengali words	40,000	40%
Tadbhava words	20,000	20%
English words	15,000	15%
Arabic words	07,000	07%
Persian words	06,000	06%
Other words	02,000	02%

If we agree to accept the tagged newspaper corpus as a representative of the modern Bangla language, then we can, perhaps, show that till date both Sanskrit (i.e., Tatsama) and Tadbhaba words constitute a major part of the modern Bangla language besides the native Bangla vocabulary, which possesses the highest percentage of use in the language. The percentage of use of English words in the language is quite high and it is clearly reflected in the table as well as in the corpus. It can be observed that the number of English words in the Bangla vocabulary is growing day-by-day as a result of new scientific and technological innovations in the western world as well as due to free global internet communication and the spread of English language and culture across international borders. On the other hand, the use of Arabic and Persian words in the language is not entirely lost, even though their percentage of use has notably decreased over the years with introduction and invasion of English into Bangla life and society. The percentage of use of words of other etymology (mostly from national and foreign stock) is quite marginal and their presence in the text does not affect much in the over-all stock of the vocabulary of the language. This observation may be cross-verified with comparative studies of some etymologically annotated diachronic corpora of the language, if available.

The table presents certain statistics on possible contribution of foreign languages to the existing Bangla vocabulary. However, the statistics is deceptive in the sense that the corpus, which is used for this study is made from newspapers texts where information of domains and sub-domains of the text is merged for the study. But we know that the stock of words vary significantly based on domains and sub-domains from where data is obtained. For example, if the domain is science and technology, one may find more English and foreign words. On the other hand, if the domain is local news, then the possibility of finding out more Bangla and Sanskrit words is much higher.

To verify if this argument is valid, one can plan to carry out similar statistical studies on some newspaper text corpora of different domains and sub-domains. In fact, one can plan to carry out statistical studies on a few Indian language corpora to trace differences of percentage of words in different languages and to measure the inter-lingual agreement (e.g., words that are of foreign origin but are now viewed as native stock by the languages, etc.) in the etymologically annotated corpora. One can also plan to carry out case studies to measure how the information of annotation at etymological level can help in different NLP activities.

In general, information elicited from the data presented in table may be used for the purpose of language planning, education and dictionary compilation. In language planning, it will give language planners an idea how the linguistic resources should be designed with clear focus on the percentage of use of words of different origin in the language. In language education, teachers will definitely look at the percentage of use of words of different etymology to concentrate on teaching vocabulary at different grades. Finally, in dictionary compilation, lexicographers will invariably take note of the percentage of use of words of different antiquities in the corpus to decide over the selection of lexical stock to be used as entry words as well as headwords in the dictionary.

Extratextual Annotation

Extratextual annotation is a process of adding representational information to corpora of different genres and text types. To achieve this stage, we can broadly classify the processes of corpus annotation into two types and try to explain different embedded layers of extratextual annotation of texts, the application of which can substantially enhance accessibility of language data in works of text file management, information retrieval, lexical items extraction, and language processing. Techniques like these expand the utility of written text corpora beyond immediate horizons of language processing to the realms of theoretical and applied linguistics. Written text corpora should be annotated at the extratextual level in a uniform manner so that they become maximally useful for various development works of language technology and linguistics.

The growing diversion in the area of corpus generation has given birth to many vital issues while dealing with rising quantities of texts; increasing varieties of texts in machine readable form; relaxation in criterion designed for text and genre representation; methods adopted in corpus annotation; and strategies followed in corpus utilization. All these issues have made the notion of 'corpus', with some predetermined matrices of text categories, an open-ended resource of natural texts. What we clearly understand now is that the diverse collections of texts that are now made available to us can hardly be analysed and utilized in proper manner, unless these are formatted properly with additional tags and labels for easy access by both man and machine. On the contrary, if texts are not adequately labelled textually and extratextually these may become less user-friendly because a corpus user may not be able to retrieve a suitable text, or a part of it, from the central corpus archive and use it for particular research in question. This justifies the argument for developing a uniform method for extratextual documentative annotation of text corpora, because we know that such information is sometimes stored sporadically in metadata. A text corpus, which contains such additional layers of extratextual documentative information, is termed as extratextually annotated corpus.

Annotation

A written text corpus, when developed in machine-readable form, generally appears in the raw state of plain text format, while an annotated text corpus after being tagged with various intralinguistic and extralinguistic information is changed in character, form, and utilities. These tags usually increase the utility of a corpus by providing specificity in text identification and information extraction, and thus making a corpus accessible to investigators interested in research and application related to linguistic and extralinguistic issues. The explicit information that is externally tagged with a corpus, although no longer belongs to the body of a text, is a repository of external information in the sense that it is able to provide relevant cues for retrieving implicit information stored in a text.

According to scholars annotation of a corpus is a practice of adding interpretative information to an existing database of spoken or/and written texts of a language, by encodings attached to or interspersed with the electronic representation of the language text itself. A typical and widely familiar example of corpus annotation is POS tagging, where specific tag is attached to each word by using some kind of attachment symbols to indicate its grammatical class or part-of-speech of the word in a particular sentential environment. Scholars have proposed several ways and methods of textual annotation (grammatical, orthographic, semantic, discoursal, anaphoric, etc.), but have not discussed much about the types and methods of extratextual annotation except those text encoding techniques and standards, such as, CLAWS (Constituent Likelihood Automatic Word-tagging System, TEI (Text Encoding Initiative), HMM (Hidden Markov Model), COCOA, DPM (Dynamic Programming Method), etc.

What is Extratextual Annotation?

Leech has proposed a theoretical-cum-application based distinction between representational and interpretative information embedded within a written text corpus. Representational information is the actual form of a language text consisting of letters, words, phrases, clauses, sentences, tables, paragraphs, images, punctuations and similar other textual elements, which are available within a text corpus. On the other hand, interpretative information is something, which is added to the basic text elements, usually by a human text annotator who has enough linguistic knowledge of the language they are handling. Here we can go beyond the scheme of classification proposed in Leech to show that an annotated corpus is actually embedded with four different components under the rubrics of two broad heads as the diagram shows.

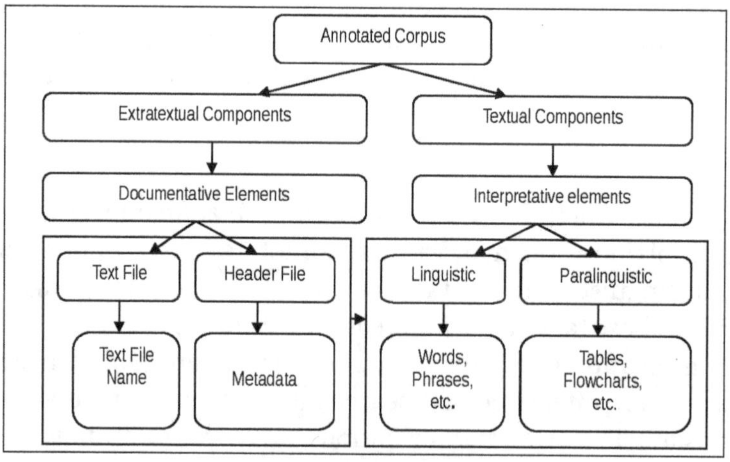

Components within an annotated corpus.

An annotated corpus, in general, contains two broad types of component: an extratextual component and a textual component. Since the extratextual component is documentative in form and nature, it is further divided into two broad parts: Text Fine and Header File. The textual component, on the other hand, is interpretative in form and nature, and therefore, has two broad parts: linguistic and paralinguistic, which are available within a written text corpus. Within textual component, linguistic elements are purely linguistic elements, such as, letters, words, compounds, punctuations, sentences, phrases, etc. without which any language text is impossible to find its entity. The paralinguistic elements, on the other hand, are tables, figures, pictures, diagrams, flowcharts, etc. which are not usually available within a text corpus containing samples of written texts only, but easily available within a multi-modal corpus that contains all kinds of linguistic and paralinguistic elements.

Paralinguistic elements are usually 'marked' using a set of tags in corpus annotation, and these are applied within a written text by some conventional set of machine-readable tags as indicators of the text features, such as, chapters, paragraphs, segments, headings, titles, images, hyphenations, diagrams, pictures, tables, flowcharts, etc. In case of spoken text corpus these are introduced via tag features like hesitations, fillers, pauses, false starts, non-beginnings, abrupt endings, repetitions, lexical gaps, utterance boundaries, suprasegmental properties, etc.

While textual information is indispensable in proper interpretation of texts stored in a corpus for retrieval of linguistic information essential in linguistics and language processing; extratextual information is required for successful identification of a text file and its direct link-up with the target texts, because without proper interpretation and understanding of extratextual elements, retrieval of linguistic information and data from corpora will fail or become ruefully erroneous. The extratextual components, in general, include information such as title, author, time, gender, nativity, publisher, ethnicity, etc., which are stored in the Header File of a corpus, as such information is indispensable in several works of sociolinguistics, ethnolinguistics, ecolinguistics, sociology, demography, language planning as well as for technical, legal, cultural, and similar other reasons.

In all practicalities, extratextual annotation is of high importance to anyone engaged in establishing a Digitally Encoded Language Text Archive (DELTA) for a language or a variety. The variables included in extratextual annotation are considered as the most credential attributes in the context of corpus generation, management and information extraction from corpus for linguistic works. Since extratextual variables are essentially nonlinguistic in nature, these are often determined without delving into textual components stored in corpus, thereby, ensuring that no linguistic judgements are made at the time of designing the extratextual tagsets. The lists of attributes, which are relevant for extratextual annotation of a text, are relevant for description of a particular language community from which the corpus is sampled. Moreover, these attributes are not only relevant for different types of language investigation, but also useful for designing methods for updating archives with new types of text not classified in the list of attributes used in the scheme.

The importance of extratextual annotation can be envisaged in diachronic corpus, which contains text samples dating over a range of periods, where it becomes useful to include information about date(s) of origin of texts and other information relating to authorship, title of work, nationality of author, and so on, within the Header File of the corpus. Such extratextual information about the content of a diachronic corpus is used for extracting data selectively from the corpus. For example, we can perform operations on small samples of text from different periods, or on all texts samples from just one period to catch the variations reflected in the usage of language across periods or different text types. Thus specified attributes of extratextual annotation go beyond the immediate domains of linguistics to many areas of other social sciences and language technology. It is, therefore, sensible to encode a text corpus in advance at the extratextual level making the tasks of corpus management and information retrieval a relatively easier and quicker exercise.

Early Works on Extratextual Annotation

The first two notable encoding projects are applied to the Brown Corpus, and the LOB Corpus, each one consisting of a little over that one million words. However, these are mainly elaborate schemes of grammatical annotation or part-of-speech tagging of the words included in corpora, for which little attention is paid to extratextual annotation of the corpus texts. Perhaps, our knowledge of that time was not advanced enough to visualize that extratextual annotation could be of indispensable significance in the acts of language text archiving, when corpus data would be of enormous volumes, varieties, and dimensions. We also failed to realize that the wide diversity and enormous amount of language data would urgently ask for a systematic and machine-friendly technique for data management in quick and easy handling of language data. Nearly two decades passed before we realized the practical importance of extratextual annotation of corpus texts, and when we realized it, we started the work in one or the other manner without following any standard or norm.

Since a widely representative and universally accepted standard for representing the extratextual information in a corpus text is yet to be developed, scholars of different corpus developing groups and text annotating agencies have adopted different approaches and methods. For instance, one well-known extratextual annotation scheme is COCOA references, which has mostly been used by the developers of the Longman-Lancaster Corpus and the Helsinki Corpus. As a standard convention, it contains a balanced set of angled brackets (< >) having two entities:

- A code symbolising the name of a particular variable.
- A string (or set of strings) that symbolises the variable.

For example, the code 'A' could be used to refer to a variable 'author', while the string would stand for the name of an author. Thus, the COCOA references, which indicated the name of author of a passage of a text, would look like the following:

< A Charles Dickens >
< A Wolfgang Von Goethe >
< A Homer >

A short representation of the COCOA format header used in the Helsinki Corpus is presented in the example below. It shows how the extratextual information could be encoded in a corpus text. The left-hand row is the COCOA format header and the right-hand row is the glossary provided for left-hand row (code 'N' represented the name of a text, while 'X' indicated that the information for that code is either irrelevant or unavailable).

Table: The COCOA format Header File.

<BCEPRIV1>	Short descriptive code	<F X>	Foreign or original
<QE1XX CORP EBUEAM>	Text identifier	<W WRITTEN>	Written or spoken
<N LET TO HUSBAND>	Name of the text	<X FEMALE>	Sex of author
<EDA ELIZABETH>	Author's name	<Y X>	Age of author
<C E1>	Sub-period	<H HIGH>	Author's social status
<O 1500-1570>	Date of composition	<U X>	Audience description
<MX>	Date of manuscript	<E INT UP>	Participant relationship
<KX >	Relevance of text	<J INTERACTIVE>	Interactive/non-interactive
<D ENGLISH>	Dialect	<I INFORMAL>	Formal/informal
<V PROSE>	Verse or prose	<Z X>	Prototypical text category
<T LET PRIV>	Text type	<S SAMPLE X>	Sample
<G X>	Foreign or original		

The COCOA reference format, as it has been shown above, is an informal system which is used for encoding specific types of extratextual information (e.g., author's name, dates, and titles, etc.). This, however, paves a way towards more formalised international standards of extratextual annotation, as it became instrumental in giving birth to the Text Encoding Initiative (TEI), nurtured by the Association for Literary and Linguistic Computing, the Association for the Computers and the Humanities and the Association for Computational Linguistics with clear aims at providing standard norms for corpus annotation both at textual and extratextual level and generating machine-readable text interchange facilities. The TEI uses a form of document mark-up system known as the Standard Generalised Mark-up Language (SGML), which is recognised as an international standard for corpus annotation because it provides clarity in text understanding, simplicity in codes implementation, and rigorousness in the act of explicit encoding formalisation. The most unfortunate thing is that, till date, we have not tried to apply extratextual annotation on the Indian languages corpora so far developed in electronic form. Moreover, we are still sceptical about applicational importance of extratextually annotated corpora in the panoramic spectrum of linguistic works in the country.

Types of Extratextual Annotation

The most rudimentary type of extratextual annotation is one, which tells what type of a text or texts one is looking for. Based on this principle we can serially depend on two kinds of extratextual elements : Text File Name and Header File. While a Text File Name gives us clues to know what kind of text a Text File actually contains. But in most cases, a Text File Name can provide only a minuscule amount of information. Information about the nature of a text also consists of much more than a title and an author and for this information, we need to refer to Header File, which stores explicitly elaborated extratextual information of a text. Therefore, it may be argued that complete extratextual data and information of a text corpus is available partly from the Text File Name and partly from Header File. In following sections, we would concentrate on extratextual (documentative) annotation including its two sub-domains: Text File Name and Header File (i.e., metadata). Other types of annotation (i.e., textual annotation) are kept out of the frame of the present discussion, as these reflect on different avenues hardly linked with the present goal of the section.

Text File Name: A Gateway

A corpus text is generally stored in a computer in the shape of different text files under different head names, which are carefully designed after the major categories of subjects properly envisaged and formalized for the purpose of corpus generation. In wider sense, extratextual (documentative) annotation includes a Text File Name, which, at the outset, provides a vital clue to what kind of a text file one has to explore from the DELTA. Thus, a Text File Name becomes the gateway to a treasure island: Corpus Database. By virtue of its brevity (it has to be confined to a limited number of characters) the form of a Text File Name is highly elusive. For example, for the Indian languages corpora of the TDIL project, it is agreed that the name of a text file should invariably be consistent for all Indian languages, and it would carry, within its length of 12 characters assigned for it, information of the following types:

- Text Category (TC): [2 characters].
- Subject Category (SC): [2 characters].
- Text Title (TT): [4 characters].
- Dot (.): [1 character].
- Number of text files: [3 characters].

Text Category Annotation

Taking into consideration all five components mentioned above, the name of each text file name (contained in large text databases), is formed in the following format:

[C_1C_2[TC]C_3C_4[SC]$C_5C_6C_7C_8$[TT].$D_1D_2D_3$[Number]]

It shows how a Text File Name is constituted with 12 characters. The first 8 characters (shown by capital 'C' that stands for a character with a subscript digit signifying number of the character) constitute the name of the text file, while the dot (constituting a single character) marks the end of the name of a text file. The last 3 characters are cardinal numerals (displayed as D = digits along with its subscript number implying the value of a numeral) used to specify the number of the text file belonging to a particular text category. Again, the first 8 characters may be further classified in such a way that they can be best representative of the text and the subject category as well as for the title of the text. Therefore, it is planned in such a way that the first 2 characters are used for a text category code; next 2 characters are reserved for a subject category code; and the last 4 characters are used to represent the abbreviated form of the title of a text. An example is furnished below from the Bangla text file to elucidate the basic idea adopted for a Text File Name in documentative annotation of the TDIL corpus of Indian languages:

- Text File Name: <LTFCKLBL.005>

The example given above contains, in total, 12 characters where the first 2 characters stands for the abbreviated code for text category [Literature], the next 2 characters constitute the subject category [Fiction], and last 4 characters constitute the code for the title of the source text where from the sample text is collected. This process is useful for accommodating the names of the major text categories, selected for data collection while developing the TDIL Bangla corpus, within the Text File Name. It also helps to divide texts belonging to various subjects under 6 major text categories mentioned below. In fact, the grouping of the source documents under 6 text categories along with their extratextual encodings minimized the effort in searching subject categories as well as text files under particular investigation.

Table: Six text categories and their codes used in the TDIL Corpus.

No.	Text Category	Abbreviation
(a)	[Literature texts]	<LT>
(b)	[Social Science texts]	<SS>
(c)	[Natural Science texts]	<NS>
(d)	[Commerce texts]	<CC>
(e)	[Mass Media texts]	<MM>
(f)	[Other texts]	<OR>

Based on the content or subject matter a text is brought into one of the six major text categories stated above. Each text category has thus included several subject categories following a simple tree-branching technique of text classification, where texts of different subjects and disciplines are divided in different text categories. Therefore, fiction, short story, essay, painting, drawing, music, sculpture, etc. are brought under [Literature]; while political science, history, philosophy, education, religion, etc. are brought under [Social Science]. Similarly, [Natural Science] includes physics, chemistry, biology, mathematics, geography, etc.; while [Commerce] includes accountancy, banking, and business, etc.; and [Mass Media] includes newspapers, periodicals, advertisements, notices, magazines, etc. Finally, [Others] includes those subject fields that do not belong to other text categories mentioned above. It contains texts from administrative documents, legislative proceedings, government circulars, legal documents, etc. This tree-branching technique provides important functional advantage to corpus developers over other techniques of text classification as well as serves primary purpose of proper representation of texts in a corpus. This method, from the name of the text file, can easily refer to which text category a text taken into the corpus actually belongs to.

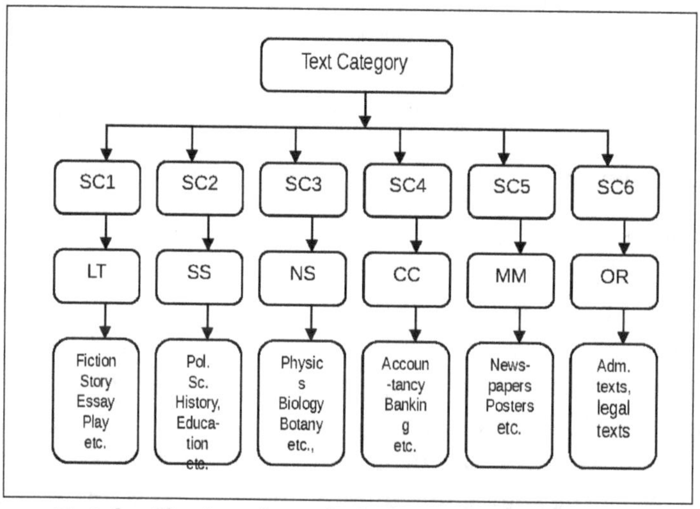

Text classification schemed adopted for the TDIL corpus.

The notable thing is that the name of different text categories is confined within two characters. Therefore, the proper way is to abbreviate the names of the text categories into two-letter codes in such a way that no code could match with other codes, because identical codes of subject categories can create severe problems in proper text identification and processing.

Subject Category Annotation

For each subject category, a unique two-letter code is used immediately after the code used for the text category. This easily makes the name of a text file different from others and it becomes easy to handle text files in corpus processing works. In this table are the codes used for subject category encoding which provides a highly systematic and effective means for data storage.

Table: Coding of subject categories of texts.

Subject	Code	Subject	Code	Subject	Code
Accountancy	<AC>	Newspapers	<NW>	Administrative	<AD>
Anthropology	<AN>	Archaeology	<AR>	Public Administration	<PA>
Architecture	<AR>	Botany	<BT>	Astrology	<AS>
Ayurveda	<AV>	Agriculture	<AG>	Psychology	<PS>
Banking	<BK>	B. Management	<BM>	Chemistry	<CH>
Biology	<BL>	Physics	<PS>	Diary	<DR>
Criminology	<CR>	Advertisement	<AD>	Cinematography	<CG>
Dance	<DN>	Child Literature	<CL>	Drawing	<DW>
Drama/play	<DP>	Essay	<ES>	Economics	<EC>
Fiction	<FC>	Short story	<ST>	Games & sports	<GS>
Geography	<GR>	Com. Engineering	<CE>	Geology	<GL>
History	<HS>	Astronomy	<AS>	Printing technology	<PT>
Hobby	<HB>	Biography	<BG>	Humour	<HR>
Journalism	<JL>	Library Science	<LS>	Folk literature	<FL>
Legal documents	<LD>	Legislative Proceeding	<LP>	Linguistics	<LN>
Magazine	<MZ>	Pamphlets	<PP>	Law	<LW>
Mathematics	<MT>	Photography	<PG>	Mythology	<MY>
Philosophy	<PH>	Political Science	<PL>	Education	<ED>
Religion	<RL>	Sociology	<SL>	Sexology	<SX>
Song/Music	<SM>	Criticism	<CR>	Veterinary	<VT>
Statistics	<ST>	Sculpture	<SC>	Travelogue	<TL>
Zoology	<ZO>	Medicine	<MD>	Letters	<TS>

Title of Text Annotation

The subjects selected for data input should have its proper representation within a Text File Name so that we can understand, after seeing a Text File Name, to which title the text belongs to. Since the whole title of a text cannot be stored within a Text File Name, the best option is to abbreviate the title in such a way that it can be suitably embedded within a code of 4 characters; and at the same time, a corpus user, by a single look, can have a clue as to which text the title belongs to. The best way to create an acrostic term is to use 4 characters allotted for the title of the text.

However, this technique of coding of title is not a very accurate practice, as in most cases, the users can deduct a false or different name from the code. The possible solution of this problem is to tabulate elaborately the titles and their respective codes beforehand (at the time of language data input or text generation) in a different file. Thus, in case doubt, a user can verify to know if a particular code is used for a particular title of the text in the language. The 3-digit extension after dot indicates further particularisation of a Text File Name. The digits stand for the number of files created from a particular title. It was seen at that time that with a fiction containing 1 million words, one cannot create more than 100 text files if each text file contains a data of nearly 10,000 words. It would have been sufficient to allot only two digits for the number of a text file.

However, to be on the safe side it was decided to allot three digits because some texts may exceed the limit of 100 text files, but not the limit of 999 text files. While this was true then, it may not be sufficient to keep 3 digits for numbering texts within a particular category. These practices change with the volume of corpus and length of texts. Working with large amounts of data or with different granularity of texts one must consider these factors for creation of a good extratextual annotation scheme. Looking at the last 3 digits we can understand how many text files are created from a particular title. Also, it provides useful information regarding a particular text file under scrutiny. For instance, the extension implies that the text file is 5th in serial number created from a particular title. Besides, if a user wants to explore texts belonging to the last part of the title, they can do that by accessing the text files tagged with last digit of the series.

Header File: A Documentary Safeguard

In general, a Header File contains extratextual data and information of the following types: name, gender, nationality, and age of author, year of first publication, name of publisher, place of publication, edition used in corpus, type of text, etc.

Table: Extratextual information in Header File.

<Header File>	Metadata Information
<Title>	<Shāmba>
<Language >	Bangla
<Genre>	Written Text
<Text Category>	Literature
<Subject Category>	Fiction
<Text Type>	Imaginative
<Source Type>	Book
<Publication Year>	1978
<Edition>	First
<Volume>	Single
<Issue>	NA
<Publisher>	Ananda Publishers
<Publication Place>	Kolkata, India
<Author>	<Kālkut>
<Gender>	Male
<Age>	60+

<Nationality>	Indian
<Total Words>	5120
<Text>	<Sample Texts>

In essence, a Header File carries basic extratextual information, which actually informs us about the kind of text one should look for in the text files. This information about the nature of a text can be much more detailed than simply giving the title and author name. Sometimes, it tells more about the content of a text file, as it gives information about the age and sex of an author, first date of writing or publication, variety of language (e.g., American English, British English, Australian English, Indian English, etc.), broad subject domain (e.g., science, literature, religion, culture, etc.), type of text (e.g., informative, imaginative), and so on, which may be used for various works of linguistics, sociolinguistics, stylistics, and discourse analysis. For example, if we look at the metadata stored in the Header File, we can retrieve a large pool of extratextual information, which is hardly available from the text itself.

Table: Format of a Header File in TDIL corpus.

Metadata	<Title : śāmba>, <Language : Bengali>, <Genre : Written>, <TC : LIT>, <SC : Fiction>, <TT : Imaginative>, <ST : Book>, <Year : 1978>, <Edition : First>, Volume : Sg.>, <Issue : 0>, <Publisher : Ananda>, <Place : Kolkata>, <Author : kālkuṭ>, <Gender : Male>, <Age : 60+>, <Nationality : Indian>, <Words : 5120>
Text	<marite cāhi nā āmi sundar bhūbane. kathāṭā āj anya ekṭi kathār khei dhariye dila. dhariye deoyā khei kathāṭi abiśyi biparīt. nā-te āche hyā. bhramite cāhi āmi sundar bhūbane.>

A Header File, when provided with information related to these fields, can be accessed for retrieving required data from the texts based on the attributes it includes. Also, a computer program can retrieve this information for the purposes of sorting and grouping. For instance, within a corpus database if we want to refer to the texts written by female writers, we can easily do this by running a search program on the lists of Header Files, which can refer to the variable where 'gender of the author' (say, X) is equal to 'Female'. Thus information fields provided within the Header File can be utilized in an information retrieval program engaged in searching and sorting all extratextual variables, thereby, the texts. Similarly, a text investigator can retrieve language data belonging to particular year, text type, genre, etc., from the large corpora based on extratextual information stored in the Header File.

Computational Lexicology

The field of modern lexicography presents a great number and variety of dictionaries of all types. Within English lexicography there are monolingual and bilingual general dictionaries, etymological and present-day English dictionaries, those which deal with jargon, dialects and slang. Modern lexicography distinguishes between historical and pragmatically oriented or learner's dictionaries. Pragmatically oriented dictionaries are those which side by side with meanings of words recorded in works of literature register functionally prominent meanings, thus giving the readers a clear idea of how the word is actually used in speech. Modern trends in English Lexicography are connected with the appearance and rapid development of such branches of linguistics as Corpus Linguistics and Computational Linguistics.

Corpus-Based Lexicography

Corpus-based Linguistics deals mainly with compiling various electronic corpora for conducting investigations in linguistic fields such as phonetics, phonology, grammar, stylistic, discourse, lexicon and many others. Corpora are large and systematic enterprises: they contain conversations, magazine articles, newspapers, lectures, chapters of novels, brochures, etc. Corpus provides investigators with a source of hypotheses about the way the language works. A large and well-constructed corpus gives excellent information about frequency, distribution, and typicality of linguistic features such as words, collocations, spellings, pronunciations, and grammatical constructions. The development of Corpus Linguistics has given birth to Corpus-based Lexicography and a new corpus-based generation of dictionaries. The British National Corpus (both written and spoken) has over 100 million words. The written part (90%) includes extracts from newspapers, academic books, school and university essays, etc. The spoken part (10%) includes a large amount of unscripted informal conversation, recorded by volunteer selected from different age, region and social classes in a demographically balanced way. The use of corpora in dictionary-making practices gives a lexicographer a lot of opportunities; among the most important ones is the opportunity:

- To produce and revise dictionaries very quickly, thus providing up-to-date information about the language.
- To give more complete and precise definitions since a larger number of natural examples are examined.
- To keep on top of new words entering the language, or existing words changing their meanings.
- To describe usages of particular words or phrases typical of particular varieties and genres.
- To organize easily examples extracted from corpora into more meaningful groups for analysis and describe/present them laying special stress on their collocation.

- To treat phrases and collocations more systematically than was previously possible due to the ability to call up word-combinations rather than words due to the existence of mutual information tools which establish relationship between co-occurring words.
- To register cultural connotations and underlying ideologies which a language has.

Some of lexicographical giants have their own electronic text archives which they use depending on the type of dictionary compiled.

Electronic Dictionaries

Computational Linguistics is the branch of linguistics in which the techniques of computer science are applied to the analysis and synthesis of language and speech. The use of language corpora and the application of modern computational techniques in various lexicographical researches and in dictionary-making in particular, have stipulated the appearance of Corpus (Corpus-based) and Computational Lexicography. Computational Lexicography deals with the design, compilation, use and evaluation of electronic dictionaries, which differ in form, content, and function from conventional word-books. Among the most significant differences are:

- The use of multimedia means: sound, animation, audio, and visual elements as well as interactive exercises and games.
- The navigable help indices in windows oriented software.
- The varied possibilities of search and access methods that allow the user to specify the output in a number of ways.
- The access to and retrieval of information are no longer determined by the internal, traditionally alphabetical, organization of the dictionary, but a non-linear structure of the text.
- The use of hyperlinks which allow easily and quickly to cross-refer to words within an entry or to other words connected with the entry.

There are distinguished two types of electronic dictionaries: on-line dictionaries which require having access to the Internet, and CD-ROM dictionaries which are usually electronic versions of the printed reference books supplemented by more visual information, pronunciation, interactive exercises and games and allowing the user to carry out searches impossible with the book dictionaries. In lexicography the developments in electronic instrumentation and computer science have revolutionized the dictionary-making process, shown new perspectives in this field, supported lexicographical studies in different directions.

Monolingual Learner's Dictionaries

According to present-day view, the learner's dictionary is a general synchronic dictionary in their coverage of phraseological units and expressions. They differ from native speaker's reference books only in amount of information about singular and relatively uncommon items which exist in 'the vocabulary at large' but do not represent the typical features of the lexicon. Learner's dictionaries develop new ways of defining words and provide information necessary for encoding. They have the following characteristics:

- Careful control over the language of definitions (to make it easier for learners to identify and recognize the words' meanings).
- The language described is the usual, everyday variety (not the formal or literary).
- Preference is given to the quality of the treatment of words rather than to the quantity of words.
- Particular care is taken in the treatment of the more frequent words.
- The provision of information on the grammar of words.
- Greater attention to lexical collocations: the learner's dictionary should supply information about the contexts and environments in which words tend to appear most regularly. They give an account of what is typical, rather than describing what is simply possible.
- The development of strategies for aiding appropriate word choice (through usage, synonym sets or information about pragmatics).
- Pronunciation is indicated by means of the IPA (International Phonetic Alphabet).
- Many examples, sometimes authentic but always representative of normal, everyday usage, are given.

Modern learner's dictionaries are instruments for the acquisition of foreign words, and of the foreign language in general. They are 'functional dictionaries'.

References

- Introduction-to-Computational-Linguistics-and-Speech-Processing, linguistics: Retrieved 03, August 2020
- Word-sense-disambiguation: scholarpedia.org, Retrieved 21, May 2020

Permissions

All chapters in this book are published with permission under the Creative Commons Attribution Share Alike License or equivalent. Every chapter published in this book has been scrutinized by our experts. Their significance has been extensively debated. The topics covered herein carry significant information for a comprehensive understanding. They may even be implemented as practical applications or may be referred to as a beginning point for further studies.

We would like to thank the editorial team for lending their expertise to make the book truly unique. They have played a crucial role in the development of this book. Without their invaluable contributions this book wouldn't have been possible. They have made vital efforts to compile up to date information on the varied aspects of this subject to make this book a valuable addition to the collection of many professionals and students.

This book was conceptualized with the vision of imparting up-to-date and integrated information in this field. To ensure the same, a matchless editorial board was set up. Every individual on the board went through rigorous rounds of assessment to prove their worth. After which they invested a large part of their time researching and compiling the most relevant data for our readers.

The editorial board has been involved in producing this book since its inception. They have spent rigorous hours researching and exploring the diverse topics which have resulted in the successful publishing of this book. They have passed on their knowledge of decades through this book. To expedite this challenging task, the publisher supported the team at every step. A small team of assistant editors was also appointed to further simplify the editing procedure and attain best results for the readers.

Apart from the editorial board, the designing team has also invested a significant amount of their time in understanding the subject and creating the most relevant covers. They scrutinized every image to scout for the most suitable representation of the subject and create an appropriate cover for the book.

The publishing team has been an ardent support to the editorial, designing and production team. Their endless efforts to recruit the best for this project, has resulted in the accomplishment of this book. They are a veteran in the field of academics and their pool of knowledge is as vast as their experience in printing. Their expertise and guidance has proved useful at every step. Their uncompromising quality standards have made this book an exceptional effort. Their encouragement from time to time has been an inspiration for everyone.

The publisher and the editorial board hope that this book will prove to be a valuable piece of knowledge for students, practitioners and scholars across the globe.

Index